Moving Blackness

Moving Blackness

Black Circulation, Racism, and Relations of Homespace

LISA B. Y. CALVENTE

Rutgers University Press
New Brunswick, Camden, and Newark, New Jersey
London and Oxford

Rutgers University Press is a department of Rutgers, The State University of New Jersey, one of the leading public research universities in the nation. By publishing worldwide, it furthers the University's mission of dedication to excellence in teaching, scholarship, research, and clinical care.

Library of Congress Cataloging-in-Publication Data
Names: Calvente, Lisa B. Y., author.
Title: Moving blackness : black circulation, racism, and relations of homespace / Lisa B.Y. Calvente.
Description: New Brunswick, New Jersey : Rutgers University Press, [2025] | Includes bibliographical references and index.
Identifiers: LCCN 2024027357 | ISBN 9781978840645 (paperback) | ISBN 9781978840652 (hardcover) | ISBN 9781978840669 (epub) | ISBN 9781978840676 (pdf)
Subjects: LCSH: Black people—Social conditions. | Racism. | Storytelling—Social aspects. | African diaspora.
Classification: LCC HT1581 .C35 2025 | DDC 305.896—dc23/eng/20240820
LC record available at https://lccn.loc.gov/2024027357

A British Cataloging-in-Publication record for this book is available from the British Library.

rutgersuniversitypress.org

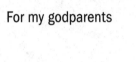For my godparents

Contents

Publisher's Note

This book contains several instances of the word n—and other profanity. Rutgers University Press does not condone usage of these words and does not reprint them without careful thought. In this instance, these terms are used in conveying direct quotes from other sources, including song lyrics and interviews.

Moving Blackness

Introduction

Story-telling
Performances

Circulation, Blackness,
and Popular Culture

I am smoking weed with my cousins in a car on 5th Ave and 120-something. A cop car blasts over the loudspeaker. "You niggers get out the car!" We kept smoking. Once again: "You niggers, get out the car, now!" Suddenly somebody knocks loud on the window. I roll down the glass and a cop shouts: "I told you niggers to get out the car!" I say: "But we're Puerto Rican." He spits back: "I don't care what kind of nigger you are. Get the fuck out the car!"
—Herbie Quiñones

Because everybody about race gets real funny. The Hawaiians. "But we're Hawaiians, we're not Samoans," and Samoans ain't nothing but Samoan niggers. The Filipinos . . . they're the real ones . . . the real ones are the niggers and they know it . . . but everybody tries to leave that out . . . the aborigines the missing link . . . they're the link, niggers. Niggers are everywhere. All my Puerto Rican friends say, "I'm Spanish," and I say, "What you say, nigger?" I don't know about the space program, but I know a nigger when I see one. Don't get it twisted . . . you are a nigger because of slavery . . . Puerto Ricans, Dominicans, Cubans, ain't nothin' but niggers that could swim.
—Paul Mooney

1

I begin this chapter with epigraphs from the stand-up comedy acts of Herbie Quiñones and Paul Mooney to illustrate the complexities of blackness, its cultural formations, and how these complexities are always and already affectively communicated. They elucidate the interplay between the major tropes found within this book: story(-*telling*) as a performative form of popular culture, racism, and the politics of blackness. Though told in different acts, at different times, Quiñones and Mooney narrate practical roles in how identity works within communities of color in the United States. For Quiñones, his identity prevents him from recognizing himself as anything else other than Puerto Rican, yet his encounter with the police officer reminds him that the signifying scope of antiblackness extends beyond race categories and its corporeal suppositions. His retelling of his altercation with the police demonstrates dialectical processes of national belonging and un-belonging that result in an affective understanding of blackness as the imagined, embodied antithesis of citizenship within the modern nation-state.[1]

Mooney's description of Puerto Ricans and the like underscores this antagonistic relationship with hegemonic western discourse and restates what Quiñones realized. He captures how signifiers of national, racial, and ethnic identity also oppose blackness and how these oppositions often bound nonwhite identities closer to the epitome of blackness and its marked anti-belonging.[2] Together, these retold stories pass along an understanding of the limitations of identity at the face of racism and its historical processes. These storied performances do not merely repeat the realities of the past but re-create them with a consciousness toward a solidarity formed under racist oppression and exclusion. Performative story-telling and the circulation of the stories told are the core of this book to take as a conscious goal, rather than a measure of opposition, Mooney's declaration, "Niggers are everywhere."

Moving Blackness: Black Circulation, Racism and Relations of Homespace is premised on the approach that a politics of blackness is inextricably linked to communication, culture, and power. The link between blackness and communication, culture, and power is not new, and it was most certainly not new to Black liberation and decolonization movements, small and large, across the globe. Such revolutionary movements articulated new formations of being and becoming that were born out of the critical understanding of colonized, and often enslaved, experiences of everyday life with the sheer determination to change the new world order. Discursive formations and regulatory processes have operated through racist differentiation established by colonialism and enslavement since the early sixteenth century.[3] That is to say, modernity as a western ideological project both relied on racism and racial discourse to exclude for capital gain and to also exist and, in turn, dominate.[4] Through new communicative technologies, early modern nations initiated overseas exploration and contact with spaces and their Indigenous peoples throughout the globe. These fifteenth-century explorations would shift power relations and spur processes of territorialization that transformed "founded" places, resources, and people into capital gain.[5]

This conjunctural moment made inextricable the connection between capitalism, colonialism, and modernity and produced new relations of domination and subjection that could not exist without the function of racism and the production of race. These colonial spaces were produced as, and with, regulatory modes of exclusion and its categorical representations based on the racialization of the population.[6] Blackness becomes vital to these power relations and the social, political, and economic production of western modern empire and thought. In line with the history of decolonization politics and theory, *Moving Blackness* approaches the politics of blackness as inseparable from racism and the function of racism in creations of violent, brutal, regulatory practices of domination and negation. It locates these discourses of negation as an integral part of the new world order brought on by colonization. As such, *Moving Blackness* brings to the forefront the necessary dependence on blackness as an included exclusion to western modernity through the experiences of Black mobility rooted and routed in storied circulation.

Blackness, as a product of the western colonial project, is the ever-present, fluid signifier of included exclusion that is reliant upon racist and racialized identification. It continues to mark multiple identity groups as those who do not belong and continues to haunt modern national consciousness even in its represented absence. Blackness is also key to the modes of deterritorialization that arise from colonial relations of domination, subjection, and subjectivity. I highlight how stories of blackness, the experience of what it means to be identified as Black, circulate to resist, renegotiate, and affirm the included exclusion experience.

By highlighting story-telling as a way in which blackness affirms itself and moves simultaneously, *Moving Blackness* underscores how communicative embodiments of belonging to blackness enable people to continue to live within marginalized conditions of both social and actual death. It underscores several key ideas. First, *Moving Blackness* centers on circulation as the technique through which resistance is articulated by the blackened, (once) colonized, and enslaved subject. It underscores how story-telling becomes the way in which blackness *moves*, both in terms of circulating the experiences of being Black and as a form of resisting the experience of limited movement and nonmovement. The focus on the function of stories as travel underscores the purposeful articulations of stories and their movements as the bodies of the storytellers are surveilled and contained.

Drawing upon critical performance ethnography and cultural studies, the book frames the act of story-telling and its circulation (its function) as performances and "the popular" rooted in the everyday lives of Black peoples of the diaspora. Second, *Moving Blackness* stresses the importance of circulation as a mode of regulation, communication technology, and signification for modernity. It examines circulation as a communicative mode of power within the modernity-coloniality relationship that determines, through political economy, modern space from colonized space and differentiates the modern human from the colonial and enslaved subject. In doing so, the book argues that circulation solidified modernity as necessarily dependent on racism and racialization and as a new world order of white domination. It highlights how power over circulation is an integral double articulation of surveillance that signifies disciplinary regulation and also ungovernable excess.

In this sense, circulation as a point of analysis to signify, honor, and retell racialized stories of blackness underscores the continued importance of story performances for communities who survive and thrive under the umbrella of included exclusion. Third, the book examines blackness, not through race and identity politics, but through racism and its regulatory and disciplinary techniques of identification. As such, *Moving Blackness* repositions communicative embodiments of blackness as products of identificatory regulations of racism as opposed to essentialist or anti-essentialist identifications of race and ethnicity. *Moving Blackness* includes Latino/a/x subjectivities as belonging to blackness and the Black Diaspora. By examining Latinx experiences as Black(ened) experiences, *Moving Blackness* reaches beyond identity signifiers, such as Afro-Latina/o or Latinx/é, and repositions the Black/White binary within the space of western/white sovereignty and its racist techniques and technologies of power.[7] As Quiñones in the epigraph makes clear, western/white sovereignty and its extended hand of direct force does not care what identity we embody aside from the specific justifications and modes of subjection and exposure to death.

With the concentration on how Black(ened) storied circulation transforms movement and space, the book introduces a futuristic approach to the Black Diaspora that is bound by a politics of identification by way of techniques and technologies of racism as opposed to one rooted in the past or to a place. *Moving Blackness* argues, instead, that a desire for homespace, a notion to belong that occurs in any space whatsoever, is the impetus for this imagined future and stems from the historical, material conditions of racism and marginalization. My aim here is not to create a hierarchy of oppression, nor is it to conflate all identities under the same umbrella of "being Black." I aim to demarcate a necessary line of oppression that is marked by the localized and consequently generalized racist acts of colonialism and slavery most often signified by race and everyday performances of what can and has been identified as blackness. In this sense, *Moving Blackness* claims that western/white sovereignty continues to identify, signify, and define those who are included by their very exclusion by way of blackness. *Moving Blackness* underscores how communication plays a primary role in both the discursive formations of included exclusion and the resistant practices that stem from these communicative encounters.

The book's primary goal is twofold: to highlight how racism functions primarily through a process of identification that relies necessarily on the fluidity of blackness, rooted in colonialism and slavery, and to highlight how performances of story-telling function and circulate. With these two central goals, *Moving Blackness* examines how the relationship between circulation and racism was necessary in the creation of modernity and demonstrates how story-telling combats the nature of mobility as it pertains to blackened subjects of modernity. In so doing, *Moving Blackness* underlines the possibilities of alternative becomings as popular, productive of the enduring processes of belonging to the Black Diaspora. These told stories and their circulation possess the ability to resist racist marginalization, oppression, and exposure to social and actual death and open the possibilities of a transformative future of social and political change.

Performing Blackness, Articulating Belonging

In 1942, W.E.B. DuBois discussed the political significance of humor in both the everyday and mediated performances of peoples of the Black Diaspora. DuBois accounts for how various performative acts, much like the above epigraphs, encompass experiences of community and signify cultural formations derived from exclusion as Black belonging. In his brief essay "The Humor of Negroes," DuBois compares Africans in the continent with Black residents of the United States and the West Indies alongside people across the globe.[8] For DuBois, performances embedded with humor and laughter are not, in fact, natural characteristics of Black people in modern nations and territories but global tactics of endurance against the daily effects of limited socioeconomic possibilities and exclusion.[9] DuBois's intervention in Black humor is in direct opposition to the proliferation of racial and racist knowledge that assists in the maintenance of white supremacy and, in turn, racial injustice and oppression.

DuBois's argument was part of a larger political commitment that positions Black American struggles against racist inequality and oppression as extensions of global antiracism and decolonization struggles.[10] For the task at hand, he was to demystify a national and naturalized representation of Black culture made possible through communicative mediums and technologies. At the same time, DuBois aimed to disentangle a politics of Black resistance and struggle that lies betwixt and between the larger realm of media culture and everyday life, a small window provided by a thick description of the politics of blackness. This thick description is comparatively what Frantz Fanon would further theorize as the lived experience of being Black just one decade later and what Sylvia Wynter subsequently described as "what it is like to be black, within the terms of the mode of being human specific to our contemporary culture."[11] Although not directly stated as a struggle over the ideological and discursive formations of the human, DuBois makes clear that the experience of being Black is rooted against a modern (multi)national (western) discourse.

DuBois recognizes the layered and engaged activities of everyday life as transformative and contextual and pushes forth a theory of communication, culture, and power that is inseparable from the politics of blackness. This inseparability echoes the history of the United States as the quintessential model of modern empire. The moment of DuBois' critical commentary was paramount as it stood in opposition to the tenets that upheld a successfully articulated postbellum, postwar(s) American modernity—a unified national identity.[12] This American national identity is not one that is static but symbolic of changes that have been struggled over and against in a continuously shifting modernization project.[13]

In contrast to its western predecessors, the young modern empire's uniqueness was tied to time, space, and ideology in several ways. Its actualized experience of revolution, rooted in a colonized past, articulated the North American territory within a naturalized teleological progression of western modernity, humanity, and democratic freedom. This came during a time in which the discourse of revolution became a signifier of European agency; enlightenment, humanity, and democratic freedom as western philosophical thought were reserved solely for the enlightened (and whitened) modern subject.[14] Slavery was not perceived as a contradiction to U.S. independence, as slave ownership served to symbolize human agency and liberty.[15] With a colonial history and democratic discourse that unraveled with time, inextricably intertwined with religious persecution and destiny, the United States interpreted itself to be *the* modernity project—a sacred space chosen to embody the new world order in the name of humanity.[16]

The success of U.S. independence as one centralized modern democratic governance depended on the proliferation of communication technology from print media to the telegraph and the railroad.[17] These forms of communication were utilized as a part of the habitual functions of the everyday as well as symbols of American consciousness as exceptional. This national consciousness became one that relied heavily on racial distinctions to distance the nation and its citizens from their other(ed) population, the embodied threat from both within and outside the perceived margins of the nation. Racialized commonsense understandings of American belonging and not-belonging circulated through print as the struggle over national hegemony grappled with "the color line." These commonsense race understandings were reinforced through everyday rituals of spatial and socioeconomic movement, which solidified the hierarchical division of the population as well as understandings of national belonging through access and law; it would also traverse the globe through varying modes of communication.

The U.S. western expansion further served the national consciousness of American exceptionalism as a divine *white* right toward relocation to the West that was rooted in anti-Black racism and acted upon through the displacement, servitude, and death of Indigenous (native and Mexican) peoples.[18] Though civil war threatened the nation-state, its disruption was temporary to the unwavering ideology of white American superiority. The primary goal of the war was less about the emancipation of slaves for democracy and human equality and more about moral and economic supremacy.[19] Reconstruction signified a new articulation of a unified national identity for the United States.[20] With strategic realignments of national ideology, communicative technology, and economic and sociopolitical infrastructure, the United States touted a reconstructed abolition democracy that in practice relied more than ever on a common enemy: the racialized and blackened Other.[21]

Mass lynching was the materialized effect of fear and threat within American consciousness that would predate capital punishment as the state-sanctioned murder of racialized others.[22] Among everyday rituals of murder, sentiments of racialized threat and criminality were communicated through print, and the moving image as counterhegemonic discourses aimed to combat them. Hegemonic constructions of racism by the mid-twentieth century tied its inception to a universal abnormality that was primarily depicted by Nazi Germany's fascism against European Jews.[23] This helped to further disconnect the link between racism, the colonized population in the United States and abroad, and global systemic oppression in the interest of white supremacy. Oppositional discourses would prevail within the terrain of politics, arts, and literature that both mirrored and influenced everyday practices and relationships well into the freedom movements of the mid-twentieth century. These feats would face both immediate and slow-forming socioeconomic, political, and infrastructural backlash in the decades that followed, which would further exacerbate the reliance of western hegemony on the blackened enemy.

Within the context of power relations and struggles over hegemony, *Moving Blackness* underscores the excess that exists in opposition and in contradiction to the forms of regulation and subjection born out of western hegemony's reliance on the blackened enemy. Black experiences and resistances have accompanied these modes and discourses of exclusion. These institutional racist experiences that make identity secondary are also memories that become part of subjectivity formations. These embodied moments of included exclusion are communicated and articulated in new cultural formations of community, solidarity, survival, and love, and it is these formations that can possibly transform into practices of social justice and change. Wynter describes these politics of blackness as the affirmations of Black peoples that attend the negating Black representations necessary to European modernity.[24]

These spillages are creations of contestation and resistance against hegemonic discourses of negation and processes of subjection. Following the works of Stuart Hall, Paul Gilroy, and Richard Iton, such struggles are what *Moving Blackness* identifies as the terrain of Black popular culture, where the battle over anti-Black hegemony can be won or lost.[25] These performative affirmations are materializations of the continuous and multiple deterritorializations of blackness that are articulated into Black positivity.[26] The possibilities lie in what Lawrence Grossberg, drawing upon the works of Louis Althusser and Stuart Hall, describes as ideological discursive formations of practices that have come into existence and whose possibilities are never guaranteed.[27] The significance of Hall's interpretation of the taken-for-granted excess of regulation and oppression as articulation is that, although these actions occur, they are not always articulated as such. Yet all these actions possess the possibilities of new becomings.

Wynter pushes these articulations further as "the imperative task of transformation, of counter-resistance to the resistances of the Real world, to the quest of the marked excluded blacks to affirm themselves."[28] *Moving Blackness* highlights such affirmations through the act of story-telling to take seriously how segments of the population are identified and how identity is always and already blackened through its relationship to the modernity/coloniality matrix of power. Its turn toward identification underscores the active function of power relations that are derived from racism and its discursive formations and ideologies made possible through the relationship between western modernity and coloniality. My critical cultural analysis centers on understanding how racism functions on the terrain of regimes of truth and power struggles that arise from blackened subjectivities who are identified by the politics of identification. My analyses of racist regulations of life highlight the ways in which ordinary people act as social agents even if that act is merely the daily affective urgency to keep on keepin' on. Because in a world where it is normal to actively resist resistances to anti-Black hegemony, the ability to continue to live and love is, as bell hooks has exclaimed, a revolutionary act.[29] *Moving Blackness* enters the conversations of Black life by emphasizing embodied epistemologies of blackness, love, and belonging that are formed through the circulation of story performances.

Politicking Solidarity: Story-telling, Stories Told

Story-telling represents a part of cultural expressive formations that have both changed and remained the same. It is connected to a particular line of communication and community building that arose within the context of power, which stems from the modernity/coloniality relationship. Stories told often in jest are part of a larger mode of communicative connectedness that is consciously positioned against the processes of marginalization and oppression. Embedded at times in humor and laughter, stories have been tactics for the systematically oppressed to endure, resist, and survive their oppression within the context of pain, terror, and exposure to death that are propelled by slavery, colonialism, and their aftermath.[30] For peoples of the Black Diaspora, humor, laughter, and down-play enable the unspeakable to be spoken, narrated in varying moments and in multiple public and private spaces.

The spaces themselves are also subjected to the modernity/coloniality relationship and underscore the significance of proximity and fluidity in the categorizing processes of blackness. These storied practices as a radical communicative tradition of the oppressed accompany the continuous changes in the everyday performances of living that transformed with the technological, political, and topographical shifts of the infrastructural spaces they inhabit.[31] Stories are embedded with how the politics of everyday life are performed and how these performances are articulated. Stories that are told, and how they are told, are significant in understanding how politics of resistance and struggles over hegemony form and are articulated. They provide the ways in which everyday practices are theorized.

As Antonio Gramsci has informed us, "all men are intellectuals" and provide life-informed explanations about the world around them and their actions within their worlds.[32] Stories preview how discursive and ideological formations affect people's common sense notions of the everyday and provide contradictions to common sense—those conscious thoughts about daily activity and experience. These stories inform us of the kinds of normalized disciplinary regulations that surround us, regulations that subject us to conform and compel us to resist. They are the conscious and unconscious formations entangled between the contradictions, located at the crossroad of interpellation and subjectification. They can provide insight into the fragmented philosophies of living that are extended by and limited to material conditions of the everyday; these entail varying understandings of processes of regulation, oppression, and subjection in any given context.[33]

These stories most importantly can reveal how popular formations of solidarity occur through strategic alliances that are rooted in given historical conditions. Of equal importance, story-telling is an indispensable part of such unification processes, specifically for those whose necks are subjected to the weight of (neo)colonial oppression. Stories are what Meaghan Morris once described as both referential and banal, yet not necessarily true.[34] Morris states, "They are oriented futuristically toward the construction of a precise local, and social discursive context" and are "functional in a given exchange."[35] Truth is secondary, shifting and transforming within a functional context of dialogic performance and exchange.

Purpose and functionality through these stories are instead enacted through mutual exchanges fostered through sincerity, trust, and respect.[36] The telling of and the told stories are tactics of re-membering, performances that are not located solely in the past but continuously engaging with the future.[37] Stories as dialogic performative acts disrupt ritualistic forms of normalization and incite alternative imaginaries of communities and worlds yet to come.[38] As D. Soyini Madison states, "The performative encompasses words and 'speech acts' that do more than name and describe but are causal in that they 'do things' and effect some form of change."[39] Stories as dialogic performatives enable embodiments of agency where agency might not otherwise exist.

These performance tactics become even more significant for much of the population who have been denied and criminalized through the technologies of communication, national belonging, and history. Because of this exclusion, story-telling and the told stories are not engaged with normalized and normalizing processes in the same kinds of ways as those forms of knowing that we have come to understand as knowledge. Gyanendra Pandey highlights how unarchived histories are those knowledges that have been actively disenfranchised in the archival processes of marking, collecting, using, and naming history.[40] Stories of this kind mark the unarchivable, not just the alternative histories that are not meant to be archived but those temporalities that are fleeting, collapsing, and enfolding and not easily marked by linear modes of time. These stories transform into acts that refuse to be archived, that is, marked as part of the past so long as white supremacy persists. Active unarchiving points to the struggles between colonial territorialization and deterritorialization, the terrain in which story-telling and stories of both the unarchived and the unarchivable lie.

The "black" in Black popular culture is the transforming signifier of embodied epistemologies that are simultaneously multiple and singular.[41] Stories told within the context of being Black are themselves articulations that materialize from the conditions of oppressive formations and exposure to social and actual death. To borrow from Gloria Anzaldúa and Cherríe Moraga, story-telling and stories told are radical acts of the everyday, embedded "in the flesh."[42] They combat systemic racism and erasure from white ignorance, what Charles W. Mills describes as a *militant, aggressive not to be intimidated . . . active dynamic that refuses to go quietly—not at all confined to the illiterate and uneducated but propagated at the highest levels of the land, indeed presenting itself unblushingly as knowledge.*[43] White ignorance as a socially constructed epistemology, not necessarily and exclusively tied to a white normative population, enables the continued insular delusion of racial supremacy at best and the perpetuation and allowance of social and actual death for the rest of the population at worst. The significance of memory in Black counterculture is antithetical to white erasure, supremacy, and ignorance that saturates western thought and hegemony.

Circulation is primary in the tradition of story-telling and its radical essence.[44] For communities of color, even for those members with access to social media, word-of-mouth remains of significant epistemological value.[45] Take for example how the YouTube commentary titled "C'mon Son!" from Ed Lover, former *Yo! MTV Raps* host and New York City's Hot 97 radio personality, grew in popularity. The show and the colloquial term were both promoted through a "pass it along" network of social media. Word-of-mouth also plays a crucial role in the significance of the platform and of the content—think of how insignificant Facebook has become. Social media forums are extensions of a word-of-mouth network with an understanding that these forums are reserved for public transcripts rather than hidden.[46] Even with the transformations of technology, the pass it along tradition of story-telling prevails and permeates every aspect of everyday life.

The seminal cultural studies piece *Policing the Crisis: Mugging, the State and Law and Order* accounts for the importance of informal channels of communication in shaping how normalized understandings about the world circulate.[47] The interplay between thick "on-the-ground" descriptions such as rumor, "word of mouth," and folk stories shapes ideologies of our world and often before mainstream forms of communication disseminate similar information.[48] The significance of word of mouth and rumor in colonized and enslaved communities has also been documented to be almost necessarily tied to imagined formations of liberation.[49] Segregated networks of talk often accompanied the murderous acts of savagery and terror exercised by whites to serve as alternative resistant knowledges that deterred from normative proclamations of innocence, civility, and humanity and perhaps saved many Black(ened) lives.[50] Story-telling networks have the power to simultaneously reinforce and disrupt normative forms of knowledge and their power relations.

Take another example of how, in her foundational piece for hip hop studies, Tricia Rose reminds readers that what is purportedly known about hip hop music consumers might not actually be the case based on bootleggers and the pass it along rate in urban spaces occupied predominantly by Blacks and Latinas/os.[51] Rose was told by an editor at *The Source*, once the most popular hip hop magazine for urban youth housed in New York City, that its "pass-along rate is approximately 1 purchase to every 11–15 readers . . . at least three to four times higher than the average magazine industry pass-along rate."[52] As word of mouth congealed into a material object, the act of passing around the magazine reveals communal interactions that both disrupt and invalidate normative discourses on hip hop consumerism, capitalist commodification, and urban youth of color. Black popular culture as articulations of the seemingly improbable, and even impossible in this sense, not only resists but also undermines the universal law of hegemonic, western (and whitened) discourse as omniscient. It exposes the very tenets of domination and resistance and turns on its head this hierarchical relationship of discursive knowledge, unveiling the mask of seemingly naturalized power as a working project that aims diligently to maintain hegemonic discursive formations and relations of power.[53]

When framing story-telling as such, it is easy to see the resistant power of this taken-for-granted act. In the same text referenced previously, Mills, through his own story-telling, reminds readers about how the memory of the 1921 Tulsa Race Riot remained, even though an official record of the occurrence did not exist.[54] Mills highlights how a researcher, fifty years later, persuaded Black survivors to publicly retell a story they had been circulating through their communal networks for decades.[55] The survivors were convinced to provide their testimony and their evidence—photographs of the event—only by way of anonymity because of the continued fear of threats to their livelihood.[56] This speaks to the terror of racism, the experience of blackness, and the perceptions of relentless and merciless power of white supremacy. This also speaks to how it is not just the content of the story that can be resistant, bursting with its own power, but the ways in which story-telling consciously and tactfully operates, also circulates, as a primary component of Black popular culture.

The oral tradition of story-telling remains and continues to be one of the most utilized weapons against racist domination and subjection. Perhaps the consistent and continuous utilization of story-telling is precisely why it is most often taken for granted. I have participated in the people's network all my life. My upbringing relied heavily on the spoken word as many of the female members of my family, including my mother, did not read English. I would listen to stories as a child that were informational, persuasive, and inspiring, and I heard warnings about the ways of the world and how my position as a woman who was not white was a parlous one.

These stories were often repeated, sometimes in the same manner, sometimes different, and sometimes with different details and results. These stories concerned the domestic and public spheres as they often helped to garner employment, housing, or education or to simply traverse the multiple obstacles of structural oppression. These stories told members of these urban communities of color about the geopolitical landscape that surrounded them: where to live, where to work, where to shop. They were occasionally accompanied by material objects that served as evidence of who cooked the best, who to buy from, and for what price; the objects were sometimes remnants of the past, both negative and positive. Sometimes these stories were to simply pass time, to entertain, or to combat the surrounding sounds. Even if the outside noise was silence, stories were told to fill the air with sounds serving as an example of the simplicity of social existence.

Context plays a significant role in the shift in form and in content, but the constant was the functionality of the story. These stories and the ways in which they were told always possessed a purpose, a goal. They interacted with communicative technologies of the context and of interest throughout the decades. The act of telling stories and the stories told affirmed one's own existence and agency, and within the context of blackness, these story performances are embodied popular resistances—affirmations of life continued. To borrow from bell hooks, story-telling is an act of talking back to the power structures from which racist oppression is derived.[57] I continue to listen to these stories, to listen to how they are told, and to tell my own stories.

Popular Black Performances: Storied Methods and Framework

Though stories are born from a particular context that is local, they possess the ability to travel; they are intimately construed through space and reform space in return.[58] As Katherine McKittrick reminds us, "We produce space, we produce its meanings, and we work very hard to make geography what it is," and Black Atlantic cultures have been implicated, they transform, and they are transformed within these spatial processes.[59] Rather than focusing on space itself, *Moving Blackness* looks at the function and circulation of stories as performative and popular acts of movement, even when the bodies that tell them are seemingly stationary. The function and circulation of these stories exist as simultaneously a theory, method, and mobile site of struggle that are necessarily tied to ideology, social discursive formations, articulations, resistances, and the people as a mass.[60] Hall's conception of the popular takes center stage for this project as he highlights that the collective "people" is at the core of the popular and its structural principle: "The tensions and oppositions between what belongs to the central domain of elite or dominant culture and the culture of the 'periphery.'"[61]

Within the context of the circulating function of story, blackness moves; it compels, and it responds verbally and nonverbally. It acts and maps and remaps space both cognitively and physically. *Moving Blackness* underscores how the circulation of stories produces an understanding of spaces that cannot be disentangled from embodied blackness. It emphasizes how blackness is set in motion even when the very bodies who are doing the telling and knowing cannot move because of spatial containment and surveillance. The stories serve as concrete illustrations of participatory performance in what is often termed as Black radical tradition, practices of conscious/collective/(and)resistant creativity that are necessarily antagonistic and embodied as Black.[62]

These stories, their function, and their circulation are underscored as a matrix of potential possibilities for social change. I rely heavily on a Fanonian framework of power-resistance relations of modernity and coloniality to explore how resistance arises through presenting these stories as a formative mode of Black popular culture. As such, *Moving Blackness*, in a similar vein as Fanon and his decolonization interlocutors, remains in conversation with western white theories of power and modernity to underscore the importance of speaking back to powers of truth but to also acknowledge and embody a dialectical process toward new forms of knowledge and knowledge production. Through this speaking back, *Moving Blackness* traces the historical conditions of blackness as a universal modern signifier and maps the agency that people create from these conditions through articulation, the glue that binds all of this.[63]

Articulation, as the connection of seemingly unrelated discourses, possesses the potential to both disrupt history and reconstitute it and is always and already grounded within the everyday. It both occurs in everyday life through the active participation of people in the world around them (common sense) and in the conscious praxis of those critical understandings of one's subjectivity into a social force/bloc/line that enacts change (good sense) and, in turn, alternative ways of spatial and temporal existence.[64] Popular culture is the terrain on which these struggles over hegemony take place, which can occur on a local scale but can extend to both national and global consciousnesses. It, too, moves, maps, and remaps. As a cultural studies project, popular culture is not just a site that is discovered but one that is made. It is made by the people via articulation within the context, the moment of conjuncture that marks this struggle of potentiality, and it also created by the author who both analyzes this possibility and calls it into fruition through the underscoring and mapping of articulations of popular cultural formations and their dialectical processes.[65]

This highlighting of dialectical processes that encompass resistances against existing power relations and the disciplinary regulation of the population is what constitutes cultural studies and the significance of the popular. Because these struggles over cultural hegemony are not wars to be won or lost but fleeting strategic positions that can shift power relations, the underscoring of these struggles becomes more significant because history as a discourse is always and already about dominance and supremacy. Through the intersections of blackness and the circulation of story, *Moving Blackness*, to again borrow from and extend upon the work of Pandey, archives the unarchivable. As Hall has argued, "The silent majorities *do* think; if they do not speak it may be because we have taken their speech away from them, deprived them of the means of enunciation, not because they have nothing to say."[66] Popular culture as a site where the struggle occurs will continue to exist regardless of the existence of cultural studies as a project.

What is at stake, however, are the power relations that marginalize the population to the peripheral, at best, through the work of intellectuals who help naturalize and solidify the discourses that maintain these relations.[67] Popular culture as a method forces us to commit to what is at stake through creating the history of these sites to disrupt these relations and create new paths—discursive formations—for these struggles to be identified and heard. *Moving*

Blackness as a cultural studies project articulates "the popular" in embodied experiences and action through the function and circulation of stories. My approach is greatly influenced by those in performance studies who have theorized on ethnography in ways that are inseparable from analytics of race and racism, which I hope is apparent in these pages.

I engaged in conversations that resulted in narratives and oral histories found throughout this book, which were collected over the course of ten years. Chicago and New York City residents in predominantly Black and Latina/o neighborhoods shared their stories and life experiences with me. I have known many of the storytellers since my youth and those of whom I did not know I grew to know through community-engaged work and through a practiced politics of blackness belonging. I also utilized the archives, social media, and literature to underscore how primary historical documents bear witness to and operate as local stories told, circulated, and rearticulated, traversing through time and space. The function of these stories reminds us that blackness is performed, and these performances help produce, reflectively and reflexively, understandings of the world around us; performing blackness is, indeed, knowing through doing.[68] Within the context of the circulating function of story, blackness moves. It compels, and it responds verbally and nonverbally; it acts and maps and remaps space both cognitively and physically.

This book consists of five chapters that move sporadically throughout and against chronological time to illustrate how movement and circulation can flow in multiple directions and disrupt naturalized modes of time and space. The contemporary and historical are interwoven to also illustrate that racist techniques and technologies shift in time as they reterritorialize modes of resistance, but they also echo specific geohistorical colonial practices marking the colonial new world order as the single most significant conjuncture. They grapple with the historical context of colonialism and slavery to understand how communication, power, and culture intersect with race and racism. Together, these chapters focus primarily on the relationship between modernity and blackness and set the stage for how blackness circulates as both a mode of regulation and as a mode of storied resistance. Each chapter showcases the importance of storied Black circulation and, in doing so, begins and concludes with told stories of racialization and racist identification.

Chapter 1 centers on the circulation of blackness as colonial regulation, terror, and death. It examines the role of racism within the colonial context by analyzing sociogenic logic to discuss how identificatory practices of racism have framed the modernity-coloniality relationship. In doing so, chapter 1 grapples with the hegemonizing of race and being and the limits of identity through the signifier of Latina/o/x and argues that such identity markers do the work of colonial, divisive categorization in the name of inclusion and western modernity. Chapter 1 argues instead that racist identification, as a technique of naming, regulating, and surveilling blackened people, provides the material(ized) conditions of blackness as a universal modern signifier and maps the agency that people create from these conditions—storied Black circulation.

Chapter 2 examines the reliance of circulation within colonialism and slavery and how the freedom of mobility as a structural and discursive formation becomes a process of differentiation and identification within modern nations. Through the politics of mobility, this chapter highlights how communication technology has been identified as white dominance and how it is disrupted. It highlights a variety of Black mobility performances that range from mobility rituals of everyday life to Black womanist authors and artists' engagement with mobility as contextualized Black popular culture from enslavement through the twentieth century. It examines how limitations of movement continue to shape Black subjectivities and subjection in our nation-state and interweaves popular representations of Black mobility to highlight how the circulation of stories matters. Chapter 2 introduces how the circulation of stories is intimately connected to relations of homespace and how they continue to play a major role in the struggle for Black liberation and solidarity.

Chapter 3 centers on the limits of Black socioeconomic mobility for Black liberation and approaches such stories of Black success through representations of hip-hop culture. In line with how chapter 2 concludes with Black mobility and Black womanist representation, chapter 3 explores how hip-hop artist Cardi B utilizes social media to speak her truth to and against the backdrop of success and media representation. This chapter showcases how storied performances of blackness rearticulate space and belonging through the failed promise of socioeconomic mobility. I frame these points of circulation as rearticulated identifications of becoming that combat modern practices of belonging and produce possibilities of becoming that go against normative formations of the human.

Chapter 4 utilizes critical performance ethnography to ground the core of the popular and to grapple with Black(ened) experiences and sociogenic life. I identify these points of identification as stemming from the excess of racism, which creates spatial possibilities of home that occur in any space whatsoever. These stories come from a different urban space at differing conjunctural moments rather than comparatively discussing geo-biopolitical life and provide experiences within the context of New York City prior to the Second World War, Washington D.C. during the Reagan Era, and also Chicago post-9/11. These stories span across temporalities and urban topographies to underscore the continuities of racism as a discursive formation and the resistances that have been articulated against it. These spaces are simultaneously unique and similar as they also share symbolic imageries of modern national consciousness alongside of and in contestation to the varying, disjointed, yet connected histories and popular memories of Black(ened) storied mobilities. As such, chapter 4 is presented as movement to highlight the extraordinary strategic nature of circulation, story-telling, and traveling throughout and beyond communities by the very bodies that are subjected as silent. The stories as travel do not follow chronological time to underscore how decolonial disorder can produce alternative epistemologies of time, space, and power.

Chapter 5 transitions to the staged performance and analyzes how performance pedagogy can create relations of homespace through the performed act of story-telling. This chapter explores how performance approaches to community-based engaged learning can be effective in alternative practices of knowing and disrupt western knowledges that center on methods of extraction, expansion, and accumulation. I argue that student-performers discover, empathize, and embody alternative knowledges through engaged learning and performance. Through the words and acts of the performers, I explore how performance workshops embody the ways in which we interpret the stories we read and the storied experiences provided by community engagement. Chapter 5 centers on pedagogical performances of disorder and the classroom caravan that moves the performers and the audience members into agents of change.

Chapter 6 concludes this book by revisiting how the freedom of mobility for blackened bodies is represented through circulated stories of identificatory included exclusion. It stresses the importance of blackness within political analyses of marginalized subjectivities and, in turn, the continued significance of Black storied mobilities that create relations of homespace. The political consciousness of the people is the segue through which this work returns to the framework of cultural studies and its political agenda to do the work that matters. It is in this spirit that my work will lend itself vulnerable to the perception of its story-tellers. Finally, this conclusion highlights what continues to be lost without the critical examination of the relationship between blackness and modernity.

1

Nation-Place

Spatial Blackness and Racist Identification

The idea of a *racialized modernity* allows us to interpret modernity as a historical and discursive "European"/"non-European" colonial process. It considers the way in which an established yet indeterminate geographical Christian entity coalesced as "Europe," becoming culturally, economically and politically marked *white* in relation to its designation and marking of a "non-Europe." From the sixteenth century onwards peoples (nations/tribes), identities (Christians/pagans) . . . histories (progressive/arrested), corporealities (superior/inferior) were embodied through Euro-Onto-Colonial structures and discourses as either "white/European" or "non-white/non-European."
—Barnor Hesse

I identify myself as a black woman. A black Puerto Rican woman. And for me what that means is that the boat just stopped in different places. And, you know, we have so much more in common than people realize, as people of the African Diaspora. And people often ask, when I say I'm black Puerto Rican, "Which one of your parents is black and which one is Puerto Rican?" And I'm like, "No, actually, both my parents are Puerto Rican, and *I'm all black and all Puerto Rican*." [italics emphasis added]
—María "Mariposa" Fernández

During the Korean War, Luis Santiago Morales served in the United States Marine Corps for two years. In 1951, he was stationed at Lejeune Base Camp in Jacksonville, North Carolina, for training. One evening, Luis and two other marines decided to go to the town's movie theater to begin their weekend downtime. After purchasing their tickets, the three marines went into the screening area to take their seats. As they settled in the middle of the empty theater, an usher interrupted them and said that they were not allowed to sit in that space. The usher gestured toward the balcony above the seating area and told them to move back there, saying, "Negroes can't sit here." Taken aback, Luis and his friends refuted the usher's claim; Luis then explained that they were Marines stationed at Lejeune and added, "We're Puerto Rican."

The usher stared at Luis and examined him from top to bottom. Luis's tall stature returned a downward glare at the usher's face. His caramel skin contrasted with the pale white of the usher and, though his hair was cut low, its texture would have only reinforced the usher's conclusion. With a second glare of examination veered toward the other marines, the usher repeated that they would have to move from their seats or wait for his boss. In anger, Luis and his friends left the theater. They did not see the movie. They did not see the usher's boss, and they did not get a refund.

This was not however the first time Luis was identified as "Negro". This kind of exclusion mirrored memories of Luis's arrival to New York City when the Italian residents forbade him to cross 1st Avenue—the same area that was popularly coined "Spanish Harlem." For Luis and many other Puerto Rican residents of East "Italian Harlem," the desire to enter the Thomas Jefferson Recreation Center and Pool just across 1st Avenue did not trump the racist brutality they would face if caught by their Italian neighbors. Luis recalled, "They would chase you and, if they caught you, they would beat the hell out of you." On those extremely hot and humid summer days, when young Puerto Ricans could not resist the temptation of the public pool, Luis also recalled, "We'd get the courage, and we'd run for our lives."

Luis's story of experiencing racism as a young migrant in New York City and as a marine in Jacksonville, North Carolina, marked his belonging to blackness. Even though he was as an American citizen before he arrived in New York City, his embodied subjectivity resided within the island of Puerto Rico as opposed to the island of Manhattan, and Luis understood his outsider position in the scenario with the Italians. Even with his outsider position awareness however, this theater experience was uniquely etched into his memory. With the official end of segregation in the U.S. military just three years earlier and as Puerto Ricans in the South for the first time, Luis and his friends never experienced segregation laws.[1] As Luis retold his story, his subjectivity as a marine, an American citizen, a Puerto Rican, a man, shifted to a phenomenological becoming.

For Luis Santiago Morales, the moment of the Lejeune movie theater was the moment he became Black. Becoming Black through racist identification can occur in any space, at any time, whatsoever, and racial and ethnic identity become secondary against the backdrop of racism and white supremacy. Even though Luis did not identify as Black, his racist encounters resulted from anti-Black racism. In his story and in his retelling of his story, Luis's identity as Puerto Rican and as an American no longer mattered but how he was identified shaped his consciousness of self and space. Luis re-membered in the act of storied embodiment that being an American, for him and for many, equated to inclusion through exclusion regardless of his service or his citizenship.

Luis's sense of self was challenged as the signifiers of being American was intertwined with his sacrifice as a marine especially as he risked his life for the nation that he called home. These experiential understandings of belonging to blackness is not about race, ethnicity, or misrecognition but racism and its purposeful identification that can be exercised, intentionally or unintentionally, within a given context. They exist through a politics of identification tied closely to the economic, political, and institutional production of truth and to mass consciousness, all of which are encompassed by western dominance and racism. Luis Santiago Morales's told stories and the telling of his stories demonstrate the limits of identity when confronted with acts of racism and white supremacy.

Racist Identification, Race-Making, and the Role of Blackness

Luis Santiago Morales was an elder in my family and my godfather. He shared his movie theater story on many of my returns home from the University of North Carolina at Chapel Hill. My godfather was from a rural town just a few hours from San Juan and was a teenager when he moved with his aunt and cousins to a Harlem apartment complex. Even though he was also a teenager during his training in North Carolina, his experience of racist segregation in the theater was told differently than his recollection of everyday discrimination from neighborhood Italians. My godfather would recall his experiences running from the Italians with laughter, which seemed to ease the threat of violence that was entangled in these racialized memories. Yet laughter did not accompany his Jim Crow recollection, and I had never heard this story before I left for graduate school.

As a small child, before my school years, I can recall my godfather picking me up high every time he greeted me. He would hold me in his arms with my feet dangling in the air, and I would smell a whiff of his black leather jacket. His short afro was as black and as cool as his leather, and his stature was only surpassed by his deep dimples, warm smile, and handsome dark eyes. For my godfather, his story safeguarded me from racist aggressions that I might encounter in the same ways his arms prevented me from falling but allowed me to touch the ceiling of my godparents' public housing apartment at which I often stayed. Though he understood much had changed since his time in North Carolina, he was also aware that racist identification and exclusion continued to exist, and my godfather's racist encounter shaped his understanding of space. North Carolina, and perhaps the South, would remain dangerously racist and specifically anti-Black, which, for him, included Puerto Ricans. His story would always begin with the question, "Why there?"

My godfather, like many others under the signifier of blackness, was excluded regardless of his achievements and identity, and his stories of racism are precisely the strange experiences of being a problem in a land that is identified as home.[2] Such stories exemplify the ways in which surveillance and regulation occur in the (post)modern nation-state and necessarily relate to racial subjectification and subjection. My godfather's Jim Crow experience informed him of his continued exclusion that was implemented by state laws and undergirded by the very tenets he was fighting for as a marine. He understood that his body then, and potentially mine, could be identified as belonging to blackness, and, in the wake of racist encounters, can culminate in dire results outside of the security of New York's urban enclave.

Subjugated moments of knowing how we belong, or do not, are produced by the everyday, localized practices of racism that occur and stem from colonial-modernity relations of power. As Frantz Fanon reminds us, the colonial world ensures that black(ened) children, "having grown up within a normal family, will become abnormal with the slightest contact with the white world."[3] Such structures and rituals of racism and white supremacy depend on both the racialization of blackness and the existence of blackness as a floating signifier. Sharon Holland describes blackness as this existential difference, "a measure of how all peoples in the United States construct an intimate idea of the self in relation to the nation."[4] The national construction of whiteness, against that which is identified under the umbrella of blackness, historically categorized racialized inclusion and exclusion into a Black-White binary, with each category shifting toward the empowerment of western white supremacy.[5]

This is not to say that race does not play a primary factor in the regulation, containment, social and actual death of large portions of the population. Through its discursive power rooted in the interrelationship of modernity and coloniality, race and racial formations remain a primary mode of classification, transforming with global structural relations to marginalize and empower. According to Fanon, colonialism divided the world into "the fact of belonging or not belonging to a given race, a given species."[6] Although symbols and representations of race and Black do not remain the same throughout time and space, modern society was built upon an articulation of racialized difference that is primary for the maintenance of power today.[7] As Stuart Hall argues, there is "no necessary correspondence" in the articulation of our species as biologically different, but these correspondences point to an "ensemble of relations" that derive from ideological and economic struggles for and over power.[8] Race was, indeed, constituted through what Barnor Hesse describes as ontocolonial taxonomies, embedded in the colonial administration, to define and interpret racial belonging; these were enacted through identificatory and behavioral management "with regard to citizenship, morality, juridical institutions, domestic arrangements, and relations of intimacy."[9] The exploits of capital are not "simply 'coloured' by race: they work through race" and reproduce the internal contradictions and struggles structured by race to maintain and ensure the division of the marginalized and exploited.[10]

To tell a story about race is also to tell a story about place and placement. As a primary function of conquest, and of colonization in general, race assemblages enabled colonial regimes to lay claim to territories, appropriate new territories through the transport of external enslaved populations, and circumvent already established rules of enslavement.[11] Along the intersection of race and place, colonial endeavors, conquest and enslavement created and defined modern space through racism and, in doing so, marked space as a racialized symbol that continues to frame the division and categorization of the population where the concept of Black takes center stage. Race as a discursive and hegemonic formation is articulated to not only bodies but also the cultural and territorial classifications attached to these bodies. It is a signifier, a sometimes dynamic and sometimes stagnant symbol, of productive strategies of power that is the core component of a naturalized world and population hierarchy.[12]

Race, racialized territories, and the Black-White binary are less about identity and inclusion and more about sociogenic structures of identification that maintain white sovereignty.[13] As such, I take a similar approach as Paul Gilroy toward contemporary politics of race in the United States and place racism in the forefront of my analysis to underscore that race is in fact the "complex, unstable product" of racism.[14] The question of "How does it feel to be a problem?" introduced by DuBois at the turn of the twentieth century frames my exploration of racist identification, the everyday experiences of being and becoming both Black and American, and the disciplinary and regularity modes of racism and white supremacy.[15] I extend Hall's identification as active strategies of community and solidarity building that point to "the emergence into visibility of a new subject. A subject that was always there, but emerging historically."[16] Locating Hall's identification historically to the significance of racism points to those material conditions that shape the sociogenic logic of power, which identifies blackened bodies that are necessarily included by their exclusion.[17]

This chapter explores the roots of racism and its practices of identification to illustrate how the moment of becoming Black can occur in any space, at any time whatsoever. It critically examines how, for those of us who can be identified as problems, as for Luis Santiago Morales, racial and ethnic identity become secondary within the context of racism and white supremacy. In doing so, the following takes seriously what Fanon once described as a significant yet hidden point of analysis of what would later be determined as the modernity-coloniality relationship.[18] This chapter frames blackness as a floating signifier that is circulated, regulated, and embodied and analyzes Latina/o as an identity strategy alongside blackness. These roots of racism begin with conquest and colonial enslavement.[19]

Products of Racism: Discourse, Enslavement, and the Limits of Racial Territories

According to Fanon, the story of colonialism is one premised on the division of the world into compartments.[20] Colonialism is a spatial-temporal world order that was established by the routes of western expansion and the roots of the West, which transformed the West into a modern empire. Western territorialization is what Édouard Glissant describes as a "predatory rootstock," totalitarian in nature, aimed to permanently control our existence, "taking all upon itself and killing all around it."[21] Colonial territorialization was not, as Oliver Cox describes, a desire for "home" but rooted in "the principal need of satisfied and exploitable people to develop the resources of a country."[22] Such exploitations resulted in growth for every sector of western economies, their intellectual advancement, and their accumulation of wealth produced and determined by the violent brutalities of colonization and native enslavement.[23] Willful mobile movements of exploitation, extraction, and accumulation became the core for this "moving transient, root" which determined global and local contact as one of force and terror rather than relations of exchange.[24]

For Fanon, contact and place-making were both an economic and ideological endeavor that produced and rested upon sociogeny, a biologized division of our species and the world that is naturalized and, to borrow again from Hall, continually rearticulated to maintain structural dominance.[25] Colonial conquests shaped the context in which Indigenous bodies became Black and western bodies became white and human, which coincided with manufacturing processes of economic inequality across the spatial globe. According to Sylvia Wynter, these sociogenic categories were supported by ontological and epistemological discourses that helped further western modernity through localized embodiments of civility and morality.[26] These roots and routes of conquest marked the moment in which the population and the world were geographically, historically, discursively, and ontologically divided into two species: the human (colonizer) and the nonhuman (colonized native).[27]

White sovereignty normalized disciplinary and regulatory practices of colonial violence to exert power over the life and death of the colonized population and particularly over the native body.[28] Through colonial violence, sociogenic power regulated the colonized to existentially expendable; their deaths were allowed, justified, and even desired.[29] The ritualistic violence and terror of enslavement extracted the body physically from place and also from anatomical placements of ideological difference as enslavement objectified the native body and permanently located it in a temporal primordial state as flesh.[30] Hortense Spillers highlights how under the conditions of colonial enslavement, "The female and male body become a territory of cultural and political maneuver, not at all gender-related, gender-specific."[31] The enslaved as commodified flesh verified their existence as nonhuman and also articulated a necessary inclusion of permanent exclusion within western white sovereignty.

With the colonizer as their Manichean opposition, the colonized native becomes the embodiment of absolute evil and destruction, an enemy against which unconditional force can be exercised.[32] This included exclusion existence for the colonized and enslaved native guaranteed exposure to various acts of "thingification" and death.[33] They were extracted, circulated, burned, roasted, severed, possessed, torn apart, pulled together, dispossessed, and utilized.[34] Practices of terror and violence were so embedded within colonial spaces of thingification and death that even performances of pleasure were brought on, demanded, and controlled through the very practices they seemed to disrupt.[35] The thingification of the colonized and enslaved was prescribed into law so much so that even when the law was no longer viable, the practices of terror, violence, and death continued as natural order.

Between the fifteenth and nineteenth centuries, a record of over 13 million Africans were subjected to the Atlantic slave trade in addition to the enslavement of approximately 9 million Indigenous throughout the Americas.[36] Colonized and enslaved Taínos throughout the Caribbean had "an estimated population decline of 7,475,000 from 1492 to 1500."[37] Additionally, "between 1520 and 1620, the Aztecs and the Incas, two of the major indigenous groupings, lost about 90 percent of their population."[38] Although Indigenous enslavement from Africa steadily replaced Indigenous labor and enslavement from the Americas, Indigenous slavery throughout the colonized world lasted longer than originally conceived.[39] Prior to the marked 1492 moment of settler colonialism, Portuguese enslavement of Africans in the 1440s paved the way for the post-Conquest surge and the "rise of Atlantic slave trade" with enslaved Indigenous from Africa and elsewhere as early as 1526 in territories of what is now the U.S. southeast.[40]

Early Indigenous enslavement fulfilled an economic need and made useful the deemed useless underpopulated islands lacking in gold.[41] The number of enslaved Indigenous peoples throughout the Caribbean during the early colonial period between 1493 and 1592 is noted to have been "from 250, 000 to 500,000," which does not include those taken temporarily.[42] Although laws prohibited Indigenous enslavement throughout the Americas, warfare provided a loophole for enslavement that worked simultaneously with illegal slave trades. Enslavement was also a strategy of colonial order to quash insurgency and alliances, as it was common for Indigenous war captives to be marked as slaves and extracted to neighboring islands.[43] The enslaved were also enlisted to fight for western territorial control and were divided further, as slave codes ensured enslaved Indigenous peoples from the Americas and from Africa were separated to prevent alliances from taking shape.[44]

Fabricated and exaggerated representations of warring and isolation among the colonized throughout the islands aided in enslavement and served to produce the imagery of western salvation and paternalism.[45] It also helped naturalize racialized depictions of Indigenous peoples as simultaneously docile and savage. However, the formation of "mixed" racial categories across the Spanish Empire indicated new points of identification spurred by colonial exclusion and strategies of security. In Mexico City, peoples of African descent, "9,000 African and black slaves alongside 1,000 mulattos," outnumbered the Spanish population of 8,000—the largest African population in the Americas in 1570.[46]

And, by the seventeenth century, although one aim of slavery was to increase the slave population, there was a rapid emergence of a free Black population primarily due to the "mixed" marriages between the peoples of African descent and Mexicans.[47] In the Spanish Caribbean, spaces identified as insurgent and free were inhabited by natives and migrants from throughout the Americas; these spaces were marked by legal and illegal slave trades and included runaway slaves of African descent.[48] Such spaces were in large part forged on strategies of survival and were indeed marked as blackened spaces of exclusion.[49]

Living under the terror of captivity, included-excluded communities created networks and practices that avoided discovery as they were often looked for and raided by slave hunters.[50] These kinds of intercultural alliances extended beyond the early colonial period and far surpassed newly formed delineations of national territory. In the southern west of the United States, enslaved Africans and their descendants sought liberation not to the North but to the South because it was easier for them to "walk south" than "run up north."[51] Demarcations of racial categories prescribed onto space officially aided in identifying and dividing exploited populations but were also utilized to circumvent the abolition of the slave trade. The time of enslavement throughout the Americas exceeded British efforts to abolish the transatlantic slave trade in the early 1800s.

Due to the trans-Caribbean illegal slave trade, particular islands reached their peak of enslaved populations after abolition. Puerto Rico, for example, reached its peak of an enslaved population in the 1830s and from 1815 to the

1830s imported its enslaved population from the neighboring islands.[52] By 1835, approximately half of the island's enslaved population were from Africa, and the number of enslaved individuals reached 40,000, which, by 1841, grew to 41,000.[53] This number of enslaved Africans in Puerto Rico was not far from the estimated 60 percent of the enslaved population in 1530.[54] Nevertheless, Puerto Rico's free Black population outnumbered the enslaved population and was almost forty percent of the island's overall population by the mid-nineteenth century.[55] In the southwestern territories of North America, Apache men, women, and children were captured and deported as slaves from Mexico to Cuba and neighboring islands; this practice continued throughout Spanish colonial rule and into Mexico's independence period.[56]

These processes of capture and enslavement lasted until the 1850s and were also applied to Mayas of Yucatan who were captured and enslaved as prisoners of war during the same time period and extracted from Mexico through the similar passages for Cuba.[57] It is no coincidence that these routes of the Indigenous slave trade parallel peaks of enslavement for Caribbean islands. Other tactics of enslavement ran rampant simultaneously and, in the late nineteenth century, "blackbirding," the illegal abduction, transportation, and enslavement of Melanesians and Polynesians from the Pacific Islands who were seen as similar to Africans and identified colloquially as "blackbirds," was enacted and popularized.[58] The Civil War, the end of the confederate economy, and racial ideologies in the United States helped spur the enslavement of these Indigenous Pacific Islanders, which ensured the profit of namely sugar and cotton plantations in Fiji and Queensland, Australia.[59]

Western expansion and development rested on colonization and enslavement, the accumulation of human capital, and this power relation would lay the foundation for contemporary neoliberal economies.[60] The ideological work of racialization made enslavement synonymous with Black and Black synonymous with Indigenous as the native symbol and divided them in nonarbitrary ways. This process ensures that the category of nonwhite, and therefore nonhuman, is sustained through continuous methods of appropriation and articulation for the maintenance of white sovereignty and coloniality. Unsurprisingly, both signifiers, "Black" and "Indian" were utilized to negatively categorize, represent, and identify Mexicans in the United States in the early half of the nineteenth century.[61] And although Mexican Americans gained their right to be legally white in 1848, they were subjected to Jim Crow laws in public spaces. Colonial space and identificatory placement demonstrate the fluidity of communicative race signifiers tied to the knowledge-power nexus of blackness and connected inarguably to enemies of the state and its rightful citizens by way of opposition.[62]

Returning to Fanon and Wynter, the nonwhite, nonhuman native is differentiated from whiteness and humanity through discursive sociogenic terms, dividing evil from good through space and knowledge and marking blackness as "the unbearable wrongness of being."[63] Blackness, as such, indeed functions as a universal signifier of fear and threat that exists across color lines.[64] It is a necessary and fluid marker of included exclusion that is racialized through visible bodies, topographies, embodiments, and performances. The categorical designation of white and citizenship becomes a precarious status that does not disqualify blackened bodies from contextual, behavioral, and juridical applications of (neo)colonial techniques of subjection. The discourse of national culture embedded in the rituals of our everyday lives articulates the loci of permanent belonging and nonbelonging within the nation-state.

Sociogenic codes have been produced and reproduced through the ideological work of coloniality and subsequently white supremacy. The remnants of colonial race-work are embedded in our everyday lives as taken for granted points of identification, signifying nonwhite with the specificities of local space. Indigenous Australians, for instance, are identified as the nation-state's Black population, and their included exclusion is reinforced in popular representations in similar ways as marginalized bodies in the United States.[65] A dear friend of mine who identifies as Mexican (American) shared a story about her grandmother and her cousin walking in downtown Los Angeles. Her grandmother pointed to the homeless people on the street and told her granddaughter, "See those people over there? They are Black like you." I was told that the grandmother does this because of her own indigenous features and how her granddaughter's indigenous features are more prominent. Her granddaughter's Indigenous features revealed her to be identified by her own grandmother as negatively Black.

In East Los Angeles, I, too, was identified as Black because of my perceived Indigenous features, but among my own Puerto Rican family in New York City, I was identified as light-skinned, desirable, and yet never quite dark enough.[66] In graduate school in Chapel Hill, I became Brown. I was often identified as an immigrant and asked to present my "green card" on more than one occasion on campus. I was no longer light-skinned, not Black, and not American, but my exclusion reminded me that I remained not-white and under the identificatory umbrella of blackness. The slippages of identification are contextual with material and affective results, however, such slippages do not erase included exclusion identifications defined and determined by, as Walter Rodney highlights, white power.[67]

Western sovereignty as white power determines racial/racist discourse and continues to ring true in our colonial world: "If you are not white, then you are Black" and will be treated as such through racist identificatory techniques and technologies.[68] Colonial methods of categorizing and regulating the population reterritorialize identities through racism, specifically antiblackness. Colonial reterritorialization reshapes the desire to belong: assimilation into whiteness, which does not require the erasure of a specific ethnic or racial culture. In fact, such differences are a desirable assemblage of colonial mimicry, "almost the same but not white,"[69] recognized, accepted, and bourgeois, but, most importantly, against blackness.

Racialized Territories of Ethnicity or *Being* (Afro-) Latina/o/x/e

The Puerto Rican and Cultural Studies scholar Juan Flores once described the focus on western and southwestern regions and their respective populations as the hegemony of Latino Studies.[70] Although population numbers appear to account for Flores's hegemony, the threat and desire of blackened populations and their growth possess a longer, more complex colonial conjunctural struggle than any of our current identity signifiers encompass. How population is communicated as discursive knowledge has played a more significant role in hegemonic formations to ensure white structural dominance and evade possibilities of solidarity tied directly to colonial blackness.[71] In this sense, Latina/o is not a signifier of identity but one of a sociogenic discursive project that attempts to appropriate and "hegemonize" intricate identification practices "to a reactionary political agenda and to harness to them the interests and fortunes" of white sovereignty.[72] The use of Latina/o, then, signifies a momentary colonial strategy of power that only appears to determine our being.[73]

Latina/o was not a popularized ethnic identity until the 1990s, the same moment that Black and Brown solidarities again took shape from popular Black diasporic culture in urban spaces.[74] As these solidarities are represented by such youth culture, mass media and the purposeful presence of "brownness" with celebrity sensations like Ricky Martin and Jennifer Lopez heightened the focus on Latina/o population growth as simultaneously threatening and desirable.[75] Following these mediated representations, "Latino" appeared in the 2000 census for the first time for counting purposes to be used interchangeably with its predecessor, Hispanic. The conflation of the realities of those who fit under the umbrella of Latina/o highlighted and fabricated historical commonalities and mediated representations reified the use of Latina/o as a racial *and* ethnic formation.[76] Although ethnic studies scholars were initially critical of the Latina/o adaptation, it was soon supported by academia and reinforced through scholarly discourse.[77]

The category "Hispanic," which first appeared on the census in 1970, was not implemented as a pan-ethnic identity until 1980.[78] Its development came on the cusp of localized coalition politics that aligned themselves as "Third World radical organizations"—the Black Panthers, The Young Lords, The Brown Berets, and The Young Patriots to name a few.[79] The use of "Hispanic" was part of national efforts to quash and control organization and coalition building of the more radical decolonization politics that were building off those aforementioned groups.[80] President Nixon appointed committees, such as the Cabinet Committee of Opportunities for Spanish Speaking People (CCOSSP), to tie together three populations—Cuban Americans, Mexican Americans, and Puerto Ricans—that were ideologically and geographically disconnected.[81] Articulated together under "Hispanic," the banner of Spanish-speaking, and the American dream, the CCOSSP solidified a pan-ethnic identity that would effectively depoliticize radical groups and prevent their coalition efforts.[82] State and corporation networks also helped to transform activist organizations into Hispanic ones, such as the National Council of La Raza (NCLR), established in the 1960s as a Chicano organization.[83]

The NCLR utilized reports from the Bureau of the Census to indicate a larger population count, gain access to resources, and channel those expenditures in ways similar to Black American organizations.[84] These institutionalized organizations aim for resources as opposed to collaborative alignment proved Nixon's deradicalization plan strategically successful. As the creation of a new identity category productive for the nation-state rather than against it was in motion, the certifications of births maintained colonial blackness as the primary sociogenic logic of the nation. As a rule, babies with both parents designated as white would be identified as white, but Black and its equivalent were the categories throughout the 1960s and early 1970s for those designated as nonwhite. It was not until the late 1970s that four racial categories were established—white, Black, Native American, Pacific Islander or Asian—and none reflected Hispanic or Latina/o.

While sharing her stories, Mrs. M, a Nuyorican, recalled how she was designated as white on her birth certificate in 1933, New York City, because her parents were Puerto Rican even though she, like her mother and her grandmother, is "Black." Mrs. M's first daughter also born in New York City, but in 1956, however was designated as Black on her birth certificate despite her light skin. Mrs. M furthered that she fought with the nurse to change her daughter's designation to white. She recalled that she gave that "fuckin' nurse hell," and told her, "I am white on my birth certificate, not Black, and my husband is white [Chilean], so my daughter is white." Mrs. M's daughter's racial designation was changed on her birth certificate that day to white.

Although Mexican Americans were legally designated as white, racial designation was illustrated to be more ambiguous for Puerto Ricans and other Spanish-speaking and Black diasporic peoples because these designations greatly depended on the local administration and individual administrators. As Mrs. M's birth stories show, Puerto Ricans and the like were randomly identified beyond corporeal understandings of race categories, falling into both racial categories of white and Black, regardless of phenotype and parental designation. Birth certification ambiguity could have extended to Mexican

Americans, especially given that institutional public records aimed to secure citizen rights for only white Americans since Jim Crow.[85] Official national racial and ethnic categories like birth certification and population recording (census) beyond the Black-White binary worked to divide the population and secure the imagery of whiteness and actuality of white supremacy. Rather than move us toward equity and national inclusion, these strategies of racial and ethnic categorization bolstered division and marginalization in the name of inclusion and representation.

Latina/o, derived from local politics of coalition building, was always strategic and "situationally specific," never meant to be an ethnic identity of its own.[86] However, similar to Hispanic, Latina/o celebrates exceptional heterogeneity that can span across the borders of nationality, color, and culture.[87] Still, Latina/o signifies a limited color spectrum of a variety of "Brown to off-white (Hispanic White)," and the so-called Latin Explosion, in turn, has served multiple white sovereign agendas rooted in capital and sociogeny.[88] These include ethnic marketing and consumer targets, crises surrounding national security and immigration control, and, most significantly, as Flores highlights, the visible "ascendency of a non-black minority."[89] Once I told a prominent African American historian from a top-tier Ivy League university about my work on Latinas/os as part of the Black Diaspora and, when I told her of my own Black Puerto Rican heritage, she responded, "That's funny. I've never seen a Black Puerto Rican."

The turn toward Afro-Latina/o marked those experiences erased from racial and ethnic brownness and signifies those who are visibly of or proclaim African descent.[90] However, it also does little to disrupt the racial and ethnic assemblages that serve to reinforce white sovereignty and operates as if those who identify as Latina/o are not also Black. Hegemonized Afro-Latina/o is another identity with collective histories and cultural practices that ignores the historical complexities of transcultural colonial resistance to racial territorialization. Latinx and Latine operate as similar sociogenic strategies and, disarticulated from its politics, are easily anglicized and maintain anti-Black/ness assimilationist sentiment. We are reminded again of Walter Rodney's call: white power only legitimizes who is Black and who is not, but it does not determine its being.[91]

Toward Colonial Blackness: A Consciousness of Included Exclusion

To argue that those of us who are recognized as Latina/o are also recognized as Black, and recognize ourselves as Black, is not new. In the late 1800s in Puerto Rico, then a Spanish colony, Arturo Alfonso Schomburg was inspired to pursue his quest of archiving Black history because of an encounter with his elementary teacher who told him, "The Negro has no history."[92] Schomburg identified himself as both Black and Puerto Rican and was heavily involved in transnational liberation for both Puerto Rico and Cuba as well as Black liberation in the United States. Likewise, in the 1920s, the Puerto Rican journalist and activist Jesús Colón once described how he was hired as a Spanish translator for silent films, but when he arrived at the Times Square office, he was refused the position because he was Black.[93] The island of Puerto Rico itself has been regulated to blackness through (neo)colonialism and the intersections of colonial discourse, regulation, ideology, and everyday practice.

Although citizenship has highlighted Puerto Ricans as an exception, the island's neocolonial commonwealth status, Puerto Ricans' depicted culture of poverty, and their supposed inability to assimilate to American culture (the former is the reason and the result of this inability to achieve American success) have depicted us as more of a problem.[94] This representation of threat dates back from early colonization and enslavement as Puerto Rico was recorded to be the first island in the Americas where an African insurrection occurred in 1514.[95] Puerto Ricans in the United States date back to the early 1800s, almost one hundred years before the establishment of Ellis Island, and there are currently more Puerto Ricans born on the U.S. mainland than on the island. After the United States took possession of the already independent island from Spain in 1898, Puerto Rican as an intranational identity made clear the island's conflicted relationship with the United States. The antagonistic relationship of citizenship, granted in 1917, can be interpreted as unsolicited at best, and the island's continued commonwealth status, as opposed to statehood, depended greatly on Puerto Ricans as "racially inferior" like that of Black citizens in the United States.[96] Puerto Rico is a tangible juridical and geopolitical example of racial exclusion, included solely as exploitable and expendable through legacies of racial inferiority, white supremacy, and colonialism and slavery.

The depiction of racial inferiority coincided with mass representations of Mexican-origin people as biologically inferior that identified Mexicans, and citizenship-bearing Puerto Ricans, as detrimental to the perceived "melting pot" of the nation-state.[97] Racial inferiority was also reinforced and replaced by culture with anthropological studies just as Puerto Rican migration peaked in urban spaces alongside population increases among marginalized groups. The American anthropologist Oscar Lewis's famed 1966 report, *La Vida: A Puerto Rican Family in the Culture of Poverty—San Juan and New York*, subsequent to, and likened to, the 1965 Moynihan report on the Black family, helped locate and naturalize Puerto Ricans within a culture of pathology.[98] Lewis's report centered on one family and their extended family members and highlighted men and women alike as sexually promiscuous with women involved in prostitution; the report culminated as a representation of transgenerational destructive values and behaviors within Puerto Rican families that crossed class and spatial boundaries.[99] For Lewis, these behaviors were less about the environment and indicative of a culture prevalent in (neo)colonial spaces.

The Moynihan report on the Black family and Lewis's report on the Puerto Rican family fell on the heels of two studies on the Mexican family: *Five Families: Mexican Case Studies in the Culture of Poverty* (1959) and *The Children of Sánchez: Autobiography of a Mexican Family* (1961), which came with heavy protests from Mexican communities.[100] One article asked, "What then can we expect from the appearance of *La Vida*? Here we find, in comparison with the *Children of Sánchez*, weaker men, more immoral women, more irresponsible fathers, and mothers all too often grossly indifferent to their children."[101] Lewis's studies added Puerto Ricans to the list of national problems of biological inferiority that transgressed class and space (as it is both urban and rural). The national crises—embodied simultaneously as the same and different in Puerto Ricans, Mexicans, and Black Americans—enforced the citizen par excellence as predicated on white and whiteness. For the (not so) new national problem, the lack of assimilability was always already established.

The longer Latin Americans live in the United States, the more likely they identify as Latina/o/x or Hispanic and, hence, not Black.[102] Similarly, other Black immigrants learn that Black equates to a negative racial category in the United States and, in turn, differentiate themselves and their children from Black Americans.[103] Opposition to Black equates to the ideological investment in hating blackness and persists as a fabricated option that supposedly pushes bodies closer to whiteness and the American dream. These mystifications reposition racial and ethnic assemblages into their original colonial order. To choose blackness is to understand that, even for those identifiable as not quite white and not Black, we remain not white. It will serve us well to remember that cultural identity, formations of Black and (or versus) Latina/o, arises from practices of colonial included exclusion; they are as much performed as they are identifiable.

In an email with the subject heading "Parece Mentira," a conference attendee addressed Flores's right to discuss W.E.B Du Bois's *The Souls of Black Folk*:

"Professor" Flores,

> I was just wondering if you are the very same individual that will speaking at the conference referenced below. I am asking this question because it seems very odd that white European, descended Puerto Rican would have the audacity to speak to the condition of "the Soul of Black Folk" anywhere at anytime. I would imagine you would be better and more authentically qualified to address the soul of Euro-Puerto Ricans.[104]

Flores printed and kept this email in his files in addition to his student's response to this email, who indicated that Flores identified as Black and Puerto Rican.

Flores's work as well as his experience highlight how blackness is more than the signifying bodies by which it has come to be determined. His experience also demonstrates how these same race assemblages, the colonial race work, continue to operate and divide even among those identified within the same (racial, ethnic, and national) categories of marginalization, exploitation, and death. In unison, they demonstrate how race assemblages do not and cannot contain the excess flows of disruption.

(Neo)colonial racial identification is precisely the signifying process of western rootedness and reterritorialization; it serves to maintain white sovereignty through the continued division of the population and the proliferation of such divisions. Mappings of racist identification are not founded or discovered but take form in the telling and retelling of stories and were/are necessary in anticolonial(ity) struggles as apparent in my retelling of my godfather's and Flores's experiences.[105] These stories help form, symbolize, and shape the often-negotiated rituals of those who live in the margins. They demonstrate the historical and interpersonal practices of engagement and resistance that stem from this past and are always embedded in the politics of representation.[106] I return to the Jim Crow south with two told stories that point to the excesses of race assemblages, the experiences, ambiguities, and exchanges that cannot be completely captured by sociogenic codes.

In her autobiography, Assata Shakur describes how her mother resisted segregation laws to allow young Shakur to enter an amusement park forbidden to Black children in Carolina Beach, North Carolina, approximately sixty miles from my godfather's experience at Lejeune.[107] Shakur recalls:

> My mother went over to the ticket booth and began talking. I didn't understand a word she was saying. The lady at the ticket booth kept telling my mother that she couldn't sell her any tickets. My mother kept talking very fast and waving her hands. The manager came over and told my mother she couldn't buy any tickets and that we couldn't go into the park. My mother kept talking and waving her hands and soon she was screaming this foreign language. I didn't know if she was speaking a play language or a real one. Several other men came over. They talked to my mother. She continued. After the men went to one side and had a conference, they returned and told the ticket seller to give my mother the tickets ... When we got home my mother explained that she had been speaking Spanish and had told the managers that she was from a Spanish country and that if he didn't let us in, she would call the embassy and the United Nations and I don't know who else.[108]

In the *Chicago Defender*, Langston Hughes captures the limits of sociogenic identifications illustrated through his character Jesse B. Semple—called Simple.[109] In "Simple Says Puerto Ricans Must Have Poro in Their Blood," written on November 21, 1953, Simple asks, "How come some of these colored Puerto Ricans have got such good hair?"[110] Hughes explains that Puerto Ricans used to belong to Spain and that the United States won it from the Spanish American War. Simple replies, "Which I know our white folks regret . . . because when they won they lost . . . Because all them colored Puerto Ricans is coming up here flooding the USA with colored blood and they got enough Negroes in the USA already—with us—so I know they don't want anymore."[111] Hughes replies, "Puerto Ricans are not caste as Negroes," and Simple responds, "The only reason they is not is because they speak some other lingo. Some of them as dark as me."[112] Because Puerto Ricans can go everywhere in New York, Simple is convinced: "Americans do not Jim Crow Puerto Ricans."[113] Hughes refutes his claims, but Simple insists that if he speaks Spanish, he will "run down to Baltimore or Washington and register at the biggest hotels." Hughes points out that Simple has confused Spanish with French, and Simple responds, "Them white folks would not know the difference."[114]

Mapping Black Becoming and Relations of Homespace

Spillers underscores a version of Black cultural practices from her childhood that could not be defined and limited by categorizations of identity, particularly sex and gender.[115] These community practices were a "democratic form" of human relations in which "people did whatever work was to be done, whether it was men's work or women's work, if it needed to be done people simply did it; to raise children, to maintain communities."[116] These bonds of love and community are the resistant acts that bell hooks describes in her notion of homeplace, a site of "renewal and self-discovery where we can heal our wounds and become whole."[117] Although such alternative practices of community are obscured through intersections of the promises of western mobility, white sovereignty, and sociogeny, they continue to exist. They are not in unknown futures but possess the practical possibilities of the unknown. These practices are hidden in the practical activities of everyday life and born out of the very necessity to live and love under (neo)colonial conditions of the included exclusion of blackness.

Extending Glissant's relation and errantry, relations of homespace are the points of affective connectedness built upon our included excluded position that is not tied to any place but to the conscious, organized investment of included exclusion that can occur at any moment in any space.[118] Rather than a site, homespace centers on the creative acts of becoming that are derived from continuous recreations of relations, progressing, retracting, circulating, and reassembling to become anew.[119] More than practices of survival, they disrupt the very territorial roots of the western world, the sociogenic codes of included exclusion, and our modernity-coloniality relationship. Relations of homespace are not a given; they must be made through the relational activities of love that encompass resistance and connectedness rooted in the excess of sociogenic violence, colonial marginalization, and white supremacy.

Relations of homespace are circulated by imag(in)ed tales and are never completely captured because "the experiences of exiles are incommunicable."[120] Storied circulations of homespace provide an awareness that the popular can arise in any space not determined by naturalized sociogenic roots but, as Glissant describes, "also in Relation. Because the thought of errantry is also the thought of what is relative, the thing relayed as well as the thing related. The thought of errantry is a poetics, which always infers that at the same moment it is told. The tale of errantry is the tale of Relation."[121] Definitively, these are relations of homespace "in which each and every identity is extended through a relationship with the Other" that is dialectical, nonlinear, noncontinuous, and multidirectional.[122]

The creation of these nontraditional traditional practices and their storied circulation of relation embody decolonial becomings that are alternative to western modernity and coloniality.[123] Those who fall under the umbrella of the included exclusion of blackness are always and already at the point of becoming, "because only a minority is capable of serving as the active medium of becoming."[124] "Deterritorialized" included excluded identifications of blackness, no longer "definable" in relation to sociogenic racial assemblages, in relations of homespace are the context that make becoming possible.[125] Fanon highlights such relational sensibilities of blackness, derived from the working and underclass within the modernity-coloniality relationship, that is grounded in the present with an eye toward the future.[126] Fanon marks this collective affect as the beginning of disalienation and revolution.[127]

Identifications of the included exclusion of blackness counter assimilation and the abject thinking that accompanies it; however, it is not the end but a mapping toward new futures. These identifications are more complex than the hegemonizing appropriations of identification that are commodified, desired, and also detested throughout western culture. Rather, circulated storied relations of homespace turn to the present taken-for-granted collective activities of loving blackness, those that my godfather's story-telling alludes to and those told truths that are circulated and embodied by many each and every day. Hall argues, "Nothing can become popular which does not negotiate the experiences, the codes, etc. of the popular masses."[128] Between the "immediate practical consciousness" of people and the possibilities of what they can become are the concrete struggles in which relation of homespace form.[129]

Resistance does not just happen, and it is not guaranteed.[130] The popular comes into fruition through the struggles of the people, and, for Hall, this struggle is never just a class-based formation but one that is, aligned with his own subjectivity, Black and diasporic.[131] It is a position of marginalization already framed by colonialism and racism, and the purpose of a cultural studies project is to shed light on these spaces and activities and map them into existence to simultaneously further these spaces of possibilities.[132] Cultural studies pushes forth a philosophy of praxis always and already aligned with the heterogeneity and transversality of culture.[133] It theorizes upon the complex cultural formations that are in opposition to universal teleological notions of humanity and are silenced, masked, and lost through and in the "fantasy" of the West, its history, and its sovereignty.[134]

This alignment of cultural studies with the popular echoes de(neo)colonization struggles where the purpose is to "dig deep" into the collective memories of our people and uncover the "subterranean convergence."[135] Following the map of cultural studies, Dwight Conquergood locates the possibility of performance studies with the people and their stories, disrupting and contesting the official mapping of the historical terrain of knowledge.[136] Conquergood draws attention to how racialized epistemologies born from colonization and enslavement have produced and practiced those rituals of knowing for survival, solidarity, and liberation.[137]

Engaged practices of knowing, the theory-practice nexus, enable us to tap into the practical consciousness that arises from the struggles of the people. Cultural studies demands open-ended theorization that necessarily depends on these external influences of the people.[138] The role of praxis and the intellectual, "the how" of cultural studies, is the radical turn in performance studies that engages with and responds to the popular call of the people.[139] The significance, then, of performance praxis is the critical engagement of "listening, absorbing, and standing in solidarity with the performance protests of the people."[140]

Conclusion

On July 12, 2019, my godfather died at the age of eighty-three. His funeral service was packed with family, friends, and neighbors. Young men who hustled in front of the building where my godfather lived that grew up knowing him and my family also came to the service to pay their respects. There were so many of us that much of the crowd eventually made its way outside of the funeral home onto 1st Avenue, the same avenue my godfather could not cross in fear of Italians when he was a teenager. The funeral home was located less than two blocks from the Thomas Jefferson Pool and I wondered if my godfather realized that the segregation laws that prevented him from sitting in that Jacksonville, North Carolina, theater would also prevent him from swimming in the public pool. This never occurred to me during any of the times he told me his stories.

On this hot summer day, we purchased cups with ice from the bodega across the street and passed them around with drinks of choice for whoever wanted one. We stood on 1st Avenue, all Puerto Rican, all Black, and nobody running. We told stories, some of my godfather and some not. Two Marines in uniform arrived to provide my godfather with service honors, one of the few requests that he had for his funeral. As we gathered for the service, there was one man, Hillary, about ten years younger than my godfather, who also shared his story. We never met Hillary, not even my godmother knew who he was, and he had not seen Luis for decades but Hillary remembered my godfather. Word of my godfather's death traveled to him even through the decades of absence. Hillary spoke of meeting Luis when my godfather arrived in Harlem from Puerto Rico and lived with his aunt and cousins. Hillary was seven at the time. They lived in a tenement, where in the summers the building was overwhelmingly hot and, in the winters, it was freezing cold. The neighbors were forced to leave their doors open because of the oppressive environment but, from this, everyone knew everyone.

Hillary's older brother, my godfather, and my godfather's cousin grew very close as their doors faced each other, and Hillary looked up to all of them. The families on the floor not only shared heat, coming from their opened ovens, and the cold fresh air blowing from their opened windows in the summertime, but they also shared food, friendship, life, and love. Hillary remembered this and even longed for it as he aged and witnessed the demographics shift and, in turn, community change in Harlem, where he still lived at the time of my godfather's death. I have never known of Hillary but, because Hillary told his memory of my godfather and their relations of homespace, I have now told his story. It is in this spirit that the next chapter will center on the significance of mobility and the affective storied relations that arise from its regulation.

2

The Limits of Mobility

Why Does the Circulation
of Stories Matter Anyway?

Situated between the matter which influences it and that on which it has influence, my body is a center of action, the place where the impressions received choose intelligently the path they will follow to transform themselves into movements accomplished. Thus it, indeed, represents the actual state of my becoming, that part of my duration which is in process of growth.
—Henri Bergson

In the case of the colonial and the postcolonial, what we are dealing with is not two successive regimes but the simultaneous presence of a *regime and its after-effects*. Colonialism persists despite the cluster of illusory appearances to the contrary.
—Stuart Hall

In Brooklyn, New York, at the Junction where Flatbush, Midwood, and Nostrand Avenues intersect, depending on which direction one would stand, a loud call for Utica Avenue can be heard projecting from the opened door of a van: "U-TEE-Kah- U-TEE-Kah- U-TEE-Kah!", the Black Caribbean young man would proclaim to inform those waiting on the sidewalk of his van's destination. In a balancing act, his body remains half visible, his feet planted inside of the van, while the top of his body hangs out of the doorway. With only one hand gripping the door as his other hand waves passengers into open seats, he would hurry his travelers, "Come on, come on, come on." His statement was spoken so rapidly that it sounded like one word and, as passengers entered the van, they would squeeze into the seats. Much like other public transport, travelers might be packed tightly or begin their ride in comfort as the driver pulls off.

While in transit, the driver would pull over at what would seem like random stops to collect more passengers, and occasionally, those who anticipated the stop by the turn of the steering wheel and the slower pace of the vehicle would respond in protest. Outcries of "No, no, no, no" were coupled with gesturing hand waves. There was simply no more room. Begrudgingly, the driver would continue on his route, taking heed of his customers' pleas without stopping for additional passengers. Before their destinations were reached, commuters would notify the driver or doorman, and statements of "Here, here, or right here" replaced the ding of a bell that is readily available on a public bus. If there were police nearby, or if he and his partner felt that it was unsafe to stop, they would simply say, "Next one," or something to that effect, which was typically only a few feet away from the desired destination. The driver would then pull over, and his partner would open the door. While exiting the van, a dollar is passed from the passenger's hand into the hand of the doorman, who quickly adds the money to the van's revenue.

Beginning in the 1980s, the dollar van came into fruition, predominantly in Brooklyn and Queens, due in part to the immigration influx from the Caribbean islands, other countries across the Americas, namely Guyana, and later from Sub-Saharan Africa. This immigration surge was a direct result of the 1965 Immigration and Nationality Act and, by the millennium, over half of the city's Black population were immigrants and their children, which altered New York's urban landscape and affected local ways of daily life.[1] Experiences of success were often outweighed by experiences of racism that greatly affected employment, housing, and educational opportunities for new Black residents.[2] They were pushed into urban spaces that were isolated, underserviced, and overexposed to environmental risks, including police brutality and murder, and became part of older marginalized communities.[3] Symbolic of alternative transportation in their places of origin, the dollar van became a way by which these new immigrants, mostly men, gained employment.

The dollar van as a vehicle of and for mobility simultaneously runs both alongside and against the Metro-Transit-Authority (MTA), the official mode of public transportation for the city. Many operate illegally and have provided a privatized amenity to zones that the city did not easily service, zones that were created to uphold a racial hierarchy that helped secure American modernity at the turn of the twentieth century.[4] As a marginal mode of transportation in New York's neighboring boroughs of Manhattan, the dollar van enabled residents of blackened, isolated spaces to move freely, for less money, and with more speed and consistency. It permitted travel at a cheaper cost for community residents who were literally contained in what was coined a two-fare zone—a neighborhood that would cost commuters the equivalent of two fares for public transportation that traveled to and from Manhattan, other boroughs, and commercial zones.[5]

As a result of the economic crisis and its neoliberal responses initiated in the mid-seventies and early eighties, public transportation was scaled back even more in these communities.[6] The dollar van's timely creation additionally fulfilled the need for more recurrent public transportation services, which were already infrequent. To reclaim lost revenue, the MTA created the MetroCard in the early nineties, which consisted of a free transfer within two hours of the commuter's initial swiped ride; it also included an unlimited transit option that promised to save travelers money with more frequent use of the transit system. The MetroCard as the direct response to the successful dollar van was premised on the two-fare zone that was now a city dilemma. The MetroCard, the city solution, was represented under the slogan of "One City, One Fare," with multiple incentives to ensure the acceptance of the card.[7]

The MTA negotiated tax-free incentives for the unlimited MetroCard, which was offered through employers who in turn received tax breaks that covered most or all the cost. These reterritorialization attempts, however, did not stop the stream of vans throughout avenues that led to major intersections like the Flatbush Junction, nor did they stop travelers from riding the vans. Instead, they opened more possibilities for commuters as perspectives of space and time, the pace at which one arrives at a destination, influence choices of transit. Congruently, the city implemented laws that required van drivers to register with the Taxi and Limousine Commission, but a majority have not done so. Police officers additionally fine and confiscate illegal vans, yet many of the owners do not pay the fines or pay to retrieve their vehicles and continue to operate their mobile businesses. This has pushed the implementation of stricter laws that would enable officers to permanently confiscate and auction off the vans for city profit. In the meantime, dollar vans continue to operate, and commuters continue to ride.

Paul Gilroy argues that the motor car was, and continues to be, significant for understanding how Black Americans negotiate exclusion from citizenship through consumer culture.[8] Borrowing from Raymond Williams's account of mobile privatization, Gilroy concludes the automobile is "associated with a privatization that confiscates the possibility of collective experience, synchronized suffering, and acting in concert. In these circumstances, the automobile becomes the instrument for segregation and privatization not an aid to their overcoming."[9] I want to underscore Gilroy's specificity of circumstance to segue toward what Adrienne Brown highlights as the collective value in Black automotivity.[10] A dollar van, as Black automotivity, is not about consumer culture as a substitute for national belonging but underscores Black radical practices that are embedded within the ordinary circumstance of everyday life.

The dollar van symbolizes Black movement against sociopolitical exclusion and economic marginalization and is a communal, conscious act of multiple blackened subjectivities who collectively move in what is meant to be a privatized, isolated experience. The dollar van symbolizes how the transnational flow of people and their exclusion from employment, space, and time can transform official topographical limits of movement into localized, ritualistic flows of access and agency. It is a symbol of and for communication that traverses the intersection of space, time, and power and exposes the position of blackened subjects within sociogenic life. The daily function of dollar vans requires that Black relationships to commodities be reconfigured as their practices demonstrate a more complex alignment with traditions of Black radicalism rather than bourgeois modes of consumption. There is, in fact, something to included exclusion, and for the commuter, the dollar van symbolizes a liminal space because it blurs the lines between unofficial and official, legal and illegal, and access where there is no access.[11]

Anyone can ride the dollar van; however, it is rare to see a dollar van commuter who is not Black and local; if passengers are not local, they are introduced to the experience by resident commuters. To ride the dollar van is a continuous process of articulation, a consciousness of included exclusion that positions Black subjectivity as being of, and on, the border of national, and western, belonging. The van also becomes a way in which urban Black diasporic communities come into contact with each other as they gain access to the promises of mobility that many citizens take for granted. Its existence has been represented as a threat to the economic revenue of the city and to the citizens themselves, which echoes how blackness is perceived and defined in our national culture. The dollar van is emblematic of how radical relations of blackness move on and around the limits of the terrain of domination and subordination, the site where power struggles take place.[12]

This chapter examines how mobility symbolizes white sovereignty in ways that link whiteness to national belonging and western modernity. It examines colonization and enslavement as the geographical canvas of racial subjugation, the freedom of movement for humanity, and the limitations of movement for the colonized. This chapter underscores how the limitations of movement continue to shape blackened subjectivities and subjection in our nation-state through popular storied representations of Black mobility. Looking at the limits of movement for the once colonized blackened subject makes clear the significance of storytelling as it escapes the policing eye of surveillance and redefines travel and the risk of travel through circulation.

Made for Walking: Colonial Mobility and the Western Right of Movement

The freedom of movement is deeply embedded in the common-sense imaginary of national belonging within the United States.[13] As part of the nation's culture, its history of dominance and modernity greatly depends on its ability to represent its conquest of time and space via communication technology. The movement of information with the telegraph and the movement of bodies and economic goods and materials with railroads both tied national belonging and nation-building with a relationship between communication and transportation.[14] The narrative of divine right to conquer both time and space is also intertwined with U.S. national culture.[15] The speed of communication and movement collapses into the notion of "one nation under God," and, through the everyday ritual of the body and communicative interactions, "God's gift" of national sovereignty also echoes the inalienable right to overcome space and time through the use of technology.

The national right of movement, technology, and liberty, reserved solely for those included in the national narrative, only exists in relation to sociogenic exclusion. Rituals of enslavement, terror, murder, and violence thrust upon the colonized cannot be divorced from the conquering of space, movement, and temporality as a primary representation of white sovereignty. The infrastructures of ports, forts, and cities came to signify and secure the very relations of colonial power and domination, and, through circulation, superimposed these geographies as white. Once built, these structures functioned as emblems of western sovereignty and an apparatus of colonial domination and violence as in the case of castle-dungeons, where the enslaved were kept before the move toward the transatlantic crossing.

In her travel account, Sandra Richards describes the contemporary structural presence of the castle-dungeon in Elmina, Ghana as "startling in its offensive whiteness."[16] Richards furthers that, with support from UNESCO, the castle is "the largest of all structures built on Ghana's coast" and "sparkles with its fresh white paint."[17] Similarly, in his travel accounts, Richard Wright describes Elmina, "Some of the walls are thirty feet thick. Towers rise two hundred feet in the air. What spacious dreams! What august faith! How elegantly laid out the castle is! What bold plunging lines! What, yes, taste . . ."[18] The castle-dungeons and walls of colonial empire, indeed, continue to signify western power, historical security, and, most importantly enclosure, but were always intended for the traversal of everyday life, centering on the control of movement and people—even as tourist sites. In their remaining grandiosity, these infrastructures of colonial sovereignty, like the Elmina castle-dungeon, reveal how space was constructed to model and enforce racial supremacy and the colonizers' diligent efforts to secure it.

Although space itself signified western sovereignty, the control of movement required hegemonizing colonial rule and sociogenic hierarchical relations. The construction of thick, high walls in port cities and within castles along the coast directly related to security and enslavement as accounts of escapes and attempted escapes justified the replacement of previous more vulnerable structures.[19] These structures were strategic investments that ensured security and demanded continued safeguarding against social and natural insurgencies; they proved to be an immense economic and time-consuming endeavor and were equally laborious to justify.[20] As city walls were no longer economically viable, and circulation could not be controlled by the opening and closing of the empire's doors, surveillance and regulation became primary in the organization of circulation.[21] The regulation of circulation demonstrated and designated power through categorizing, controlling, and "maximizing and diminishing" good and bad circulation, which included the movement of people.[22]

The legitimization of conquest and governance over space, circulation, and, thus, colonial and enslaved subjects shaped the organization of western urban space.[23] These infrastructures of modernity communicated symbolically and complexly "the point of no return" for subjugated parts of the population and "the world's end" for others who imagined safety within the fortified chimera of their empire's security. For the colony, temporal spaces were constructed to represent western superiority, and the extraction of its resources ensured the material development of western modernity.[24] Walter Rodney highlights how not one form of communication and mobility infrastructure developed during the colonial period was for the needs of the colonized.[25] Roads and railways all "led down to the sea" for the movement of territorial goods that were circulated in one-way flows.[26]

Through the mechanisms of violence and terror, spatial, structural, and social conditions and practices were created to support capitalist claims of liberty, which established the freedom of movement in the form of extraction and accumulation for wealth (upward mobility and western empires) through territorialization. Space in this sense plays a primary role in coloniality and the terror formation that simultaneously produces colonial subjectivities. Colonial occupation compartmentalizes space and categorizes people, which centers on the implementing of new "boundaries and internal frontiers epitomized by barracks and police stations;"[27] it is a space that is "regulated by the language of pure force, immediate presence and frequent and direct action."[28] The colonial space is what Michael Taussig refers to as a "space of death" brought on and maintained through regimes of terror and violence.[29] Colonial death spaces, such as the port cities and castles (where the enslaved were kept), the ship, and the plantation, became where the colonized native often blurred the line of who possessed the absolute right to live and who was regulated to the state of death.[30]

As the last chapter highlighted, enslavement was a necessary factor in the economic, political, and ideological creations of western modernity and its necessary opposition on which it depends: coloniality. The portability of people for enslavement was integral to controlled and surveilled extraction as it mirrored colonial spatial infrastructures. Death marches toward the coast by captured Indigenous from the Americas and Africa served to represent white supremacy, modernity, and terror, an imagery of compulsory movement that would later be mirrored by displaced Indigenous Americans as well as enslaved and free Black Americans who were forced to walk the trail of tears.[31] Death marches were often conducted in stages "with sales to various intermediaries" and the speed of these marches also depended on "whether the enslaved were also made to carry goods to the coast."[32] The dual function of the virtual and material within ritualized acts of one-way circulation was performed and embodied through the colonial relationship. Death marches symbolized white supremacy through the subjection and expendability of the colonized and were integral to the colonial machine of production for economic and political capital through the extraction of goods.

Paths of death were not absent of smell as remains of the dead were simply dumped into the marshlands to rot and added to the communicative landscape of conquest.[33] Although the death rates during the slow march to the sea varied and were primarily based on modes of capture, distance, diet, and environmental disease, the marriage between death and extraction helped establish the sociogenic foundation of white sovereignty.[34] The ritual of enforced portability and extraction superimposed western dominance and served to thingify Indigenous bodies who were reduced to quantifiable resources of and for transferrable goods. Slow movement as a form of control articulated the colonial population distinction and vacillated to and from limited to no movement. Enslaved Africans were contained in dungeons by the numbers to await their fates in detention ports, and as insurrections occurred, colonial strategies of controlled movement increased to limit the success of struggles for freedom.

As a form of security, shackles limited movement: "'short irons' binding captives' wrists ensured that slaves could not raise a hand to strike their tormentors nor seize a weapon, open a door, or scale a wall without great difficulty; 'long irons' around the ankles likewise held captives fast."[35] Iron shackles around the limbs of the enslaved physically disabled the captives from escape.[36] They also served as visual signs to differentiate the slaves who were charged to maintain the castle from those who were marked by the iron chains for export.[37] These stages of colonial displacement and extraction, in one account, attributed to approximately half of the deaths of the enslaved, which are not counted in the death toll of the Middle Passage, a death rate that has far surpassed both the Black Death and the Great Famine of Ireland.[38] When coupled with the genocide of Indigenous populations in the Americas, killing was an inevitable component of western circulation (extraction, expansion, accumulation) and aided in the thingification of the colonized and the savagery of their colonizers.[39]

Shipping was one of the flourishing industries for western capitalism whose marked success solidified the ship as the symbol of western communication, sovereignty, and sociogeny.[40] Parallel to the slow-moving death march, slave ships, prior to departures to sea, "coasted" often for "months along the African shore acquiring their cargoes, and many slaves bought early in this process died during the period after purchase by slavers but before the ship's departure."[41] The "packing" within the ship added to the controlled movement of enslaved peoples as their bodies were counted, measurable resources by the shippers and their ledgers.[42] If the death march, detention, and the coasting period were survived, the enslaved would experience the Middle Passage itself.

By the eighteenth century, the ship as a mobile space of death was acknowledged by its captives as "the floating tombs" with the shippers as "the bearers of the tombs."[43] The ship of death was, as Stephanie Smallwood describes, the "site of a relentless accumulation of incomplete deaths, each one holding its own tragic meanings. Entrapped, Africans confronted a dual crisis: the trauma of death, and the inability to respond appropriately to death."[44] Incomplete deaths illustrate how the temporalities of life and death for the colonized and enslaved were disrupted and reconfigured through the ritualized terror of western circulation. Because movement on the ship was controlled by the moving vessel, the enslaved were unchained once the ship sailed far enough to ensure no escape.

The ship in transit became a multilayered, multifunctional discursive signifier, the means and modes of transportation with containment, death, subjection, torture, and capital. The portability of people as a routine strategy for western empires distinguished its citizen population from its colonial subjects, a juridical order that continued well after the abolition of the slave trade.[45] The ship in transit, like the death spaces before it, also marked the excesses of power: new productive methods of communication that shaped interactions among the enslaved and were foundational in tactics of survival and strategies of resistance. The enslaved forged sociality even under the most constrained conditions, and ship captains affirmed enslaved sociality through accounts of nonverbal gestures of sharing food, nurturing the ill-stricken, and comforting those who expressed need;[46] these sociality formations also fostered insurrections.[47]

Plantation life also reflected the violent rituals of colonial circulation that were often implemented and strengthened to quash solidarities and resistance, a continuous mounting fear of western empires and their colonial extensions. The seemingly isolated plantation, much like the larger-scale colony, was greatly dependent on colonial circulation and its regulation.[48] Wealth accumulated by colonial empires was inextricably linked to the production in and exportation from colonies and their plantations as well as colonial consumption of produced goods, and the plantations depended on such goods imported to the colonies.[49] The structure of the plantation and its ability to thrive also depended on strategic limitations of movement; their fortifying boundaries and methods of surveillance on enslavement mobility were bound to the disciplinary rituals of plantation life. Enslaved movement was limited to repetitions of forced labor and diversions of pleasure naturalized as banalities of everyday life to ensure the daily cycles of production under the stringent acts of discipline and terror.[50]

Surveillance, inextricably linked to colonial circulation, regulated sociogenic codes on the plantation and throughout the colonized territory with the keen, seeing-eye as white and the surveilled as the enslaved and the colonized—not white.[51] Even the double articulation of surveillance through colonial mimicry was performed officially for white sovereignty.[52] Each plantation was "defined by boundaries whose crossing was strictly forbidden, impossible to leave without written permission or unless authorized by some ritual exception."[53] The written permission and the authorization of ritual exception accounted for the comings and goings of the enslaved and became a symbolic shackle as it grounded the enslaved to the plantation and, in turn, articulated these bodies to the institution of slavery. Documents of surveillance extended to "the publication and circulation of newspaper advertisements for runaway slaves and truant servants," which applied to those who went missing from plantations and other private and public spaces.[54]

These documents of surveillance were essential as prerequisites for controlling the movement of people in general and tracking blackness specifically.[55] Death spaces ritualized methods of colonial mobility such as, but not limited to, controlled movement, repetition, and surveillance. They served as quintessential models of western sovereignty and naturalized the discursive differentiation between the colonizer, the modern whitened subject, and the colonized, enslaved blackened other. If infrastructural change was central to metropolitan privileges of ease, for example, the mapping of highways, tunnels, and expressways, the exclusion of blackened people layered with the protection of white as literal property and value was inextricable to the environmental improvement of national space.[56] Black popular constructions of mobility, rooted in and routed from the ever-present communicative techniques of colonialism and enslavement, as well as the means and modes of communication technology, circulate to tell stories of movement possibilities, limitations, and included exclusion.

Moving toward the Future with Storied Black Mobility

Black popular constructions of mobility are a glimpse of how Black life centered movement technology and its politics of freedom under regulations of circulation, surveillance, and erasure. As their storied circulation confronts white sovereignty through presence, their told stories emphasize mobility struggles and conformities within the sociogenic positionality of being and feeling Black.[57] As Black and popular, these stories begin to showcase the circulation of stories that are rooted in the historical network of those "who do not travel," but whose knowledges are conveyed through affective relations of homespace.[58] Black consciousness of communicative movement often interrogates western freedom, its modern subject, and the sociogenic codes that stem from it and, in these acts of conscious interrogation, creates the possible terrain where new subjectivities may arise and real movement can take place.

Struggles of Black mobility, homespace, and their storied circulations accompanied conquest and enslavement from the start. In fact the account of enslaved Africans and other Indigenous in the contemporary U.S. southeast in 1526, "escaped from a Spanish settlement" and then fought against their recapture.[59] Official records of accounting for the colonized and the enslaved were understood to be skewed as it was known that escaped Africans and other Indigenous would flee to the mountains, neighboring islands, and other parts of the Americas away from the purview of western rule.[60] Letters from colonial governors described how they were unsuccessful in finding those who fled and how the creation of palenques, maroon societies of Africans, "Amerindians,"[61] "Mulattos, and Mixed Bloods,"[62] were formed.[63] They also described how such palenques organized strategies of attack and how colonizers were killed with unsuccessful retaliation.[64]

The blackened body as the mobile vehicle for liberation and resistance was also conveyed in nonconfrontational ways. In his narrative of enslavement, Frederick Douglass shares that as an infant he was separated from his mother, Harriet Bailey, who was forced to work as a fieldhand, twelve miles away from him.[65] Even though she would suffer a whipping for her absence from the field at sunrise and she did not have permission, Bailey would travel during the night "the whole distance on foot after the performance of her day's work."[66] Douglass never recalled seeing his mother in the day; Bailey would come to see him at night, hold him, lie with him until her death ended these visits.[67] Much like the promises of liberation that are exercised through travel on-foot, even if momentary, the train as a public mobile forum also encompassed mobile liminality for Black subjects, who oscillate between possibilities of the freedom of movement and its limits.

In 1884, 20-year-old Ida B. Wells filed a discrimination lawsuit against Chesapeake, Ohio, and Southwestern Railroad for an incident that occurred the year before when Wells was assaulted by the train conductor with the help of two white passengers.[68] With a first-class ticket, Wells was on her way from Memphis, Tennessee, to teach in Woodstock, and she refused to move to the other train car when asked to do so.[69] Of the assault, Wells highlights,

"Everybody in the car seemed to sympathize with the conductor and were against me."[70] She recalled that she "resisted all the time, and never consented to go," even as her "dress was torn in the struggle."[71] Although her case was overturned by the Tennessee Supreme Court, which sided with the railroad company, Wells initially won her suit.[72] Her in-transit experience and lawsuit would strengthen her positionality and shape her future agency both as Black and as a "lady."[73]

In *Their Eyes Were Watching God*, Zora Neal Hurston captures the symbolic value of mobile liminality through the train's liveliness paralleled with Janie Crawford's journey of Black womanist subjectivity.[74] Hurston writes, "The train beat on itself` and danced on the shiny steel rails mile after mile . . . the train shuffled on to Jacksonville, and to a whole lot things [Janie] wanted to see and to know."[75] Janie is in movement as she becomes her own subject, and the train becomes a vessel that provides her with the liberated act of seeing the vast terrain of a larger world and a future yet to come. Juxtaposed with Janie's hopeful move toward freedom, Hurston tells another story in which the train symbolizes limited hope and death through Janie's reflection of Annie Tyler and Who Flung.[76]

Janie recalls how the town saw Annie Tyler off and onto the train after Who Flung persuaded her to sell her house and move with him to Tampa, only to see Annie return two weeks later.[77] Who Flung left with all of Annie's money after two days and, as Annie was forced to beg on the streets, a hometown neighbor who saw her paid for her return ticket after she told him that she was robbed on the train.[78] Shortly later, Annie's daughter "took her away to die in peace," and Janie concluded that Annie "had waited all her life for something and it had killed her when it found her."[79] Finally taken away from the very space that she wanted to escape, though not of her own accord, the doubled-telling of Annie's experience becomes a metaphor for stolen freedoms to travel beyond the repetitive cycle of an entrapped life. Hurston's conflicting trope of the train embodied through Janie's telling and told stories marks the often invisible intersections of western patriarchy, blackness, and the complex affective relationship with motivity.

Fewer than thirty years before Wells' assault, Frederick Douglass traveled by train and boat to New York City with a free sailor's identification papers, a trip that, according to Douglass, was smooth and uninterrupted.[80] In his told story, Douglass pushes forth a promise of mobility that mirrors national liberty but articulated to Black (and) liberation. The secretive methods of Douglass' escape from bondage nonetheless marked Black mobility and freedom as life threatening. Douglass further explained, "The *salt water slaves* who hung in the guards of a steamer, being washed three days and three nights—like another Jonah—by the waves of the sea, has, by the publicity given to the circumstance, set a spy to the guards of every steamer departing from southern ports."[81] Douglass warned of white craftiness toward capture and recapture and of the regulation of Black movement that aided in sustaining white supremacy.

Douglass recalled how railroad and steamboat regulations were "so stringent that even *free* colored travelers were almost excluded. They must have *free* papers; they must be measured and carefully examined, before they were allowed to enter the cars; they only went in the daytime even when so examined."[82] Even free, Black travelers limited their movement to the day in fear of those who earned "the accursed award of slave hunting."[83] The complexities of Douglass's transit stories helped circulate strategies of escape and an awareness of its surveillance just as Wells's transit narrative circulated to inspire consciousness of struggle. Against the backdrop of signified blackness, colonial mobility existed within the regulatory confines of surveillance and containment and made clear that any*body* in motion and identifiable as Black was exposed to the terror of enslavement and its afterlife.

Much like identification forms during enslavement, labor visas at the turn of the twentieth century limited mobility through the compression of time and space in ways antithetical to the mobility freedoms awarded to white citizens. The train served as both transportation and an ideal space for teaching by Americanization instructors for laborers from Mexico.[84] In 1917, a railroad company transformed their boxcar into a mobile model of an "American" home, and national cultural narratives moved freely throughout the enclosed railcar as it literally contained laborers.[85] The train also served as a vehicle of colonial extraction and transported people to work camps who were, at times, transported to neighboring cities without consent.[86] By 1961, there were "fifteen thousand Puerto Rican migrant workers, plus other thousands from Jamaica and the other West Indies. Plus, thousands from Mexico" as well as Black and white workers from the south.[87] Alternatively, blackened citizens were often subjected to enclosed work camps that often held them longer than they were permitted to—and under inhospitable working and living conditions.

Through infrastructures of transit that bordered according to sociogenic codes, Black citizens were confined to their communities, unable to move freely without exposure to violence and death. Richard Wright recalls how, as a young boy in Arkansas, train tracks separated his home from working-class whites. He and his friends were met by broken glass bottles thrown from white boys across the tracks; one bottle hit Wright and resulted in three stitches on his neck.[88] Wright's recollection underscores the train track as delineated sociogenic space that would not protect him from antiblack racism and white people who were "an overreaching symbol of fear."[89]

In the subway car at Penn Station in New York City, the fear of anti-Black racism by white people in public space shaped Jesús Colón's experience as he watched a white woman struggle with a baby and two additional children.[90] As Colón exited the subway car at the same Brooklyn stop as this woman, he wondered, "Should I offer my help as the American white man did at the subway door . . . how could I, a Negro and a Puerto Rican approach this white lady who very likely might have preconceived prejudices against Negroes and everybody with foreign accents, in a deserted subway station very late at night?"[91] Much like the train travel stories before him, Colón's travel story moves against erasure and grounds his Black body within the politics of movement. Colón illustrates how W.E.B. Du Bois' veil and double consciousness "suggest that there is a predominant mode for seeing race that engenders an awareness of looking while being looked at through the distorting prism of the veil."[92] His consciousness cannot be separated from the public surveilling eye of white dominance.

Colón's experience of double consciousness is, as Riley C. Snorton theorizes, "a critical optic for black people in negotiating the condition of hypervisibility."[93] Colón continues, "Perhaps the lady was not prejudice after all. Or not prejudiced enough to scream at the coming of a Negro toward her in a solitary subway station a few hours passed midnight. If you were not that prejudiced, I failed you, dear lady. . . . I failed myself to myself."[94] His acknowledgment of sociogenic effects exposes both his invisibility and hypervisibility as Black *and* Puerto Rican riding the train to and from work every day. Much like Hurston's story of Annie Taylor and Who Flung through Janie, Colón's told story grounds his Black body against erasure within the politics of movement. When contextualized with blackness, the limits of colonial mobility are complicated and become unbound.

In Hurston's earlier autobiographical work, she limits dominant western mobility as she turns the ethnographic gaze upon white residents and tourists who traveled through her childhood town of Eatonville, Florida.[95] Hurston states, "The native whites rode dusty horses, the Northern tourists chugged down the sandy village road in automobiles . . . The front porch . . . was a gallery seat to me . . . Not only did I enjoy the show, but I didn't mind the actors knowing that I liked it."[96] In her reenactment of her childhood pastime, Hurston embodies a Black female subject that refuses the normative western roles prescribed to her with an understanding that they do not apply to her blackened body always and already rooted in and routed from a colonial past. Hurston pushes a liminal invisibility-visibility to the forefront, one that is defined by her Black and female body, and limits white freedoms of movement with *her* watchful eye.

Hurston demonstrates how surveillance can be accessed through the combined excess of national investments in mobility and ethnography, a formal mode of knowledge reserved historically for whites and performed strategically during colonialism, enslavement, and their afterlife. This subversion of the "seeing eye" as white challenges modern discourses of knowledge and colonial mobility. It also challenges white as the modern qualifier of an all-seeing and knowing subject and transforms erasure, invisibility, and hyper-visibility into agency that is defined, located, and embodied as womanist and Black.[97] In Ann Petry's *The Street*, set in primarily Harlem during the early 1940s, the automobile as an extension of western mobility symbolizes Black success and mobility but, much like the dollar van and the other modes of transport, the links between capitalism, blackness, and mobility are complicated and countered by the very practices of included exclusion.[98] Practices of consumption align with performances of Black critical consciousness and sociality (double consciousness and the veil) and encompass an understanding that success and national belonging do not apply to blackened bodies in the same ways.

Petry writes, "From the red leather upholstery to the white walled tires and the top that could be thrown back when the weather was warm . . . this is the kind of car that you see in movies . . . that swings insolently past you on Park Avenue, the kind that pulls up in front of the snooty stores on Fifth Avenue."[99] Boots Smith's car is described by Lutie Johnson, the protagonist in Petry's narrative, who, like Hurston, turns her watchful eye onto western sovereignty and patriarchal mobility. Her description as the seeing and knowing Black woman provides an often-absent viewpoint in the politics of mobility and communicates that she too understands and acts upon the normative interpretations of Black consumerism and automobility. Lutie's critical awareness presages the exclusivity of Boots's Cadillac, a symbol of success not to be admired but guarded against. It informs us that womanist blackness disrupts western sovereignty and mobility even in its colonial confines of erasure, exclusion, and containment.

Hurston also challenges western car culture through Janie's love affair with Teacake who teaches Janie to drive in a borrowed car.[100] It is not the car itself but the ability to drive, which, for Janie, is a symbol of independence and liberation from the gendered role she was expected to embody. Learning to drive in a car that neither of them own is a stark contrast to western freedom mobilities and its ties to consumer culture and bourgeois sensibilities. Hurston advances circulation, the practice of passing along automobiles and stories alike, as integral to Black sociality and consciousness. Against the extension of western car culture as national belonging and Black success, Hurston redefines car culture through Black circulation as relations of homespace.

Similarly, through Lutie riding with Boots, Petry underscores relations of homespace through the speeding of the car and concurs that it is not car ownership but "the swiftly moving car" that made Boots "feel he was a powerful being who could conquer the world."[101] Preceding Ralph Ellison's oft-cited essay "Cadillac Flambé," Petry notes that it is the loss of "all sense of time and space as the car plunged forward into the cold, white night;"[102] the speeding, moving car driven by Boots allows him to escape the realities of his included exclusion as he places his mobility (both himself and his car) on display. For Petry, white people also "sensed that the black man had to roar past, had for a brief moment feel equal, feel superior; had to take restless chances going around curves, passing on hills, so that they would be better able to face a world that took pains to make them feel like they didn't belong, that they were inferior."[103] The spectacle of blackness becomes a spectacular performance of agency, and driving while Black is doubled as Lutie's experience of moving fast and freely is intimately and empathetically connected to Boots. The racialization of space proves significant as Boots takes Lutie out of Harlem to white suburbs to freely and quickly move in order to maintain control of his always and already invisible, hyper-visible body.

Petry continues, "She stopped staring at the road ahead to look at Boots. He was leaning over the steering wheel, his hands cupped close on the side of it. Yes, she thought, at this moment he has forgotten he's black."[104] Lutie's watchful eye as the passenger grounds her in her womanist blackness and her reflection of black automobility positions Lutie as the subject who articulates a dual form of talking back. She controls the knowledge of Black spectacle and transforms it into a moment of Black sociality and freedom. Lutie's position as the mobile subject with the ability to see, know, and empathize is the pivotal moment of possibility in a space where possibilities are grim. Freedom through automobility proves to be fleeting as Boots and Lutie are stopped by a police officer, however Boots' lack of surprise demonstrates his awareness of included exclusion and the anticipated reaction to it. As Boots pays off the officer, Lutie acknowledges that money can make only a slight difference in the contextual confines of sociogenic racism.

Conclusion: Black Temporal-Spatial Realities in Motion

In 1970, Ike and Tina Turner added their rendition of "Proud Mary" to their album titled *Working Together*. The song, as explained by Tina Turner, was from their stage performances and was added due to the lack of songs when they initially completed the album.[105] The impromptu inclusion of "Proud Mary" became one of Ike and Tina's most popular songs, so much so that it was released as a single just one year later. The song itself is popular in its own right; it was covered by dozens of artists in 1969—the very year it was released by Creedence Clearwater Revival (CCR), and has over one hundred renditions to date.[106] Although I am referring to the song's success in the common definition of the term "popular," I want to highlight how Ike and Tina's performance of the song articulates Black womanist mobility, one that is simultaneously embodied, social, and spatial.

Ike and Tina Turner begin with the sound of Ike's signature plucking of the guitar followed by Tina's address to the audience. She speaks about how the band will perform the song: first, nice and easy, then rough, Ike begins to sing background while the plucking of the guitar sets the tempo for the rest of the band. Tina's voice carries over Ike's singing as their doubled, nonsynchronized voices repeat the first few lines of the CCR song. As Tina's sung words gesture to the movement of the riverboat, we hear the Ikettes for the first time, strengthening Tina's voice as Ike continues his solo refrain. The Ikettes weave in and out of the song as Ike and Tina sing, synchronizing their voices only with Tina.

The voices of the women as one, however, do not overpower Ike's deep, steady sound. Instead, their voices together are reminiscent of a church song with multiple tones and voices purposely woven together. As they slow their pace, singing the refrain one last time, the Ikettes begin to echo Ike. The echo, as opposed to synchronization, showcases Tina's solo voice. This restaging of "Proud Mary" pushes to the forefront a Black sociality produced by an expressiveness of sound that is derived from traditions of Black radical performance.[107]

Foregrounding the possibilities of the future while calling upon the past and present, Ike and Tina Turner's performance of Black sociality is intertwined with movement in both form and content. The play on speed parallels the lyrics' emphasis on mobility. Unlike the original, Tina's spoken word address, Ike's guitar, and the slow tempo help transform the original song into one that encompasses a sound that bridges rhythm and blues with rock and roll. The shift from slow to fast provides a dual sense of familiarity both with the original song but one that would also resonate with Ike and Tina's fans. Tapping into Raymond Williams's "structures of feeling," the new sounds of "Proud Mary" affectively register as both Black and rock and roll, a sentiment that was less congruent with the mainstream representations of rock and roll of the time.[108]

The video recordings of Ike and Tina's performances of "Proud Mary" typically begin in similar fashion, with the camera switching between close-up shots of Tina and Ike until both images are imposed onto one another so the audience views the performers simultaneously singing their parts. Though their costumes differ in each performance, the style of dress and hair remain part of their trademark look, marking both a belonging to blackness and a conscious display of sexuality. In unison with the slower pace of the last "nice" refrain, the camera changes from the imposed close-up shots to a wide shot of the Ikettes and Tina with a close-up of Ike as their background; this quickly changes to a medium shot of Tina with Ike's close-up remaining. The wide shot mimics the voices of the Ikettes demarcating a togetherness with Tina and demonstrating their slow, corresponding lower body motion. The medium shot of Tina provides a view of her more exaggerated winding hip motion, which visually complements her words of movement.

As the song transitions to its rough stage, Ike is no longer in view. Tina and the Ikettes are now the central image as their dance speeds up with the music. The mid-song transition to a quicker tempo provides an imagery of speed-movement that parallels the moving bodies of Tina and the Ikettes. The performance by Tina and the Ikettes both accentuate sexual desire and actual movement as the arms and body gesture mobility technology. As they sing of big wheels turning, the women's bodies perform a turning of their own. The tight and short costumes of Tina and the Ikettes display their bodies, accentuating their curves and legs that are emphasized further as they gyrate to the theme of movement.

The conscious performance of sexuality and mobility demonstrates the restricted representation of blackness and its limitations within colonial mobility. The song takes on new meaning for Black subjecthood and creates the potential for affective alliances based on alternative possibilities of mobility that counter and critique the past.[109] As affective alliances relate to rock and roll, Lawrence Grossberg argues:

> The rock and roll apparatus affectively organizes everyday life according to three intersecting axes: 1) youth as difference: the social difference of generations is inscribed upon the phenomenological field of social relations; 2) pleasure of the body: the celebration of pleasure is inscribed upon the site of the body; and 3) postmodernity: the structure of uncertainty (the fragment) is inscribed upon the circuit of history and meaning.[110]

Here, Grossberg's analysis of rock and roll as an affective apparatus is derived from a specific context, one that is absent of Black bodies who created the very musical tropes of the genre.

The three intersecting axes, however, persist with the affective power of "Proud Mary," especially as the sound remained consistent with the original and popularized fan base of rock and roll. The complexities and contradictions of Black culture, however, become a necessary fourth axis that continues to exist in "Proud Mary," even when the appeal of youth culture fades as Dick Hebdige once emphasized.[111] In line with identifications of blackness, Tina Turner added, "And, I said let's do it, but let's change it. So in the car Ike plays the guitar, we just sort of jam. And we just sort of broke into the black version of it. It was never planned . . . it's just that we get it for stage, because we give the people a little bit of us and a little bit of what they hear on the radio every day."[112] Turner's own position on "Proud Mary" marks the transition of the song into one that references Black embodiment and positionality in relation to mobility.

According to John Fogarty, the lead singer of CCR, "Proud Mary" was meant to be about a woman who worked as a maid. He envisioned her as someone who "gets off the bus every morning and goes to work and holds their lives together" and then must return home.[113] The origin of the song, focused on domestic labor, repetition, and controlled movement, possesses some significance here as it interestingly remains one of the many layers of mobility, not as CCR sang it, but as Turner reclaimed it visually and sonically as both Black and female. This sounding image of womanist mobility reflects upon a relationship to unlimited movement that exists and has yet to exist at the same time.

Tina Turner's performance of "Proud Mary" affectively underscores Black womanist mobility, Black womanhood as embodied empowerment unified with the possibilities of movement. The affective relationship with the riverboat queen symbolically references histories of slaves' escapes to freedom, and the call for the continuance of the moving boat on the river rings true of the active persistence of freedom struggles. This imaged past is also imposed by an imagined escape from patriarchy, an escape made possible through Black womanist becomings. With Ike out of the mise-en-scene, Tina and the Ikettes exude an empowering image of Black movement toward something else, a possibility of sorts, pushed forth by womanist bodies moving in unison.

Alongside the Ikettes, Tina transformed the song to necessarily refer to Black female subjectivity and liberation so much so that later renditions of the song depended on Black women's voices to carry the performance.[114] As Hall reminds us, Black popular culture is not a space where we find our true selves but an "arena that is *profoundly* mythic. It is a theatre of popular desires and a theatre of popular fantasies. It is where we discover and play with the identifications of ourselves, where we are imagined, where we are represented, not only to the audiences out there who do not get the message, but to ourselves for the first time."[115] These stories both mark time and place with their presence and, most importantly, are free from the confines of controlled movement with the ability to travel further than the bodies who tell them. At times, such stories also possess the ability to move the storytellers and their audience toward movements of freedom. Through the complex layers of the telling of stories, the told stories and the representation of stories perform counterassimilation, the revolution of and toward blackness. They, indeed, provide the "oxygen which creates and shapes a new humanity."[116]

3

Movin' on Up

Mobile Traps and Mapping Performances of Homespace

> One is reminded of the words of
> Langston Hughes in *Ask Your Mama*,
> where he says that the African visitor
> finds that in the American social
> supermarket blacks for sale range from
> intellectuals to entertainers. Thus, it
> appears that the price of the slow
> integration which the Negroes are
> experiencing must be bought at the price
> of abject conformity in thinking.
> —E. Franklin Frazier

At the sixty-first Grammy Awards in February 2019, Belcalis Marlenis Almánzar, better known as Cardi B, won in the category of Best Rap Album for her first studio album, *Invasion of Privacy*. The honor seemingly came as a shock to the Bronx rapper when she heard her name announced as the winner. As she took the stage with her husband, Offset, of the rap trio, Migos, an excited and anxious Cardi was comforted by her husband's whispers of assurance and her fans' supportive chant of her name. Once she composed herself enough to speak, she quipped perhaps she should start smoking weed to calm her overwhelming nervousness; she then thanked everyone involved with her album.

She especially thanked her baby, Kulture, explained how difficult it was to complete her album and accompanying videos while pregnant, and she credited her husband for pushing her to finish.

Cardi B's win was a historic one. Although five other female rappers have been nominated for the Grammy's Best Rap Album category since its creation in 1996 (Missy Elliott, Eve, Rapsody, Nicki Minaj, and Iggy Izalea), Cardi's win was the first for a female solo artist.[1] Her album won over Pusha T's *Daytona*, Nipsey Hussle's *Victory Lap*, Travis Scott's *Astroworld*, and Mac Miller's *Swimming*. Cardi is the first female artist, and third artist since the digital era, to have all thirteen songs on her album certified at least gold.[2] She is also the first solo female rap artist in nineteen years, since Lauryn Hill, to climb the Billboard Charts to number one with her lead single "Bodak Yellow (Money Moves)."[3] The Grammy win itself arrived after Cardi's reconciliation with her husband, whose adultery was exposed a few months earlier just after their daughter was born. It also came amid her off and ongoing feud with Nicki Minaj, another top-charting female hip-hop artist from New York City.

The celebration for her achievement was short-lived, however, as Cardi received much criticism for the honor, criticism that began the very moment her name was announced as the winner. Mac Miller died the September before from an accidental drug overdose, and his ex-girlfriend, Ariana Grande, tweeted "literal bullshit," "fuck," and "trash" in separate tweets during the announcement and during Cardi's acceptance speech.[4] Even though each tweet was promptly deleted, fans of Grande, Mac Miller, and Cardi immediately circulated the sentiment alongside their own comments. Although some responses only insisted that Mac Miller should have received the award, others bashed Cardi and identified *her* as trash, using Grande's tweets as verification for their disdain. At the same time, others stated the opposite in support of Cardi.

Cardi took to social media and responded directly while backstage at the Grammys, saying, "You wanna know something? I read an article that Mac Miller's family said that if he don't win, they wanted me to win, so I'm sharing this Grammy with you."[5] Grande later explained that she was not referring to Cardi with her tweets but the Grammys itself for not honoring her ex-boyfriend, whose parents attended and were invited by the Grammys.[6] The controversy over Cardi's win did not end with Miller. At the same time that Grande's tweets were circulating, a representative for BET tweeted, "Meanwhile, Nicki Minaj is being dragged by her lacefront," and although that post was quickly deleted, Minaj reposted a screenshot of it the next day with the caption, "Young Money will no longer be a part of the BET Experience or award show."[7] She also added that her fans should request refunds from the network because she was no longer performing. BET posted a public apology to Minaj; however, Minaj stood by her initial sentiment, which prompted more posts against Cardi and her win.

In response, Cardi again took to Instagram to address the opposing views.[8] She chastised the BET post that disparaged Minaj during her win and restated how hard she worked. Cardi added:

> I remember last year when I didn't win for "Bodak Yellow," and everyone was like "Cardi got snubbed. Cardi got snubbed." Now this year's a fucking problem? My album went two times platinum, my nigga, and every chart there was, my album was always top ten. Number one album as well. I fuckin' work my ass off. I locked myself in the studio for three months, my nigga. Didn't went to sleep in my own bed sometimes for four days straight, pregnant. . . . Niggas couldn't sleep, niggas couldn't do shit while everybody was harassing me like, "You not gonna do it. We know you pregnant. Your career is over. That shit dwellin' in my mind while I'm workin'."[9]

Cardi deactivated her Instagram account immediately after her address, however, she made one final post that stated, "I used to want this shit foreva. Ya can have it back!"[10]

I begin this chapter with Cardi B as she picks up where Black womanist mobility concluded in the previous chapter with Tina Turner's performance of "Proud Mary." How does the sounding image of Black womanist mobility negotiate the possibilities of movement and reflect upon these possibilities that simultaneously exist and do not exist? In the performative arena of Black popular culture, how do we locate the desired movement toward freedom? An argument could be made that Cardi's musical sounds call upon Black radical traditions underscored by her identification as Bronx, Black, and Latina, but I am less interested in her music and more interested in her performances of Black womanist mobility through social media, which call upon those magical processes of connectedness: relations of homespace.[11]

Black popular culture as a space that is magical and mythical, performative, and self-reflective extends to Cardi's communicative performances within her new (and old) media platforms. It is in these local stories and practiced Black circulation that we gain a glimpse of alternative forms of being and becoming made possible. Along these lines, this chapter explores relations of homespace to grapple with how experiences of mass mediated racist identification circulate. I frame these points of circulation as rearticulated identifications of becoming that combat modern practices of home, bound to white sovereignty and sociogenic assemblages. Re-presentations that exist outside of the frame mark the ways in which hip-hop culture remains the space in which critical consciousness, derived from and against sociogenic relations and white sovereignty, is made possible.

To echo Édouard Glissant, nonrooted relations of identification, homespace, are inseparably linked to blackness and are how sentiments of included exclusion are circulated.[12] Cardi B embodies and represents the conjoining hegemonic imagery of hip-hop culture of both black success via socioeconomic mobility and Black pathology and criminality. She embodies the excess that cannot be contained by the regime of visibility and hegemonic sociogenic discourse. As such, this chapter explores how storied representations of hip hop articulate spaces and performances of belonging to and loving blackness through the limits of western mobility, attached directly to the accumulation of wealth. It analyzes how these limits are shaped by coloniality and white sovereignty and, in turn, how they shape Black popular representations of hip-hop culture.

As touched on in the previous chapter, the intersecting affective axes of difference, pleasure, uncertainty, and racist identification organized within and through everyday life align and inform Black popular culture, in this case hip-hop music, as an affective apparatus. Much like rock, its complexities of feeling are masked with discourses mediated and articulated through new cultural technologies that help shape and repackage historical ideology. Hip-hop self-representation through multiple mediated platforms offers a glimpse of the often-masked structures of feeling Black and embodying and loving blackness.[13] Through localized embodied and storied practices that have circulated in the nonplaced communicative technologies of entertainment and leisure, these points of identification underscore different stories of unassimilated and unassimilable blackness.[14] In line with the last chapter, hip-hop culture speaks back to sociogenic common sense and its own implication within racialized ideology and discourse.

These stories of Black mobility, including those of colonial restriction, expose the political limits of hegemonic regimes of visibility and their conceptualizations of blackness that frame and power it. Hip hop continues to provide insight to alternative practices of being and becoming that go against coloniality and ongoing processes of neoliberalization. It remains a site where the struggle over hegemony continues to take place and where stakes can be won or lost.[15] The performative re-presentations of Cardi B that center her blackness consciousness through her Instagram and Twitter feeds are demonstrative of such struggles. They tell a different story that parallels her fame, musical performance, and recorded representational success within hip-hop and popular culture. They also combat how racialized neoliberalization proliferates and normalizes difference as an emptied signifier that reinforces the status quo rather than disrupts it.[16]

Media Traps, Neoliberal Opps, and Hip-Hop Culture as Unassimilable Blackness

The self-proclaimed "trap Selena" identifies as a "regular degular shmegular girl from the Bronx" who danced and hosted parties to fulfill her goal "to make shmoney and turn everything up" prior to her hip-hop success.[17] Although Selena references the departed Tejano singer Selena Quintanilla and positions

Cardi as Latina and American, "trap" has many meanings but is tied characteristically to the making and selling of illegal drugs. Unlike the terms that are aligned with it, for example, gangster, hustle, and hustler, trap directly refers to a place, usually a house, where drugs are made and sold, and it traps people associated with this lifestyle as it is difficult to escape. The trap genre is a subgenre of hip hop that, much like its predecessor gangsta rap, is known for its particular sound and is criticized for its content.

Although the use of trap alludes to the self-reflective and reflexive position of blackened youth, the popular categorization of Cardi as a trap artist reinforced by her Bronx locale shapes her and her behavior as naturally criminal and pathological even when she is symbolized as a success. To echo Herman Gray, realistic representations of Black pathologies juxtaposed alongside of representations of Black success work together to reinforce the ideology and discourse that all and any can succeed if they try hard enough;[18] these representations together naturalize poverty and failure as Black culture.[19] Such common sense understandings mystify structural and institutional marginalization and racism and their effects on those who fall under the umbrella of blackness.[20] The popularization of hip-hop music, culture, and its representations becomes the sole source for this understanding and traps those artists who seemingly simultaneously succeed and are represented as pathological. Trap, along these lines, highlights how colonial mobility, the accumulation of wealth, and its sociocultural circulation bounds Black liberation, particularly for those who fall under the umbrella of unassimilable blackness, as does Belcalis Almánzar.

Cardi's rise to fame began with her social media persona that is described by many of her fans as "real" and "naturally funny" with a "bigger than life personality."[21] Cardi's display of self, circulated through social media, called upon previous claims of hip-hop authenticity closely linked to the urban underclass. Her self-crafted native-Bronx imag(in)ed identity helped distinguish her as a racial, spatial, and temporal brand rooted in hip-hop culture. As Sara Benet-Weiser suggests, such brands explain the self within particular social and cultural contexts and are shaped by an overarching neoliberal framework.[22] Almánzar already built a strong social media presence with her videos, first on Tumblr and then on her Instagram, with approximately two million followers before her debut on VH1's reality television series *Love & Hip Hop New York* (*LHHNY*). Cardi's social media success prompted Mona Scott-Young, producer of *LHHNY*, to add her to the New York season six cast in 2015.

After her first season on *LHHNY*, Cardi B released her mixtape *Gangster Bitch Music, Vol. 1*, which had at least one song ("Foreva") directly tied to content from *LHHNY* in addition to songs written before her reality television premiere. The song referred to a scene where Cardi and DJ Self, from New York's Hot 97 radio station, were discussing a physical altercation that involved Cardi and Self's girlfriend. Represented on the show as a love triangle, Self attempted to resolve conflict between his girlfriend and Cardi to avoid jeopardizing future business endeavors with Cardi. As Self attempted to quash the tension, Cardi turned around in a complete circle, tilted her head as she peered at Self, and responded, "A girl got beef with me she gonna have beef with me, foreva."[23] The episode cut immediately to Cardi addressing the audience, not uncommon in reality television, however, it was her unapologetic performance that demanded attention.

Counter to bourgeois civility and uncommon to the typical regretful reality television performance, Cardi's song solidified her stance. "Foreva" highlights the aforementioned line from *LHHNY* as the chorus and also reinforces Cardi's brand: unapologetically urban, authentic, young, and Black with no expressed desire to conform to "industry professionalism." After two seasons of *LHHNY*, Cardi B left the show to focus on her music career, released a second mixtape, *Gangster Bitch Music, Vol. 2* in 2017, and signed with Atlantic Records, where she debuted her aforementioned studio album in 2018. In seemingly Godspeed, just three years since her premiere on *LHHNY*, (Ba)Cardi B(elcalis) rose to success, a journey represented in the media as a contemporary fairytale. Portrayed as a hip-hop Cinderella, she embraced and reinforced this image through her social media accounts.[24]

Her origin story of the American dream fulfilled, however, is not one that is unique to hip-hop, especially since the 1990s; the representations of Notorious B.I.G.'s *Juicy* and Sean Puff Daddy Combs's label Bad Boy helped popularize this imagery, and fellow Brooklyn hip-hop mogul Sean Carter, aka Jay-Z, perfected it. Since its *move* into mainstream pop culture in the late eighties and early nineties, representations of hip hop became synonymous with Black urban youth and have helped reinforce a global perception of blackness that is necessarily included and excluded. Representations of hip hop continue to be utilized to articulate the neoliberal logics of equality, individual responsibility, reform, and choice and reinforce mythologized pathologies of blackness: discourses of Black and Brown—often urban—criminality.[25] This double function rests on representations of hypercommodification, nihilism, and crime; it justifies the hypersurveillance and policing of all blackened bodies, as well as their exposure to death, and masks processes of sociogenic victimization and marginalization.[26]

Mediated representation, directly and necessarily linked to the modernity-coloniality relationship, continues to play a primary role in how blackness is imagined, policed, and exposed to terror, violence, and death. Sociogenic discourse and common sense, as the previous chapters have shown, have been embedded in our national culture since before our nation's inception. These racialized knowledges shifted and continued in multiple forms, symbols, and signifiers, and hip hop is no exception as it brings to bear "an already available stock of meanings" in "linguistic and visual form."[27] Accordingly, representations of hip hop—one of the most popular musical forms in our contemporary moment—are packaged and appropriated to help reconstitute conflating imageries of Black, urban, and poor. These representational imag(in)aries echo Walter Rodney's distinction that Black incorporates all other identifications not included in the category of white and function in nonarbitrary racist ways.[28]

Motivated and shaped by racism, threat and fear as common-sense modes of territorial security are equated to blackness, which is inarguably the quintessential symbol of enemies of the state and its citizens.[29] These reconstituted conflating imageries of classed and spaced blackness are in turn applied to all Black people regardless of class status, socioeconomic mobility, and respective bourgeois performances.[30] Cardi's Grammy wins were not excluded from the media frenzy, social and otherwise, nor were they excluded from the signifiers of unassimilable blackness. Although Cardi B's Instagram address was not unique to her social media and (reality) television persona, media representations and public reader comments on news websites highlighted how her behavior illustrated her lack of deservingness for her Grammy honors.[31] Cardi's Instagram address followed by her disappearance from social media only reinforced the very sentiment she aimed to disrupt.

Headlines centered on her post as a "foul-mouth," "expletive-filled rant" against those who did not believe she deserved her Grammy.[32] These depictions reinforced Cardi as undeserving, and the continuous use of the term "rant" from multiple headlines further positioned her as impassioned and wild. Negative comments, ensued from the "Conversations" sections of the news websites, social media posts, and channels, reinforced racist sentiments from headlines and called upon these depictions. One conversation section included Carol, who stated, "Well honey. You didn't deserve a Grammy. Terrible voice. Awful music" and later followed with "Rap music is an oxymoron."[33] Carol's sentiment toward hip-hop as not music and undeserving of honorable recognition reinforces this generalized sense of "enemy within" applied to both the genre and the people who partake in it.[34]

Death and containment do not conclude with representations of enemies within the nation. Comfortably Numb wrote, "What a class act. lol. . . . . . . Oh, and how about learning to speak proper English," and Mark Olsen stated, "What a nasty mouthed dog."[35] The identification of Cardi as a "nasty mouthed dog" who does not "speak proper English" redefines her as both animalistic and alien. The demand "to learn to speak English" directly refers to how ethnolinguistic common sense defines citizenship and national belonging against the imagined other whose very accent is a threatening characteristic.[36] Immigration discourse and representation police the enemy from outside national borders and help establish the national imaginary of belonging.

Discursively militarized law and order both within and along national borders in the name of security remain one of the primary methods of articulating sociogenic national belonging as one that is identified within standards of whiteness. Immigration discourse and juridical order serve to police anybody that poses an invading threat against white sovereignty. Such ideological and structural repressive processes are imbedded in the national imaginary and have been apparent since the Immigration Act of 1882, which was uncoincidentally implemented shortly after the Fourteenth and Fifteenth Amendments. Cardi's identification as both Black and Latina from the Bronx with immigrant parents from the Caribbean (Trinidad and the Dominican Republic) intensifies the articulation of subhuman alien enemy—one that is within the nation haphazardly because of immigration and one that refuses to disavow her belonging to blackness, and cannot, because of her identification.

Representation depictions demand receptive circular responses that call upon racist discourses to articulate hip hop and/as blackness as antithetical to western and national belonging, expendable, and unassimilable. When Cardi B returned to Instagram, her initial address was deleted and replaced with congratulatory posts from the same rap artists who were mentioned in the media backlash such as J. Cole, Chance the Rapper, and Nipsey Hussle. In addition, she posted the headline concerning Mac Miller's family that she mentioned backstage at the Grammys. The formal and informal modes of embodied racist ideology depicted against Cardi B, and hip hop in general, achieved their purpose. They silenced and policed the young artist as apparent through the erasure of her address and the appearance of its acceptable replacements and communicated regulatory practices for the rest of hip hop.

The managed and maintained continuance of racist common sense made apparent in news websites, print, social media, and television coverage alerted audiences that blackness and Black-identified people must be silenced and contained. Calling upon racist knowledges of blackened urban pathologies, symbols of wild specifically have been utilized and circulated through the media to articulate hip hop as synonymous with urban, Black (synonymous with Brown), and violent and illustrate the subhuman, alien, enemy of the nation-state. These kinds of sociogenic representations position blackened bodies as more primal than human. They have been utilized to demand and justify the mass and hyperincarceration of Black bodies, the heightening of police presence, and police and civilian killings, terror, and brutalities against such bodies in predominantly urban spaces.

The term "wilding," for example, became a defining signifier in the Central Park Five case, in 1989, where young Black diasporic boys were falsely convicted of the assault, rape, and attempted murder of a white woman in Central Park. Wilding was used throughout media outlets to describe the acts of these Black boys, which, according to the New York chief of detectives at that time, were "unrelated to money, race, drugs, or alcohol."[37] Wilding simply meant "they [Black youth] were going to raise hell."[38] The lack of motive underscored the sentiment that "wilding" was a natural act of savagery connected to being Black, young, and urban. The wilding threat intensified as it moved across a space historically considered a marker of bourgeois civility and leisure emblematic of "white civilization" and western modernity.[39]

Wilding was in turn connected to hip hop, linked to urban slang and the top-charting crossover song "Wild Thing" from Tone Loc, even though the slang term "wil'in'" (the "d" and "g" are silent), had nothing to do with the song or its title nor did it necessarily possess a negative connotation.[40] The link to hip hop and other subhuman imagery such as "animals" and "wolfpack" continued as media coverage heightened. One 1989 study counted 406 news items, which consisted of a total of "3, 415 column inches of print coverage and 4.25 hours of television coverage" from "only five newspapers and six television stations within two weeks of the incident."[41] Inspired by the Central Park Five case, on May 1 that same year, Donald Trump spent $80,000 for full-paged advertisements in four newspapers and demanded the reinstatement of the death penalty to punish and execute "roving bands of wild criminals."[42]

Trump's advertisements also demanded the reinstatement of police power against claims of police brutality in the name of safety and security.[43] Trump stated, "Unshackle [the police] from the constant chant of 'police brutality' which every petty criminal hurls immediately at an officer who has just risked his or her life for another's. We must cease our continuous pandering to the criminal population of this city."[44] Indeed, there did exist a constant chant against police brutality during this period in the New York City area. There was the Thomson Square riot of August 1988, in addition to the deaths of Michael J. Stewart in 1983 and Eleanor Bumpers in 1984 and the beating and torture of Mark Davidson in 1985.[45] In February 1989, just a few months before the assault and rape in Central Park, in Morristown, New Jersey, 22-year-old John (Tony) Jackson died while being held in police custody for failure to appear in court for a motor-vehicle violation.[46]

Trump never racialized the criminal population of New York City in the ad, however, the context of the Central Park Five case and the protests against police brutality already mark the "wild criminals" as belonging to an unassimilable blackness. This sentiment was not Trump's alone. Just a little over three months after Trump's advertisements, 16-year-old Yusuf K. Hawkins was shot and killed by a group of white teenagers in Bensonhurst in Brooklyn when he traveled to the predominantly Italian neighborhood to view and possibly purchase a used car. Hawkins was killed for coming to and moving through white space, precisely a re-imag(in)ed marker of Central Park's significance juxtaposed against his alienated Black body. This sociogenic imagery of alien enemy articulated to colonial mobility proves deadly in the regulation of blackened bodies in transit. It justifies brutality and murder against those who are identified under the umbrella of blackness under the guise of justice, civility, and security.

Nonhuman images, such as "bear-like," were also called upon to describe Rodney King during the trial of the acquitted Los Angeles police officers who were recorded brutally beating King during a routine traffic stop in 1992.[47] On June 11, 2000, during the Puerto Rican Day parade, approximately fifty women were sexually assaulted in Central Park by youth who were identified as predominantly Brown and Black.[48] These assaults occurred while police officers stood watch, reportedly ignored complaints, and were even witnessed to smile, laugh, and ogle the young women.[49] Immediately, media coverage, which did not occur until a French tourist was assaulted, identified the attacks as similar to the 1989 Central Park case. The coverage again highlighted the youth as "wolf-pack," "hoodlums," "garbage," and "rampaging," with the acts described as a "super frat party," "gang assaults," and "wilding attacks."[50] Police officers absolved themselves of blame as their inaction was justified as a response to public outcry against police crimes and stringent policing laws that targeted Black diasporic city residents.

Anonymous New York Police Department officers claimed that they were under public and political pressure to approach the parade or any other public minority event with a "hands-off attitude."[51] This was in fact "pay-back, they hint, for the police brutality protests" this time for the shootings of unarmed Amadou Diallo and Patrick Dorismond as well as the unlawful "stop and frisk" practices overseen by then Mayor Rudolph Giuliani.[52] The refusal to aid nonwhite residents serves as part of the same power relations that promote and produce police crimes and hate crimes against these same residents. Additionally, the refusal of aid reinforces Black and Brown residents as enemy-opponents rather than citizen-residents who demand and deserve police protection and service.

The conviction of the boys who were imprisoned for assault and rape of then 28-year-old jogger Trisha Meili was vacated in 2002 when another man confessed to the crime, and his DNA and testimony matched the evidence. The representation of hip hop, articulated and circulated as evidence of Black urban pathology and nonhuman, however, remained, and media coverage continues to play a primary role in the demand for law and order and in violence against perceived threats of embodied blackness. In his testimony on shooting and killing Michael Brown, Officer Darren Wilson, who was not indicted for Brown's murder in 2014, described Brown as a "demon," and the "Incredible Hulk."[53] In response to Black Lives Matter protests for the police killing of Brown, a Ferguson store owner stated, "Guys on drugs, the rapper attitude, nothing political about it for them."[54] For 17-year-old Laquan McDonald, the embodied threat of blackness justified Officer Jason Van Dyke's claim of fearing for his life. In October 2014, Van Dyke shot McDonald sixteen times while the teenage boy was seen in dashcam footage walking away from police officers right before Van Dyke shot and killed him.

The perceived and accepted embodied threat of blackness has given legal aid to killers of Black and Brown children and, in Van Dyke's case, helped reduce his conviction from first-degree murder to second-degree murder and sixteen counts of aggravated battery. In fact, a 2017 study found that "since 2005, 82 police officers have been charged with murder or manslaughter for on-duty shooting," an occurrence that happens approximately "1,000 times each year."[55] However, since 2004, "Only 29 officers have been convicted," and many of them received lesser manslaughter offenses; only one officer was convicted of intentional murder.[56] Although the study does not reveal the racial makeup of the victims of police killings, it makes clear that "a cop is justified in using deadly force if the officer has a reasonable fear of an imminent threat."[57] In stark contrast to police killings, the Black and Brown boys in the Central Park jogger case were found guilty of rape, assault, riot, robbery, and sexual abuse; one boy was charged with attempted murder, evidenced only by solicited, unsupervised interrogations that resulted in his recorded confessions.[58] The boys' guilt was also shaped, supported, and pushed forth by circulated media representations.

Four of the teenagers who were tried as juvenile defendants served six to seven years each and the 16-year-old, who was tried and sentenced as an adult, served thirteen years in adult prison before all were exonerated from their charges and conviction.[59] The stricter sentencing without evidence beyond the threat of blackness is also a far cry from the plea deal of first-degree manslaughter and one count of burglary given to Robert Chambers, the "preppy killer," just three years earlier in the same space. Chambers brutally murdered 18-year-old Jennifer Levin, whose half-naked body was found bruised, bitten, and strangled in Central Park in 1986. Chambers admitted to killing her accidentally after, according to his testimony, Levin demanded rough sex. Rape was never established by the state,[60] and the deal was only agreed upon after the jury was deadlocked for nine days.[61]

Although Chambers did serve much of his sentence, this was not without the continued effort of Levin's mother, who petitioned against his parole and Chambers' numerous infractions while in prison.[62] Unlike the Central Park Five case, it was the victim, Jennifer Levin, in the Preppy Killer case who was to blame in media perception. While the imagined threat of blackness gives legal aid to the killers of Black and Brown children, the imagined promise of whiteness also gives legal aid to killers of children. As such, identified acts of sexual violence and murder within Central Park and public space in general are contingent upon the sociogenic logics and colonial motivity practices of white sovereignty.

In June 2016, the now retired police commissioner of New York City, Bill Bratton, conveyed his perspective of the problem of urban violence after a shooting occurred at a TI concert. With the same sentiment toward hip hop as Carol from the commentaries section on Cardi's Grammy win, Bratton stated, "The crazy world of the so-called rap artist, who are basically thugs that are basically celebrating the violence they lived all their lives . . . The music unfortunately oftentimes celebrates violence, celebrates degradation of women, celebrates the drug culture."[63] Hip hop is the quintessential signifier of unassimilable blackness and, in a world where blackness is a universal measure of opposition and signifier of fear, representations of hip hop help uphold blackness as a cause for death.

Yet unassimilable blackness within hip hop and the music genre's popularity underscores Fanon's claim that the "unpoetic," corrupted "white soul" needs blackness as "an insurance policy on humanness. When the whites feel like they have become too mechanized, they return to the men of color and ask them for a little human sustenance."[64] Paul Mooney furthers Frantz Fanon's modernity-coloniality relationship and states, "Everybody wanna be a nigga but nobody wanna be a nigga."[65] Indeed, hip hop, Cardi B, and the like remain popular despite failures and refusals of abject conformity.

Expelled from structural and self-governing processes of recuperation and resiliency, blackness remains the normalized exception within the neoliberal order and the universal measure of modernity.[66] Sociogenic discourse has reassembled colonized bodies as primitive, nonwhite, pathological, and third-world, arriving too soon or too late in the spatial and temporal ontological order of western modernity.[67] The only depicted resilient characteristic of blackness is its threatening pathologies, even as privileges of economic mobility have been achieved. These mediated and disseminated sociogenic signifiers are apparent in the headlines of Cardi's response to the Grammy critics and in voluminous mass media coverage of hip hop's Cinderella.

Talking Back to White Space and Circulating Conscious Included Exclusion

As with early hip-hop culture and young people's use of technologies of their time, new forms of technological engagement have been utilized by hip-hop artists to embody, tell, and circulate the local experiences of being young, Black, and poor in an urban space. Cardi resembles this form of engagement as many other artists have done to circumnavigate institutionalized obstacles of censorship and share their voices beyond the musical sounds and visual imagery of their craft. In contrast to these artists who were made famous through their music careers, a large part of Cardi B's success stems from her new and old mediated performances that exist outside of her music. Cardi's ability to *tell* her story on various communication platforms turns the constraints of sociogenic logic on its head.

Although these stories became part of her brand, Cardi offers a glimpse of her perspective in fleeting moments not often framed within our sight of hip-hop representation. These stories told in turn are circulated through various social media platforms and speak a truth—the paradoxical excess embedded in the modernity-coloniality relationship—that is often expressed in hip-hop culture and masked through its representation. One of the most popular representational points of contention has been Cardi B's unrelenting feud with Minaj. Coverage of this feud underscores both the dual function of hip hop and the impossibility of unassimilable blackness to achieve western motivity through socioeconomic success. In line with colonial sociogenic blackness, these representations are simultaneously ungendered and sexed, and although both rappers received criticism and headlines for their ongoing feud, Cardi received much disdain for her behavior.

On the night of the Harper's Bazaar ICONS party for fashion week, Cardi confronted Minaj, which resulted in a scuffle that was recorded by multiple people. Cardi was escorted out of the event with only one shoe (the other was thrown at Minaj), her gown ripped, and a large bump on her forehead due to a physical altercation with Minaj's security and entourage. On Instagram, Cardi claimed she confronted Minaj for talking about her daughter and her mothering skills and added to Minaj that "all bets are fuckin' off!!"[68] Disapproval for Cardi heightened when news covered Minaj as "mortified" and embarrassed of the altercation while Cardi refused to perform the same remorseful demeaner.[69] Although hip hop is contained as a representation of unassimilable blackness, it continues to encompass neoliberal logics of western national belonging.

According to E. Franklin Frazier, Black bourgeoisie sensibilities are the unconditional acceptance and overemphasis of "the white bourgeois world: its morals and its canons of respectability, its standards of beauty and consumption."[70] Cardi B's active refusal of apologetic shame disrupts Black bourgeois sensibilities and its performances of inclusion but not without consequence. Frazier underscores how Black bourgeoisie performances "are rejected by the white world" and, despite their limited triumph, they sustain affective investments against blackness.[71] As Richard Iton forewarns, such bourgeois investments "on the part of blacks to distinguish themselves from 'those people'" reinforce the difference between citizen-subject and the blackened body, and bound "quite oddly and inevitably, Breer Rabbit even closer to the tar baby in the bordered and disciplined otherworld of subaltern existence."[72]

On her *Queen Radio* program, Minaj performs Black bourgeois sensibility as well as its limits and said:

> The other night I was a part of something so mortifying and so humiliating to go through in front of bunch of upper echelon—and it's not about white or black—it's about upper echelon people who are you know people who have their lives together, the way they pass by looking at this disgusting commotion

I will never forget. I was mortified. I was in [an] Alexandre Vattier gown, okay, off the motherfucking runway, okay, and I could not believe how humiliating it all felt because we—and I use "we" loosely and I'm going to clarify "we"—how *we* made ourselves look.[73]

Toward Cardi, Minaj stated she would never talk ill about anyone's children because "that's clown shit" and then stated:

> You just had the biggest blessing of your life with a child, and in two weeks, you have attacked three women, one at fashion week?! And left looking the way you left looking so that people could point their fingers at our culture and our community and laugh at us some more. . . . You came into my fucking culture. I never had to fuck a DJ to play my songs. You calling black women roaches, you been getting girls beat up because of what your man's doing? Real bitches never do that. You never attack the woman. You never attack the woman! You take that up with your fucking man. Fuck out of here. You're angry and you're sad, and this is not funny, and this is not about attacking. This is about get this woman some fucking help. This woman is at the best stage in her career and she's out here throwing bottles and throwing shoes?! Who the fuck is going to give her a fucking intervention?[74]

Minaj also offered her listeners $100,000 for a copy of the altercation that revealed who gave Cardi a blow to her head and the visibly massive lump.

In response to Minaj, Cardi took to Instagram Live with an over eight-minute confrontation spoken directly to Minaj:

> This is my thing Nicki Minaj, right. How you saying that I got ragged by Ra Ali when there is so many footages of that night from every single angle and where am I getting ragged at? Why would I be sitting here online saying, "Oh yeah, I did this or I did that," knowing that the next day, there's gonna be so many footages of that same night? And, second of all, how you say that I was the wild animal, that I attacked you, that you was mortified, that you was humiliated, playing the victim, but now ya the gangsta? You need to pick a side.
>
> Do you wanna be the victim or do you wanna be the gangsta? You lie so much you can't even keep up with your fuckin' lies. First you say that you got the footage, your cameraman got the footage, but now you talkin' about you wanna pay somebody a hundred thousand if they get the footage? Yo. Make sense when you talkin'. I thought you were the victim. I know what there's footage of, you standing on the wall talkin' bout, "I'm standin' right here." Miss Chung Li, the street fighter. Get the fuck outta here. . . .
>
> Let's talk facts now, okay. . . . Then you talk about suing and shit because you claiming that Ra Ali beat me up. Sis, I don't gotta sue nobody because of

a fight. I'm a street bitch. That is called snitchin'. You know, but, since you wanna talk about suing, maybe I should sue you for defamation of character since you wanna claim that I am using something illegal, called Payola, 'cause you don't understand why I'm so fuckin' successful. . . .

Since you say you tired of talking about it, I'm tired of talking about it, too. I'm tired of the whole internet shit. I'm tired of the interview shit. If you really wanna talk about it, you know where to link me. We can always link up. You know who to reach out. You know. We could settle it however you want to settle it. We could talk about it, or we could fight it out. I'm with whateva. . . . [75]

Cardi addressed not just the Harpar's Bazaar confrontation but also Minaj's dissatisfaction with being forced by the record label to change her verse on "Motorsport," Migos's single that featured both Cardi and Minaj. Cardi reveals that Minaj waited until immediately before her album release to revisit her dissatisfaction with "Motorsport." Cardi used her phone to show evidence of her claims that contradicted Minaj and showed how her phone number was leaked, convincingly speculating that it was Minaj and Ra Ali who leaked it. Cardi also showed how Minaj encouraged violence by liking posts that called for the death of Cardi and her daughter, Kulture.

Cardi indicated she would fight if necessary, and especially to protect her daughter, but also extended an understanding of camaraderie and addressed Minaj as "Sis" (with the exception of the Kulture situation). Cardi also said that she always looked up to Minaj and showed her love and respect, but now Minaj is ruining her legacy and "lookin' like a hater."[76] Cardi's use of her social media platforms to talk back to opposing representations and voices provides a space where she is seen and, most significantly, heard. Audre Lorde reminds us that discursive racial difference creates a continuous "unspoken, distortion of vision," and "Black women have on one hand always been highly visible, and so on the other hand, have been rendered invisible through the depersonalization of racism."[77] Cardi's truth-telling moments, as Lorde identifies, are bridges toward self-revelation and transformative action.[78]

Cardi's affective performance of her lived experiences and truth demonstrates an authenticity that has less to do with essentialized acts of Black urban culture and more to do with what Stuart Hall identifies as popular culture, the nonessentialist practices of agency and survival that arise from particular historical conditions of the excluded.[79] A direct ode to urban political practices, Cardi "keeps it real" through her shared intimacy and direct honesty. Before her introduction to reality television, for example, her Instagram was deleted for obscenity when she wrote that she would remove her back teeth so she could "suck dick better."[80] Of course, Cardi did later get her teeth fixed, along with her buttocks, waist, and breasts, but verified she did not get her back teeth removed.[81] Cardi also received pushback for her cosmetic surgeries, which, given their prominence (think of the Kardashian-Jenners), masks the issue of Cardi's forthcoming approach toward her surgeries.

Cardi again responded on social media to critiques of her dental work:

> You know what really be fuckin' pissin' me off when people be commenting like, "Oh my gosh, Cardi, why did you fix your teeth, Aa, Aa, Aa." Bitch you know why I fixed my fuckin' teeth. What is you talkin' about? And you know what really be pissin' me off when people be like, "Oh my gosh, Cardi, I miss your teeth. I miss your old teeth." Bitch, you and my teeth were not fuckin' friends. What is you talkin' about? Like, Like you act like you personally knew my teeth, like you act like you been in my mouth before, like what is you sayin'? "I miss your teeth." Bitch, ya'll was not friends. You and my old teeth was not friends! What the fuck is you missin'? Go miss you man's nuts![82]

Regarding her other cosmetic surgeries—her ass and breasts in particular—Cardi replied in another video,

> I remember before everybody used to talk shit about my teeth, right. Well, I fixed them, so now it's like, uhm, well, your titties look mad fake . . . and it's like, bitch, ya'll never used to talk shit about my titties, now you wanna talk shit about' em. . . . Ya'll bitches is mad. You're mad, bitch [in a West Indian accent], and I don't wanna hear, "Oh but they do look fake." Cause, THEY *ARE* FAKE, BITCH![83]

In response to people like Comfortably Numb who demand she "speak English," Cardi said,

> You know what I don't understand. You know what my question is, when niggas be like, when I do a video, and people be like, "Oh, talk English, bitch," or "Learn how to speak English," and it's like (Cardi makes a nonverbal gesture with her mouth and tongue, seemingly for dramatic pause) my question to you is, WHAT FUCKIN' LANGUAGE AM I MOTHERFUCKIN' SPEAKIN' THEN, BITCH? ISN'T THIS MOTHERFUCKIN' ENGLISH? 'CAUSE IT AIN'T FRENCH. IT DAMN SURE AIN'T NO MOTHERFUCKIN' SPANISH OR PORTUGUESE. IT'S MOTHERFUCKIN' ENGLISH, URrr-KAY.[84]

Cardi's story-telling speaks back to her followers, and her circulated told stories labor to provide a record of localized subjectivity performances that often get re-presented through their circulation. Many, for example, took offense to Cardi calling a woman "roach" and argued it was because the woman was a dark-skinned Black girl; this was also stated by Minaj's podcast address. Cardi reposted an older video on Twitter to disprove such claims. Accompanied with the video, she stated: "I called MY OWN self a roach before so stop it! It's a

word I use ALOt Bronx bitches use a lot stop trying to make it into some racist shit."[85] She then said she was a roach that transformed into a butterfly.[86]

On Instagram Live, Cardi spoke for fourteen minutes on the limits of identity, how she identifies, and how she is identified, talking back to those who
question her identity:

> A lot of people don't know the difference between nationality, race, ethnicity,
> and that's not nobody's fault. That's actually the school's fault because schools
> don't be teachin' this to people. You know what I'm sayin' like this week
> somebody told me in California they was talkin' about Mexico and everything
> and they was like, "You should be out there, you Mexican." And I was like,
> I'm not Mexican, bro. I'm not Mexican at all. First of all, I'm West Indian and
> I'm Dominican. I speak Spanish because I'm Dominican. And so, it's like so,
> "What's the difference between Dominican and Mexican?" It's like everything.
> Everything. Like, everything.
>
> Then they ask me, "Do you understand, Mexican?" And I was like, uh,
> whatchu mean if I understand Mexican? Uh, I understand what they be sayin'
> but sometimes I don't understand what they be sayin' because everybody got a
> different lingo. It's just like people, people from the United Kingdom, they
> speak English but Americans, they won't necessarily understand them, and
> they won't necessarily have like the same culture as them, and that's the same
> thing as every, uh, Latin, Hispanic countries that speak Spanish.
>
> We just don't have the same tradition, like, and I feel like people need to
> really understand because people just don't be understanding shit. Like, it's
> like, "Oh Cardi's Latin; she's not Black," and it's like, bro, my features don't
> come from fuckin' white people fuckin', okay. And they always wanna race-bait
> when it comes to me. That's why I have Afro features. It's that "oh, but your
> parents are lightskin, your parents are this." All right, but my grandparents
> aren't . . . people from the Caribbean islands, they all, it's a mixture, you know
> what I'm saying. It's like the first places where, um, the first places where, uh,
> the slaves were taken to . . . and people don't be knowing that shit and then they
> be just so confused and they want to dictate your race so bad, and it's like, bro,
> pick up a passport or pick up a book so you can fuckin' know.[87]

Her spontaneous addresses to fans, followers, and oppositional posts reflect
many issues that have previously faced hip-hop artists, but Cardi's responses
are often uncensored and create a sense of shared intimacy between herself and
her audience. In another video, Cardi shares with her viewers,

> You know what I hate? I hate when people give me a compliment and short
> me at the same time. Like, you know what, I be getting a lot of haters on my
> Instagram, or on my social media, but I appreciate when they just play me and

that's all they do. I really hate when people be like, "Cardi, I love you, but
I think you look funny. Cardi, I love you, but you're stupid." Like, no. Stop
with that fake love shit. I don't like that. Like, do your mother be tellin' you
I love you but I should've aborted you? Get the fuck outta here with that shit.
I don't like that. It's either you fuck with me or you don't. Don't give me that
fake ass compliment, cornball.[88]

In answering back in real-time, which is often witnessed in her video posts,
Cardi builds similar bridges of communicatory intimacy significant to those
built in localized space. These circulated bridges of communicatory intimacy
mimic relations of homespace created and shared through the expressed awareness and alternative ways of living, being, space, and time that arise out of the
intersections between sociogenic racism and the included excluded position of
blackness.[89] These spontaneous moments reinforce Cardi's performed authenticity, not as a substantiated identity rooted in sameness but as mobile, dynamic,
performed acts of identification that are a foundational part of hip-hop
culture in terms of both communal allegiance and speaking truth to power.
These points of identification "cannot be reduced to a purely biological order
based on blood, race, or geography. Nor can they be reduced to a custom to the
extent that the latter's meaning is always shifting."[90] Cardi's circulated storytelling also provides a clearer glimpse of popular culture that is muddled by corpo-
rate influences and capital.

In the seventh season of *LHNNY*, Cardi's second season on the show, the
first episode shows Cardi reunited with her sister, Hennessy Carolina, and they
drive around New York City in a Bentley.[91] Hennessy tells Cardi that she loves
the new lifestyle Cardi's success has brought them and says, "You better keep
going until you reach the top."[92] Cardi responds, "I ain't gonna lie though,
sometimes I do miss the hood," and Hennessy immediately laughs, which
appears to redirect the conversation.[93] Cardi's sense of longing for the hood is
demonstrated again while touring in Dubai on social media only a few days
after her BET nominations for Best New Artists and Best New Female Artist
were announced.[94]

Cardi addresses her audience and shares her perspective on success in the
industry. Initially looking away from the camera, Cardi begins:

I can't believe I'm nominated for this shit and, like, I was so happy. I was so
happy when I found out I had that award, and there's so many people took that
joy away from me. . . . Evidently, I'm good enough because I got nominated and
for people to try to take that shit away from me that shit really hurt me. . . . My
brain been so fucked up, and another thing that fucked me up is that I noticed,
that I noticed that these niggas in the industry, ain't no love in the industry,
like, you can really buy these niggas loyalty.[95]

Cardi turns toward the camera and looks directly at her audience: "I'm BRIM you know what I'm sayin'."[96] She turns away and continues:

> I'm a hat girl, and I've been jackin' Brim since I was sixteen, and I took an oath when I was sixteen, and loyalty means so much to me, and loyalty should mean so much to anybody. . . . Evidently, ain't no loyalty to these niggas. These niggas, a bitch with a bigger clout or a nigga with a bigger clout bum through your way, and they dick get hard or they pussy get wet. Like, this industry that I'm in, it's so fake. It's so wack. It's so hard for me to adapt to because I'm not used to this shit, my nigga.
>
> I'm not used to this. I'm used to livin', I'm used to livin' my life under an oath. Like, I've been livin' under an oath ever since I was sixteen. I've been livin' under laws, of my 5–9 Brim laws, laws of life since I was a youngin' so when people do funny shit to me it's either I eliminate them, or my heart gets broken. . . . This shit is wack to me. Like, I really hate this industry, like, I hate this industry so much but I got to fight it. I gotta deal with it. . . . Everybody in this industry is an opp. They only lookin' out for themselves. They not lookin out for you or nobody. . . . Ya'll niggas is like fake.
>
> Ya'll niggas ain't about that life. Ya'll niggas ain't real. Ya'll niggas went through the same struggle as me, and ya'll actin like you didn't. That shit is wack, my nigga. I hate that shit. I really hate this fuckin' fake-ass life, like, I'm grateful to you know experience all of this but, then again, I'm not.[97]

It is no coincidence that gang subsets arose in New York City at the same time that the city endured the results of Reaganomics. With the vast reduction of social and public services and the expansion of Richard Nixon's War on Drugs in the mid-1980s, the mass and hyperincarceration of primarily Black and Brown urban youth in the 1990s and 2000s created the conditions for new gang formations. The Mac Baller Brims arise from this context and are a subset of the national Bloods gang; they are predominant in the Bronx and are also located across New York's boroughs and in Rikers Island, the location of one of the largest correctional and mental institutions in the world. The history of Black and Brown gangs, however, does not stem from crime and prison but, as John D. Márquez highlights, were formed primarily to protect their families and neighbors from white ethnic gangs and racism in general, and it is this history that illustrates foundations of a decolonial turn derived from these organized youth.[98]

The violence and death that arise from these gangs both mirror the violence that has been an integral part of creating and sustaining white sovereignty within the modernity-settler colonialism relationship and the suffering that persists within coloniality due to the lack of decolonial resistance.[99] Nevertheless, the foundation for decolonization remains masked with representations of American upward mobility and threatening discourses of blackness in addition to the real effects of law and order. For youth who are simultaneously invisible and hypervisible, targeted as enemies within the nation-state, the bonds they build with each other is more often than not the only socialized love and belonging they experience. And, as many scholars have acknowledged, in a world constructed to hate blackness, loving blackness is indeed a revolutionary act.[100] It is a source of agency. It is an affective practice and alliance that trumps those aligned with upward mobility and success.

In the same post, Cardi continues when someone outside of the frame suggests that her complaints about the industry are the result of success:

> Fuck success, my nigga. I rather have no success and have real niggas around me . . . but, like, these people that be comin' to me, my nigga, and suckin my dick, they mad fake. All these niggas that wanna fuck me, all these bitches that wanna heehaha with me, ya'll never was doin' that when I was a stripper, so get the fuck out my face with that shit, my nigga. Everybody wanna suck my dick now cause I'm a fake ass somebody. . . . Now that I'm older, I don't wanna be in this shit bro. I just wanna live my life regular. . . . Shit is crazy.
>
> In order for you to live this type of lifestyle, and see all these beautiful views, you gotta be a fake-ass person, bro, and I hate being fake. I was never a fake bitch but now, now I gotta act like shit don't bother me. I gotta act like shit is so cool. I gotta act like I don't give a fuck, and I do give a fuck. I definitely give a fuck. You wanna know why I give a fuck? Because I'm a fuckin' human being, and I'm not used to people talkin' shit about me.
>
> I'm not used to people talkin' shit about me, and I don't do nothin'. I'm the type of person a bitch talkin' shit about me, I punch her right in her closure, or I'm the type of person if a nigga talkin' shit about me, I send my niggas out, but I can't even do none of that. I feel like I'm a prisoner. I'm a prisoner to the fame, bro. I'm a prisoner to the fame. I'm a prisoner to the money, like, and that shit is wack. I'm making so much money and I'm mad fuckin' miserable.[101]

Upward mobility and its accompanied lifestyle is not worth the price of abject conformity to whiteness, which demands that Cardi surrenders her codes of loyalty, integrity, and dignity developed through the street. The sentiment of belonging to and loving the community of young people, "the real niggas" around her, when she was Brim echoes that which she expressed when she was filmed talking with her sister. Her storied experiences, however, navigate around the limits of representation through her story-telling and intimacy building. Cardi's lived experience of being Black and loving the sense of solidarity created by communities shaped by marginalization, racism, and white sovereignty appear in moments of these spontaneous reflections. Cardi illustrates how such culture is about spreading love as opposed to individualistic and privatized approaches to access.

The "tensions and oppositions between what belongs to the central domain of elite or dominant culture and the culture of the 'periphery'" are certainly the "structuring principle of the 'popular.'"[102] Indeed, the collective "people" is at the core of the popular, and "popular" culture is a matrix of potential possibilities for social change.[103] As such, the streets, corners, clubs, and other localized spaces that encompass productive affective investments are momentarily and sporadically revealed on a larger scale with Cardi's use of social media to express her everyday politics of included exclusion. In another post, Cardi states, "I don't be understandin' how a lot of these niggas wanna be the only nigga in they team eatin', like, ya'll wanna be the only nigga in they team makin' schmoney. Ya'll don't wanna put your bros on and it's like, my nigga, what's what's fun about being the only nigga in your team makin' money? Like ain't you tired of paying for everybody's shit . . . I don't get it."[104]

These investments disrupt colonial assemblages and aspirations to realize the American dream. They express an identification that is something more. Such storied moments position Cardi and her role in hip-hop culture within a long history of New York hip-hop artists who, as the Notorious B.I.G. reminds us through a sample of Martin Lawrence, need to talk, speak on how they feel and on life with how they see it.[105] In the same post on identity, Cardi discusses how points of identification operate between the intersections of space, racism, and the police:

> Nah, 'cause it's crazy right, because people, some island women, some, some artists that are from the same islands as me, people will be like, "Oh, they Black," but because Cardi speaks Spanish she's, to people, she's not Black even though we have similar features, same skin complexion, but no, they, they wanna, they wanna not put Cardi in it because I speak Spanish. They wanna act like when Cardi use to walk in stores, these white bitches wasn't behind me like, "Can I help you? Can help you? Can I help you? Can I help you?"
>
> Like if Cardi didn't come from a hood that's continuously ghetto-pressed, that people get treated like shit and I didn't grew up with. I didn't grew up on somethin' like a certain group of people hanging out with a certain group of people, a certain group of people hangin' out with a certain group of people.[106] I'm from New York, like, we don't do that; everybody just fuck with each other. *Everybody have the same enemy and the enemy is the police.* Everybody gets oppressed where I come from by the same people.
>
> Everybody over here gets, everybody here, whether they Puerto Rican, Dominican, Jamaican, Haitian, African American. Every single time, when a guy or a woman gets harassed, everybody have each other's back here. It's not like, oh, well they ain't my peoples so we ain't takin' up for them. That's not how it works out here. That's now how it works in the Bronx.[107] [emphasis mine]

Although I have focused on Cardi B and how her social media circulates truth to power, these embodiments and investments have always and already been produced. Cardi's embrace of her included exclusion of unassimilable blackness is not hers alone as particular representations and circulations have shared these articulations. In circulated footage of Tupac Shakur and the Notorious B.I.G.'s live performance at Trafalgar Square in 1993, Tupac addressed the crowd:

Thug life is not what these white folks are trying to peg it to be. I'm not tellin' niggas to go and kick sistas in the ass, ya know, and just cause ruckus. I'm just saying for all you broke niggas, you ain't got to be broke no more in '94. If we all got together and used the fear that these white people have for us any muthafuckin' way, we might have somethin'.

One nigga can't do shit, but a million niggas, we'll run this mutha fuckin' country. I mean, work this mutha fucker. Just like there's niggas in New York, there's niggas in Texas, niggas in Oakland. We'll all rip this whole muthafucker up till ya'll is dead.[108]

The crowd cheered emphatically to his call.

Tupac's words and the crowd's responding sentiment echoed fictional gang leader Cyrus from the now cult-classic *The Warriors*.[109] In his address to the multiple gangs across the boroughs in this fictional depiction of youth gang life in 1970s New York City, Cyrus addresses the young urban crowd:

Can you count suckas? I say the future is ours. If you can count. (A voice from the crowd responds to Cyrus: "Come' on Cyrus, we're with you." Another voice is heard: "Come on, bro.") Now look what we have here before us. We've got the Zarsens sitting next to the Jones Street Boys. We've got the Moonrunners right by the Van Cortlandt Rangers. Nobody is wasting nobody. That is a miracle, and miracles is the way things ought to be. (Member of the crowd responds with cheers.)

You are standing right now with nine delegates from a hundred gangs, and there's over a hundred more. That's twenty thousand hardcore members, forty thousand counting affiliates, and twenty thousand more not organized but ready to fight: sixty thousand soldiers. Now there ain't but twenty thousand police in the whole town. Can you dig it? Can you dig it? CAN YOU DIG IT? (The roars and cheers in response and do not quiet down until Cyrus gestures to do so.)

Now here's the sum total: one gang can run this city, one gang. Nothing would move without us allowing it to happen. We can tax the crime syndicates, the police, because we got the streets, suckas. Can you dig it? (The crowd responds again in louder cheers.)[110]

Communicated traits of authenticity and truth-telling as linked to the popular help combat negative mass media representations and, equally important, they illustrate that abject conformity to bourgeois sensibility and civility derived from modernity-coloniality relations is not the only means of survival or even being. Most significantly, they spread an alternative act of love that extends beyond discourses of western mobility and its contemporary neoliberal logics of privatization and reform.

Conclusion

After her first mixtape and her popularity on *LHHNY*, Cardi's Instagram was deleted again when during her performance in Flint, Michigan, she stated, "Fuck you, Trump. Fuck the government," and got the crowd of hundreds to chant "Fuck Trump!"[111] When Flint was brought up on an interview with The Breakfast Club on Power 105.1, Cardi then said she was not going to talk about the government anymore because "She didn't want to get Tupac'd out" in reference to the murder of Shakur.[112] Her expressed concern of Black killings, however, has yet to stop her. Cardi has been outspoken against police murder and torture that occur on the street and inside correctional facilities; she has continuously critiqued the state policies that unduly affect marginalized communities and has gone against patriarchal perspectives reinforced in the music industry, for example, Jermaine Dupri's critique of female rap artists and body-shaming celebrities such as Lizzo. She has also been forthcoming about her antiracist stance, for example, turning down the 2019 Superbowl half-time show to stand in solidarity with Colin Kaepernick to democratic senators publicly contemplating if they should retweet Cardi's post on the government shutdown the same year, where she replied via Twitter, "Why am I trending?"[113]

These spontaneous communicated performances labor to make apparent critical practices of revolutionary consciousness. As C.L.R. James reminds us, the colonized leaders and elite did not pave the way for revolt immediately before the first decolonization revolution in Saint Domingue.[114] James states, "All the educated ones, all those who were not so educated but who had sat for a while in the seats of power, they were prepared to submit to any indignity in order to remain, not with power, but merely the symbols, and to enjoy the profits of power."[115] It was the people, what Fanon would identify as the lumpen-proletariat, who would ignite the spark of complete and fundamental change.[116] James argues, "It took a man like Dessalines, an absolute barbarian, to lead the people finally to their freedom. Dessalines could not write: the name of many a Haitian general had to be traced for him in pencil for him to trace it over in ink. But he, Dessalines, was the one who could lead the rebellious mass of the population."[117]

For those of us who have never or no longer experience these affective collectivities of the popular, Cardi is a reminder that they do in fact continue to exist, even and especially in the direst times and spaces. Moreover, as Fanon, has underscored, violence is inevitable in the decolonization process as it is the colonizing sovereign that will exercise the right to kill and quash insurgency and threat.[118] As such, to paraphrase John D. Márquez, perhaps the problem is not the violence of urban youth but who they target.[119] The young people in these urban spaces, in the front line as marked included exclusions, understand this and often articulate it as they did in Flint, prompted by Cardi.

The empathy and organized affective investment in localized groups are built upon shared understandings of included exclusion. These potential points of becoming circulate through social media, spreading their affective investments in relations of homespace beyond any particular site. These moving acts of articulated agency circulate through both actions and stories, even while those who do it and tell it are regulated to various forms of immobility. As in hip-hop culture, we respond to the call.

4

Mobile Stories and Bounded Spaces

Stories Told and Telling Performances

I have come to believe over and over
again that what is most important to me,
must be spoken, made verbal and shared,
even at the risk of having it bruised or
misunderstood. That the speaking profits
me, beyond any other effect.
—Audre Lorde

Particularly for people of color, life lived,
whether on the concrete pavement of
inner-city streets or in the backwoods of
a rural southern community, is the root
of our beginnings and the root of our
understandings.
—D. Soyini Madison

On a hot and sunny mid-August day in 2017, as I was opening my curtain windows to let the sun shine into my living room, I saw a police truck parked across the street by my neighbor's driveway. One officer was outside of the truck, and the other was standing crouched over by where the grass separated the narrow concrete walkway from the curb. I stood up on my tiptoes and stretched myself as far up as I could to see what he was peering down at. As I was trying to see what the officer was looking at, the second officer got out of the vehicle and walked slowly over to stand about three feet from his partner. He was facing down but seemingly in another direction. Once I moved to the side, I saw legs moving about. Where the second officer was positioned, a man was rising from the ground. He was shirtless and in his late twenties or early thirties; his hair was brown, and although a bit shaggy not very long, and he had a goatee. He was white.

Because I was inside, I could not hear what he and the officers were saying but they were all talking to each other while looking every so often on the ground toward the direction of the original officer's peering eyes. As they talked, another police car pulled into my neighbor's driveway and parked vertically, halfway on the driveway and halfway on the street. The rear of the truck was positioned to be protected by the parked car at the front of its side, and the other police car was stationed at the back of the truck's other side. The officers in this second vehicle were sitting in their car as I watched the second police officer move his leg as if nudging something on the grass. Nothing. He nudged again and then turned to the young man; they were talking. Then, the young man directed his head toward the grass, saying something. He bent down out of my sight, and the two officers were now also facing and talking downward.

The two other officers stepped out of the second vehicle but were in closer proximity to their vehicle than to the location of the other officers. The young man then stood up and, as I suspected, another young man slowly rose up. This second young man was also shirtless and responded as if abruptly awakened from a deep sleep in his room. He stretched slowly as they were all talking with the original officers at an arm's distance from this second sleepy man. This second one was blonde with hair much longer than his friend's, and his beard was longer than his hair. He was taller than his friend but much thinner. He, too, was white.

After a few minutes of talking, it seemed the officers directed the two young men to go. The two men began to walk slowly away in the opposite direction of the officers and from where they were sleeping. The blonde one stopped to smell the flowers that protruded through my neighbor's fence. As his friend tugged on his arm to continue walking, he ripped some flowers out to take with him. The officers did not say a word; they watched the two young men walk with the flowers in root, in hand, and then talked among themselves before they returned to their police vehicles and drove away.

On the same block just two years before, William, a longtime Chicago resident, recalled a confrontation between a police officer and a young boy, which he observed from inside his enclosed porch. Unlike the exchange I witnessed,

William was in ear's range and had heard the encounter. According to William, he was on his porch bringing some things inside when he saw a police officer approach a young boy as the boy was crossing the street. William said the police officer stopped the boy and asked him where he was going. The boy told the police officer that he did not have to tell him where he was going, and the officer then said that he wanted to see the boy's identification. He moved toward the teenager until he was less than an arm's length, blocking the boy's path. The officer repeated, "Show me your I.D.," and the boy responded, "Fuck you. I don't have to show you nothin'. I'm not doing nothing wrong. I'm just walking."

William continued, "The officer quickly threw the boy onto the side hood [of the parked car] in front of them, and that's when I saw the boy look toward me. When he looked, the officer turned around and saw me just staring at him. At this point, my arms were crossed, and I was just standing there on my porch, staring at him. I didn't even blink, and I was lookin' like, 'go ahead.' The officer turned back to the boy and brought the boy to his feet." As he said this, William gestured with his arms to demonstrate the police officer holding the boy's shoulders and literally placing the boy back on his feet. William watched the officer's demeanor toward the young boy change, and, for William, the shift was because the officer knew he was being watched by William who was inside of his home. The officer moved from the boy's path and left him with a warning: "'The next time someone asks you for I.D., you show it to them,' and then he started saying why he as an officer had the right to stop him and ask him for I.D. When the officer stopped talking, the boy walked away, and so did the officer. Neither of them looked my way." William is Black American and was in his late 30s at the time he shared his story; the teenager was also described as "Black and about 17 years old."

These two police exchanges occurred on the same block in the Rogers Park neighborhood of Chicago, a neighborhood that represents one of the most racially diverse neighborhoods in Chicago and one that is not nationally publicized as a high crime area for the city. Rogers Park is, however, a neighborhood that possesses blue lights for security, a heavy police rotation, and exists alongside a high rate of undergraduate and graduate students from the neighboring universities. It is in the northside section of Chicago that is adjacent to Evanston, the suburb where Northwestern University is located, and also has a strikingly large percentage of professionals and those who work for nonprofits as residents. This neighborhood has seen much change in the last decade due to gentrification, including a rise in white residents and public and commercial investment, related to Loyola University, which occupies the lakeside at the beginning of Rogers Park. Although this chapter in not about Rogers Park, it will highlight experiences from this Chicago neighborhood that were shared during my work for a northside nonprofit's pilot program that centered on young residents documenting shared experiences of police brutality.

As preparation for engaging with their neighbors, youth who participated in the program would also attend training workshops twice a week that consisted of ethnographic and community engagement methods and themes of racism. The program's purpose was to empower the storytellers and active listeners to disrupt isolation, marginalization, and erasure that haunt the people who are victimized by such traumas. I chose to include these stories to contextualize the experiences of being identified as Black in a space that is not considered a high crime area in Chicago. Although the disparity of the experiences might be unimaginable for some, it does not even scratch the surface of how urban space is policed, surveilled, and terrified under the law. These encounters suggest that space is marked as white and that the duty to protect and serve within those spaces, especially public space, is reserved for those who are not marked as Black. Along these lines, this chapter centers on the experiences of those who are identified as Black and the stories they tell about those identifications.

The telling of these identifications is multifunctional. They are told as active expression, allowing the teller to embody herself as an actor in her own life and empower herself through the act of telling. They are told with a purpose to not only empower but also to keep those who are part of the exchange "in the know" as a primary part of community formation and as shared acts of trust and love. These acts of communicating and life-told are positive productivities of life lived and living life, as the epigraphs illustrate, even as the content encompasses experiences of race-based terror, torture, and marginalization. These told stories are, indeed, relations of homespace, aimed to share knowledge, and are derived from love despite the conditions of included exclusion.

All these stories have been collected from New York City and Chicago. I had originally meant for these stories to be a tale of two cities, but as the storyteller, I cannot control the flows of the stories told and their origin. As such, some of these stories include residents who are not originally from these cities but whose experiences resonated with being identified as Black in an urban space. For instance, I listened to Malcolm's stories while visiting him near or at his Brooklyn apartment; however, many of his childhood experiences happened in Washington DC, where he was raised until he finished high school. Together, these stories span the urban spaces of New York City prior to World War II, Washington DC during the Reagan Era, and Chicago post-911. Some of the story-tellers spoke for long periods of time and desired to continue the conversation across multiple days, but others spoke for less than one hour.

Some story-tellers chose to continue our conversations on the phone after our visits and my departure from New York City. Many were born and raised in their neighborhood boroughs with their families for generations. These narratives are retold as disorder, and not represented chronologically, to highlight how articulations of time and space are primarily discursive, ideological formations in the struggle over hegemony. All these stories are from residents who exemplified included-excluded identifications of blackness through the told stories and their telling of their stories. Repeated here, these told stories in circulation possess the potential to become relations of homespace, just as they do each time they are shared.

Each story within these varying contexts enters the conversation of what it means to be marked as Black in a world that is taught to hate blackness. I have heard some of these shared stories often, some I have heard only once, I have been a witness to others, and some have been given to me. Even the stories that have not been directly shared with me have been a product of dialogic exchange and racial sincerity by way of living and working closely in communities in which they are told, and, most importantly, through community members who have entrusted me with these shared memories. Not all of the storytellers felt the need to be anonymous, but some did and, because of the nature of some of what was discussed, I have maintained anonymity for all of the storytellers involved, using only first names, pseudonyms, and initials for all storytellers.

To honor the taken-for-granted act of storytelling, the storied performances in this chapter are displayed as a dialogic exchange and call attention to human action and the voice of the story-teller rather than the author.[1] Written as such, I aim to mirror how stories are shared and circulated and how they function as moving and mobilizing modes of care, community, consciousness. These narratives attempt to visually provide a description of how they are told and underscore how "words are alive with sounds that condition their meanings" in the contextual moment.[2] In unison, these stories span over seventy years and touch on the many temporal and spatial shifts that have occurred in the local and national space.

The skylines of New York City and Chicago mirror each other as they both were created to exemplify the United States as the quintessential model of modernity; as the capital of the nation, Washington, DC, additionally reinforces these ideals. The discursive and symbolic formation of movement (the speed of time and the navigating, i.e., conquest, of space) is key in these urban models as the hope from national myths that center on upward mobility have been strengthened by the spatial infrastructure. The three cities together function as symbolic of movement in a variety of ways; for example, they are connected to multiple, realized Great Migrations of African diasporic peoples, and each possesses the most frequented public transit systems in the United States. These cities quite literally encompass the primary mode of capitalist communicative technology: the conquest of both time and space. These spaces are simultaneously unique and similar as they all also share symbolic imageries of modern national consciousness. These spaces alone, however, do not share how the people who live and experience these temporal spaces also shape them through their active conscious existence, traversal of space, and their creative relations of homespace. The following performed stories attempt to capture how the stories shared, performed, and experienced move those who tell, in the act of telling, and those who listen.

Moving Bodies

Harlem, New York City, early 1920s

Your mother's from Puerto Rico?

MRS. M Yes, my mother was born in Puerto Rico, and my father was born in Puerto Rico. My mother was from San Juan, I think, if I'm not mistaken, and my father was also from there, but my mother came here when she was young. Because she fell in love with my father over there and my grandmother didn't want them to get married, 'cause she thought she was too young, so they sent her over here and then my aunt sent her mother, which was my mother's mother, over here. 'Cause then, my mother, she came over here and then my father followed. He came over here 'cause she was here. He found her and they got married, and then my mother had a child every year because my father believed in having children. Until the time they killed him.

My father was stabbed to death. They say he was uh, playing cards (pause) You know, in those days, you played cards in people's houses; everything was in the house, and, um, they say some men, a guy that was there was talking about his sister and he didn't like what he was saying, and he told him look, you're talking about my sister. You know, he was degrading her, so they started arguing, and my father, then, when he walked out, when he was walking in the street, they threw a knife in his back. But it, you know, it cut him, but it wasn't serious, so when he turned the corner, they threw another one, and it took him by the heart (pause); that's what killed him. That was (pause), I was very young at the time.

His sister. My father's sister, Nereida, she was the tall one that used to live on Madison Street. She used to live here. Um, she was very pretty, very pretty, very elegant. She looks like [my second daughter's] mother. If you see her and you saw [my second daughter], you would swear that was her mother. Just like [my second daughter]. Tall, very elegant, beautiful features, beautiful jet-black hair. She had the most gorgeous hair you can see. And um, he, my father, had, Nereida, Consuelo, and there was another one in Puerto Rico (pause); it was a family of about six or seven kids. You know it—it was a big family.

Who's the oldest?

MRS. M Leon, then me, then Mary, and my brother Jesus is the youngest. He's the baby. He was my baby brother. When they killed my father, my mother was pregnant of my baby brother Jesus. She had been about eight months pregnant when the funeral (pause). My mother was so small and thin and skinny. She was always very tiny.

My father was a big man, he was over six feet. Husky man too! He looked Italian. So, my brother, Paco, I mean we call him Paco for short, but they named him after my father and my father's name was after his father; it went down the line. But, instead of naming my brother, Leon, which he was the one that was supposed to be named after my father, they named him after a nurse that took care of my mother, when she was having him. And, my mother fell in love with her because she was so good, you know, took care of her, so well, so she named him, William. So, my baby brother, they gave him my father's name.

Washington DC, late 1970s

MALCOLM Moving to DC was no accident. As I said previously, my mother provided me with a type of countereducation, so moving to DC was a way to provide me with a frame of reference that was different. Ya know.

Different in what way?

MALCOLM Ya know, different in the sense that I would get a diverse range, a wide variety of Black folk, poor, middle class, Black folk in suits, those who aren't. Like that. Ya know, it was kind of like those different stories and songs, my mother wanted me to see different things, different ways of life, ways about the world. She provided me with the guidance, or you could say knowledge, that was indicative of the man she wanted me to be. She wanted me to think critically.

So, where did you move from?

MALCOLM We moved from New Orleans, Lou-eaze-ee-ann-a. (He says it in song in a kind of drawl.) We moved to DC when I was two. My mother was in graduate school, gettin' her master's at Tulane University. Being in DC helped to develop me in a certain way. We often took trips to the Frederick Douglass Museum, the National Mall. I remember Saturday and Sunday we would be at the museums, 'cause, you know, the museums are all free in DC, so there I was with my mother. My mother gave me an outlook on the world politically. Movin' to DC, teachin' me about myself. Well (pause), the first thing is my name, Malcolm, after Malcolm X, so in a sense you could say that since birth I was pigeonholed into it. (He slightly laughs). It's, it's like that rapper said: I was born into it, not sworn into it. (He laughs again). So, I had my hair locked before that was even in style and dudes were like, "Yo, whatsup with your hair?" You know, and after that my mother taught me things that kind of, ya know, went against the education that we get taught. Some may call it countereducation.

Brooklyn, New York, 2005

ASIA We moved from Brooklyn in 1999. James, our two kids, and his mother, all of us moved to North Carolina. His sister came with her family, and I sent for [my older daughter] once we got settled. James joined the army to get us out and start over. It was bad for a few years. We couldn't live with his mother in [housing], and we couldn't live with my family either. They were tired of James and I fighting. The time he knocked my front teeth out, it was done for my family. Same thing with his mom; she was done. I mean, of course she blamed me for the fighting but whatever. We lived with some of his relatives in [housing] in Coney Island; they said we had to leave after the baby was born, and we did when he was like a year. We went from shelter to shelter with the kids, and then I got the apartment by [the projects]. But, we lost that.

Why did you move with James? I mean [after the abuse].
ASIA (She laughs). We're married, and this was our chance to start over. When he's home (pause), he don't hit me no more. We still fight, but he never hit the kids. You know (pause), my life is better; it's easier, here. My kids, too.

Traps

Brooklyn, New York, early 2000s

ERIC Now you KNOW I've BEEN hustlin, but seriously, when they tried to kill me was when I was trying to get out. I actually was already movin' to Florida.

So, they tried to kill you? Who?
ERIC DICK, niggas (pause) tried (pause) to kill (pause) me (pause)! Mothafuckas who wanna see me dead (Eric bends his face toward where I was sitting and points to two bullet scars on his forehead, one right above his left eye and the other slightly just left of the first above his eyebrow). They shot me. They shot me in my head! Yeah, nigga (pause), I almost died. I was in the hospital for months and, and I was already sayin' I was getting out and movin' but, yeah, they shot me and my baby mother, my son, my family they were coming to the hospital, and that's when I told my baby mother that if I get out this hospital and survive this shit, I'm out.

So, did they try to kill you because you were getting out?

ERIC (Eric smirks with his lips out and scrunched together, shaking his head). Nah. (He does not answer my question) So, yeah, nigga, I was in the hospital, and I'm getting better. I sent my son and his mother with money to Florida, house, rides; she set everything up, and my son was doing good in school and shit. So, then I sell my phone to that fuckin' dick over there (Eric points a few feet over to his friend), and I'm out. (Eric responds to my facial expression that I unknowingly communicate to him.) Right, nigga (pause), and let me tell you somethin'. I go over there. Shit is ALL set up with MY money, and I'm ready to do ALL THAT SHIT. No bullshit. No more of this. No more bitches. Nothin', nothin' and she's like, "I'm good." Dick, you believe that shit? I'm good. So, what do I do? I fuckin' run back here (Eric does a running gesture with his hands) and call that nigga (he acts as if he is making a phone call) like, "Yeah, I'm a need my phone back." (We laugh) Dick. Crazy right? I gotta buy back my own fuckin' phone, and here I am (Eric gestures to one of his friends who passes us on his way to the restroom) with these dicks.

Harlem, New York City, mid1940s

MRS. M I could remember when I was in public school, and um, about fourth or fifth grade, yeah, and at that time this area was divided. You know. At that time, this area was divided. Like um (pause), on Third Avenue, we had a trolley and the train. But you could not cross on this side of the street 'cause this side was just for the Italian people. (Mrs. M points and gestures, creating a map of the streets with her hands and showing how the divides were made not by the official maps of Harlem but by the residents.) So, we were not allowed to come on this side; on that side from Third, Lexington, Park and Fifth was the Puerto Rican and the other side was the Black ones. So, I went to a public school 'cause uh, like how, you know, I didn't have my father, my mother there, so we were poor, I'm poor.

So, I went to public school, and it was on 111th Street between Fifth and Lennox. And we were living at the time (pause) 113th, 114th, and Fifth. And, as a matter of fact, I still know the number of my building. It was 1367 Fifth Avenue. Um, it was hard because you know, it was public school and, and it wasn't as bad as it was now because public school now is (pause). It, it, but it was, it's uncomfortable, you know, it was hard for us because we were poor. Uh, that when you could go to the store and buy with a quarter, a quart of milk, bread, and you still had two cents or three cents to buy candy, to buy little kisses or Mary Jane, you would get maybe five for a penny (pause) in those days. YEAH! Um, at lunch time, I had a girlfriend, who her name was Emma, and we could go to eat at a fish n' chip. Which that fish n' chip would cost us maybe twenty cents, but they gave you so much fish n' chip that we would share that for her and I. It was delicious.

Um, the teachers were good. The teachers were, you know, they helped you. Ohhh, how can I explain this, um (pause), the area was not the best 'cause it wasn't a, a very nice area where we lived, because there was, you know, um, in those days they had a lot of prostitutes. And they would be like in the corner. But these girls were young girls 'cause I would talk to, you know, I went to school, and I would see them and say hi, hi, and they would talk to you like. And my mother of course didn't tell us, she told us one day, you don't talk to these women. But they were young, they look so young, they looked like maybe twenty years old and nice-looking girls, and they were so sweet and friendly. Really nicely dressed you know, nothing under, exposed or nothing like that. So, we would go to school, come home. Did my work, my housework, do my homework, and then you stayed home.

MRS. M   Okay (Mrs. M gestures again toward outside). From there, from Fifth Avenue to Lennox that's where only the Puerto Rican and the Black people used to live, and then from Lennox all the way to the West Side, there was just Blacks. From Fifth to Madison and Park and Lexington was Puerto Rican and Black, but, from Third all the way to Second, this was all Italian. That's when we had the trolley on Third Avenue. You was not allowed to walk on this side of the street. 'Cause if the Italians catch people or the kids whatever, they'll beat you up. That was a no, no, you know, and the kids, because they were raised that way, you know, they didn't mingle with the Spanish kids or the Black kids. So, kids were being brought up in that area where the kids hated Puerto Ricans or Blacks. That's the way it was in those days, you know.

So okay, the neighborhood was divided. Did you ever cross into the other side?

MRS. M   Oh, yes, I used to cross every Saturday to buy my mother her chicken. Right there, on 112th.

But you weren't supposed to be there?

MRS. M   Oh, no, honey, and you better run, 'cause if they catch you, they beat you up.

Why did your mother send you there?

MRS. M   Well, my, to my mother, she told you to do something, you're gonna do it. That's the way it was. She knew that this was a prejudice side, that you were not supposed to be here, but she figured if you run from there to there get my chicken and then you run back. (Mrs. M. points and gestures to her impromptu map.) Once you get on that side of the street, I was safe. It was just this block here, because from there to there, it was all Italian. Yeah, I mean, it was ALL and a lot of mafia, a lot of mafia. You bet.

I r'member one time, I went to the pool because I would go and I went to Jefferson. Now, that pool belongs to the housing, you know, that Jefferson pool, Jefferson. I went to the pool, and um, I went to the pool with my friends. When I went to get in the water, they took my bathing suit off, so I had to walk out of the pool without clothes. No bathing suit. I was maybe what 10 years old, very little. You know, yeah, but they took my bathing suit off, they sure did, and then I had to get out of the pool, otherwise, they would have drowned me in there. And then somebody threw me a towel. I took my, you know my stuff, I go into the locker, got my clothes, and then I had to come home (pause), run home.

And where were your friends? They ran too?
MRS. M Oh hell! EV-ER-Y-BO-DY ran. EVERYBODY ran. You better run, 'cause if not, they beat you up. They would beat, for no reason, they would beat you up. It was horrible (pause), it was.

Washington DC, late 1980s

MALCOLM I was CONSTANTLY being trapped. I don't know if I told you, but my mom never stressed grades.

No, I didn't know that. In the eighth grade?
MALCOLM Yeah. Yeah. Exactly. At that moment in time, I was ready for more work. Now, I was like, "Oh, okay, I could do this." Like, this ain't half bad (he laughs). I wanted to be challenged more. And, you know, they had different tracks: the academic, comprehensive, and special ed, and I was in the comprehensive track. I had asked to be in the academic track, right. Now, this is the first time I had asked this question to be challenged more, and nobody picked up on it. I had asked to be in the academic track, and I remember the teacher who was in charge of placing the students, Mrs. Sommers was her name, and ya know, Mrs. Sommers was like, "Nah, we're not gonna be able to do this, Malcolm." I think this is pretty common for young people of color.

For the most part, I think it is ESPECIALLY common from what I have experienced in terms of myself and my work for Black boys who want to be smart but are not allowed to. They are consistently being ignored, or not challenged, and, ya know, my research is primarily on these assaults on the intellectual and identity development of Black boys within the everyday. You know that's why it's important for us to begin examining these assaults and to begin to establish and institutionalize countereducations, if you will. And, ya know, I am hoping that my work does that and continues to do so (pause). But, ya know, now that I am telling you this, ya know, now that I think about it, it, it's more than an assault.

For me, it was more than an assault. It was a denial. 'Cause, ya know, ya have to think, what would've happened if she would've said, "Okay, Malcolm, let's put you in the academic track." Ya know, we don't know those potential the possibilities. I just would have no idea.

And what kind of grades did you have at this point, around when all this happened?

MALCOLM I had all A's and B's. Yeah, it would've been interesting to see what could've happened. But, you know, I was actively denied access to intellectual development; there was an active resistance to me being smart. And another story of this active resistance. Now, this one, my mother flipped. I don't know; I must've told her or something. I don't know; I don't quite remember, but I remember some cats came around givin' tests. They created some kind of career aptitude test, and, when it came to my turn, I was like, "Oh, I don't know exactly what I want to be but I kind of like to talk to people, and I like workin' with people. I most definitely wanna be communicatin' with people," and they were like, you know, "Oh, you could be a barber, and my mother was SO MAD. She went up there and was like, "HAVE YOU ALL LOST YOUR DAMN MIND!"

Like the other night, I was watching *Malcolm X*, and you know the part where the teacher asks Malcolm if he's given his career goals any thought, and Malcolm was like, "I wanna be a lawyer," and the teacher is like, "Nah. That's not realistic for a nigger. You SHOULD be a carpenter." Tsss. (We both uneasily laugh a similar disappointed, yet unsurprised expression). And ya know, it's the same thing. Tellin' me I should be a barber. It was as if I was actively prevented to really claim smart. You know, they might as well say it to me like they said it to Malcolm. AND I'm not sayin' there's anything wrong with these professions or that being a barber takes less skill and smarts than being a lawyer, but what I am sayin' is that you have kids that are being actively discouraged or even encouraged to claim particular categories and identities. I'm at a point in my life where possibilities should be unlimited and, you know, they were like, "Nah, that's a wrap."

So, yeah, with good right, my mom had to flip on my behalf. 'Cause you know, it's like it begins at such an early age where you are constantly being trapped into particular categories, and it's these people in authority, who SHOULD BE guiding you toward multiple possibilities, that are like, "No, you need to be a carpenter," or "No, you need to be a barber," or, or, "No, you need to be an athlete." So, what you have is exactly what you created, and you have a bunch of kids whose potential abilities are focused elsewhere. This is why I give praise to my mother; I give praise to people within my cultural community. Ya know, I give praise to the people I was in contact with when I needed a kind of guidance or, or a countereducation.

Brooklyn, New York City, 1989

ASIA I remember I was with Rose, my older sister, Judy, and Lisa, visiting Jax in the hospital. We were spendin' all this time over there because of Rose [Jax's girlfriend], and we were already told that he didn't have long to go with the leukemia. (She takes a deep breath and sighs). So, I go outside to get some air and have a smoke, and, uh, instead of standin' right outside the hospital, I walk further up the block almost by the bus stop. (She gestures with her hands to show me where she is a how far she is from the hospital entrance and the bus stop.) I'm standin' there and smokin', and this guy comes over to me and starts talkin' to me, this grown man, and it's dark out. And, uh, you know, I don't, I don't know, I don't (pause).

At first, I kind of half smile and let him say what he's gotta say, but then he starts gettin' a little TOO close, and he's lookin' at me all (pause), I don't know, uh, dirty and shit. So, I'm like, "Yo, can you give me some space? I really wanna be alone right now." And, uh, instead of doing what I tell him, he comes closer to me, and he's still talkin' and, honestly, I really don't remember what he was sayin'. But he comes so close and touches me. I mean, like, grabs me (she gestures to her arm), and I'm like, "GET THE FUCK OFF OF ME," and he doesn't. So, my other hand's been in my pocket since I flicked my cigarette, and I, uh, push up my boxcutter and I cut 'im. I was fourteen when they sent me to a [juvenile detention] home for cuttin' his face.

How did they arrest you if he attacked you?

ASIA They said that, because I was by the hospital, I could've went back to where I was, and there was security and there was also security just the opposite way from the bus stop, too. They said, if I couldn't run from 'im, I coulda easily screamed for help, but I didn't. (She looked at me and smirked.) I spent eighteen months there [at the detention center] and, when I came out, I got with this older guy, Bobby. I got pregnant with my daughter a few months after that.

Northside, Chicago, 2011

RICHARD I was driving home from work and a guy started chasing me from behind in his car. He was blocking the lane, and I blew my horn. I went around this guy, and, when I went around him, he started chasing me in my car, from lane to lane, down several blocks. It (pause) not just one block; this is down several blocks. I'm switching lanes and he's just chasing me. So, I pull over.

When I pull over and double park, this guy gets out his car and walks up to my driver's window. Just by the way he approached my car (pause), it was just danger; it was danger, so when I get out of my car, I didn't talk. I get out of my car with a golf club, and then, this guy, we got into it. I mean, now he's at my window. I'm not at his window. He followed me. He pulled up on me and walked over to me like, like he has a BADGE. Like, he has a badge. He is at my driver's window, standing over at my driver's seat, so I'm worried. I'm nervous. I get out to protect myself; of course, I get out. We was in each other face. It was all (pause), but I wasn't (pause), he was (pause) after me.

Do you think he was trying to hurt you? Do you feel like he was trying to hurt you physically or something like that?

RICHARD Of course, and I wasn't waiting. I just (pause), it was, it was, I don't know how you put it; it was a car, and I wasn't pursuing him. He was pursuing me.

Was this guy, like, white, Black, Brown?

RICHARD The guy I argued with? I don't, I didn't even remember his race. I knew his race when we started to go to court to fight the case. He was Korean. The officer that came to pick me up at my house kept asking me do I know what race he was. You know, every time they questioned me, they asked me about race, and race didn't have an issue here. I was being chased by some guy.

I didn't care about race; that made me feel way uncomfortable. When he was standing over the steering wheel. I was just uncomfortable, meaning scared. Nervous. Shook up. Like, guy, why are you chasing me? What are you doing? I wasn't getting out of that tank. Why are you chasing me? I get out with the club. At that point, we was in each other face. When I got out my car, he was already in, standing out my window. I don't think it was much more for him or me to do with it, but he was after me. I was in front going home. I was being chased by a Korean. I didn't know he was Korean though, so it didn't matter about his race. It was just how the system wrote it up. The system set it up after he told the court. He came and told the state he chased me down. He came and told that state he walked up to my window, so all I wanna know from the state is: what am I supposed to do when a stranger come to your (Richard, clearly upset, does not finish the sentence). Strong-willed, after chasing you from lane to lane, state, court system, judge, whoever wanna listen to this (pause), just as a man (pause), if I'd ever did that to another man, and I got hurt, I would've went home, and I would've thought about what I did wrong.

The system found what I did wrong, but I was the one being chased. And I'm 49 years old. I'm not a kid. I don't cotton to being pursued by anybody, by anybody, without a badge or without some type of authority. And, I don't get the state, my lawyer, the judge, the conviction call. Nothing.

So, do you feel like if you woulda got into a scuffle with a Black guy (pause), you don't think it woulda been a problem with the authorities?
RICHARD No.

And you were recently convicted of battery?
RICHARD Aggravated battery. It's DEAD WRONG.

Terror

Northside, Chicago, mid-2000s

JOSIE I was in junior high school and already gettin' into trouble. You know, fightin' and cuttin' school and what not, so. I was with my friends, and we were outside of school during school hours. We was by my school, but not too far, and this detective comes up and he stops us. He tells me to come with him, so I just go. I actually thought it might've been about this girl I was fightin' with 'cause the last time I was into trouble with the police, it was about her. And it wasn't that long before (pause). So, I go with him, and he takes me to an alley, not too far, but it's quiet, and (she looks at me while she pauses then looks away), he rapes me.

The detective?
JOSIE Yeah. I mean I don't think he was a detective. I mean, when he showed his badge (pause), I'm not sure if I saw a real badge. I don't think he was a detective. I think he was just sayin' he was (pause), pretending (pause) to get me to go with him.

Why do you think he wasn't a detective?
JOSIE Because if you're the police, a detective, you don't do those things (pause). No, that's just so bad, just. (She stares at me and shakes her head, and I stare at her. We don't say anything.)

Brooklyn, New York City, early 1990s

CONSTANCE I was fifteen the first time I was stopped by police. I was coming from my boyfriend's house in Sunset [Park], and I showed my bus pass to the guy in the booth. I knew I wasn't supposed to use my bus pass to take the train, but there was no Metrocard yet, and the school either gave you a bus pass or a train pass. It's crazy, 'cause it was actually easier and quicker for me to take the bus to the train, but I couldn't do that unless I hopped the turnstile. I needed two passes to do that, and the school wouldn't give you two. It was one or the other.

'Cause I had a pass, I would flash it and go through the doors. That's when you could do that. Anyways I hopped the train, and the guy in the booth said, "Pay your fair," and three or four cops came out of nowhere and stopped me. It was crazy, you know, 'cause at that point I was doin' this like a year and never had a problem! So anyways they gave me a ticket and I remember that the only thing I could think of was hiding the ticket from my mom and being able to pay for it. (She begins to laugh.) Well (pause and more laughing), my boyfriend paid for it, and my mother never found out. (She ends with a laugh but takes a five second pause.) Because I was so concerned about my mother, I never thought about how I was treated by those cops. They could've just stopped me and gave me a ticket, but they didn't. They frisked me.

They made me stand against the wall with my hands on the wall and my legs spread and they (pause) frisked (pause) me. There was no female cop. My face was lookin' at the wall while this male cop frisked me with his friends standin' there. It was a busy time. People saw. It was so embarrassing. But, I remember, all I could think about was my mother. Even at that point! And what she would do if she found out!

She never found out.

Harlem, New York City, mid-1940s

MRS. M My mother and my sister Mary and my brother Jesus and my brother Leon. So, all four of us. And from there we moved to West 113th Street and then from there, I went to school on 111th Street. 101 Junior High School, and then, you know, both my brothers, they went to their school, too. He went to um (pause), what the hell was the name of that school? It was 120th Street and, uh, Cooper. That was the name of that school, that was its name, Cooper. And which every day, Leon, my oldest brother, got beat up 'cause he was Puerto Rican and that was a Black school, so every day he got beat up.

But Leon is Black.
MRS. M Yeah, but he's Puerto Rican. You know.

And they could tell, or no?
MRS. M Well, of course! You speak Spanish, come on, they're gonna beat you up. Yeah, he was getting it from the Black guys.

So why did he speak Spanish? He couldn't speak English? No?

MRS. M No, he spoke English but not as, you know, when we were small my
mother, everyone in the family spoke Spanish, so, basically, we spoke
Spanish. When we went to school, then that's when we started learning
how to speak English. We learned, you know, at home.

So, they knew from the beginning?

MRS. M Yeah, from the accent. Uh, when you're at home, everybody (pause),
the whole family used to speak to us in Spanish, so, of course, you know,
we learned Spanish.

Northside, Chicago, early 2010s

MARCIA I had one experience with the cops where I was walkin' down the
street with a friend. They just kind of stopped us all crazy and got out and
threw my friend on the hood and started searching his pockets and body
and everything. And, I made a little smart comment about, "Oh, police are
bitches," and, "All ya'll," you know, "you're thirsty." And then, the female
cop turned to me, and she hooked me and said, "Well, I'm gonna take you
in for being a prostitute."

Was it a white cop?

MARCIA Yeah, it was a white lady.

Do you remember her name?

MARCIA I don't but I remember her face (pause). Um (pause), yeah. She hooked
me and then looked at my friend and said, "Yeah, you were. She was trying
to sell herself to you, wasn't she? Wasn't she?" And he didn't make any
comment, and they ended up lettin' him go. They end up taking me in for
absolutely nothing. Yeah, and I was screaming in the paddy wagon. She
came by the paddy wagon and called me a nigger, and I just like (pause),
and, believe this, I was embarrassed. It was one of the worst experiences
I had with the police.

Did you get convicted?

MARCIA Um, no, but I really didn't say, argue, or say anything about it. They
just kind of dropped it. I wasn't satisfied or satisfied or was just like (pause).

Have you ever seen that cop again?

MARCIA Um, I actually did see her again. She actually, like maybe a month
later, she seen me in the taco shop. Came in. Straight into the taco shop and
arrested me for nothing, again, and said that I was loitering. After those
two experiences, I never seen'd her again.

Brooklyn, New York City, early 1990s

CONSTANCE It was a couple of years later the next time I was stopped and
frisked by police. This time I wasn't jumping the turnstile but was in the
train station, the Church Avenue stop, and there was about seven or eight
of us. Graffiti and taggin' was popular in Brooklyn, and I was hanging out
with a bunch of taggers. We were on our way to the city [Manhattan]. We
saw some police officers, and we were being messed up, you know, and we
started shoutin' KRS One's "Black Cop."

Two of the cops was Black, and the other two was Spanish, and there
were four of them. We definitely outnumbered them. I remember we were
shouting the lyrics and laughin'. They came over to us and, uh, tell us, to get
against the wall (pause). All of us. Two of them was asking the questions:
"Where are you going? Do you have any weapons on you?" They frisked
all of the boys and told them to move to the side. I couldn't see because I
was facing the wall, but I heard, "Move to the side, stop, move to the side."
Then, they told the other girls to move to the side where the guys were, and
they frisked me.

It was crazy 'cause (pause) there, there was two other girls but (pause)
they only frisked me (She laughs and looks up with her eyebrows raised).
I remember he patted my whole body, my arms, chest, backside, and
between my legs, and I had to just stand there. My friends were yellin' at
the cop that was pattin' me down and sayin' that he couldn't do that, and
that I was a girl and what not. They were saying that I wasn't doin' nothin
wrong and, I remember, I turned my face to look at them, and the cop told
me to turn my face back to the wall. The other cops were tellin' them,
"Back up," and "Shut the fuck up or it's gonna take longer."

When the cop finished pattin' me down, I'll never forget after he patted
me down, he said, "You know, I'm really disappointed in KRS-One. That
song is wrong. I was a fan." The Spanish cop said we could go, and we did.
When the train came, they were comin' down the steps. So (pauses then
laughs), when we were leavin', we stuck our fingers up at them through the
train doors (continues to laugh).

Brooklyn, New York City, mid-1990s

ASIA You know. It was tough livin' [in the housing projects]. I got so tired of
the shit there.

What shit?

ASIA Jealousy. You know how it is when your pretty. Girls don't even know you,
and they don't like you. Guys, too. One time, I came out my building and
I'm walking, minding my own business, and the girls from the building

right around this one (gestures toward inside the housing complex) are ALL lookin' in my face, sayin' shit. Talkin' out loud, and they don't even know me. I just kept it movin'. I went to the store across from my building, and when I came back, one of them was really in my face. I had to fight her before I could even go in my building. My sister was there and shit, so I didn't get jumped or nothing like that, but DAG, I'm like, seriously? Can a bitch live? Even when I was at the mall wit' MY daughter. I mean she's in the carriage, and bitches are tryin' to play me. Wit' my daughter there! I mean, you believe that shit? I had to get into it at Kings Plaza [Mall], and they was blocking my way and shit, and I'm with the carriage.

Did anything happen?
ASIA No, but still (pause), that's what I had to fuckin' deal with. Fuckin' jealous bitches.

Chicago, late 1990s to 2010s

When you were coming up you say you lived on the west side and the south side.
Tell about the experiences with the young people and the police you seen out there.
RICHARD Oh, the police out there; they constantly badgered. I watch them badgering.

I've been lucky enough to get passed it myself. I ain't got no tore up record or anything, but I watched them badgering. Badger the teenagers for the last fifteen years, you know, because of their belts, because they don't like belts, because they walking in groups of eight or ten. They don't even have (pause), it's not a matter of 'em being a threat or, or, they don't have a call on these young men, and they keep they hands in they pockets. They keep they hands on the hoods of the cars.

They don't have a call saying, okay it was six young men; they don't even have a description. They (pause) touch (pause) young Black Americans today at will. They don't have no cause, probable cause to touch 'em; they don't have no call, no description of this character or anything, and, over again, I ride down the street, and I see 'em. I call it, "practice." What they do, they get practice until they get lucky. That's what they targeting. But that's targeting. They targeting. They get practice until they stop enough groups of Blacks. Of course, they gonna find a gun; of course, it's making the community safer but, if it's not targeting, I'll EAT MY HAT.

They targeting people with sagging jeans; they targeting people with long braids. They target people with dark skin. They not targeting the kids going off quaaludes at Loyola, by the campus, you know what I'm saying.

They not doing that, and believe me, those kids don't have guns, but they have PLENTY of DRUGS on campus.

Brooklyn, New York City, late 1990s

CONSTANCE I was with my friend, Missy, and we bumped into a couple of guys we knew from the block. Henry and Hector were brothers, and they were good guys, you know. Not corner guys, not hustlers, but had jobs, stayed out of trouble, those kinds of guys. We get to talking with Henry and Hector and (pause), and uh, instead of goin' to where we were plannin' on going, we stayed right in front of the bodega. We were drinking. Missy and I had twenty-two ounces of [malt liquor] and they had forties of [malt liquor]. They lit up, but I had quit smokin' [weed], so I just chilled. Awhile later, Miro comes up and we're all hangin', talkin' shit, and havin' a good time. Henry leaves 'cause he gotta go meet his girl, and now it's just the four of us. Hector says he's gonna go to the corner and see whose over there. Cool, so it's me, Missy, and Miro, and we are all just talkin' shit.

This guy comes over and asks for a light, so Missy's like, "Oh, you got a cigarette? Give me a cigarette, and I'll give you a light." She gets a cigarette from this guy and lights up his and her cigarette. Now, he's just standin' there with us. I'm lookin at Miro like, "Look at this shit." So, he's just talkin' and getting in our conversation but, whatever, no harm no foul kinda thing. Hector comes back and we're all just chillin', and this guy is still there with us. Now, he's comin' in and out of our conversation, and we are makin' faces at each other. He's lookin' at Missy like he's wantin' her or something. I forgot what he said, but he's basically tryin' to get with her. Imagine. We are all young (pause), in our early twenties. I'm only nineteen, twenty, and this old man is trying to hang with us and get with Missy!

Miro tells him to chill. He does (pause) for a while but keeps at it and even asks Missy if she knows where he could get some coke [cocaine] and if she wants to do some wit 'im. Then, I don't know, I don't actually remember what we're talkin' about or what he said. But Miro's like, "Yo, chill man." And Hector's like, "Com'on man, I don't even know why you standin' here." The guy says something turns and walks a few steps. He actually turns in the middle of the street and comes back. He starts talkin' some shit and then says he's a cop. He starts actin' like a cop, ya know, like he's gonna arrest us or something, and Miro's like, "Oh word? You're a cop?"

He responds, "Yeah. I'm a cop." And he's lookin' down at Miro 'cause Miro's shorter than him, and I saw it coming. It happened so quick, but it seemed like it was slow motion. Miro responds, "Oh word" again, and his arm goes all the way back and down, and he punches that cop. I mean, this guy goes down in ONE punch. We're all like, "OH SHIT!" And Miro's all calm, and he's standin' over this guy and he's like, "Now, you a cop that just got knocked out. Mutha fucka." And we're all like what the fuck. We are like, "Yo, Miro, we gotta get the fuck outta here right now." Hector's like, "Yo, I'm out." He goes home, and Missy, Miro, and I catch a dollar cab.

Northside, Chicago, early 2010s

MARCIA Um, yeah. There was one time I was out there trying to start some trouble (pause) with a girl, and the girl was out there and called the police, and the detectives came up. They automatically just snatch me into the car, and I'm like being resistant and, I guess, when he handcuffed me and threw me in the back, I must have kicked him between his legs or something. And he just came in there, and, into the car, and started punching me all in my face, and I couldn't do anything because I was handcuffed. After he did that, they drove me around the corner around from my house, and then they just let me go, and told me to say that this never happened (pause). Well, they just told me, "This never happened," and they let me go and drove off (pause). Yeah, I remember that cop, and he actually ain't a detective no more. He is a regular cop.

Northside, Chicago, 2012

You are very active in the community, helping young people in the neighborhood. Do you see a lot of harassment going on with the police and these young people that you be around?

RICHARD Yes, yes, yes. Uh, one young man was out here, and he was using this hanger. This was his car; he came to get a hanger from me. This is his car; his car is parked. It's him and one more individual. The whole 24th district came. For one, somebody called from one of these windows. Apparently, it's not just the police but that, that's, that's got these kids targeted. It's the community and the nervousness because if it had been five Loyola students with the hanger. Whatever neighbor made that call to the 24th district, and that neighbor know who that neighbor is, so we know what I'm talking about. It's not just the 24th district; it's Rogers Park. It's pretty much prepped out. It's preppy. It's, uh, segregated in its own little hidden freakin' pockets.

[Violent police encounters] It's gonna be a lot more to come. It's just like the measles or a sneeze. If you get a child with a gun, a teenager that feels that it ain't gonna be justice, [justice] won't be served properly; it goes, well, [it's] something to do with the community he living in, well, uh, these young men, they constantly, you know, if he's been in and out of jail and he got a gun, there gonna be a high probability yeah he's gonna shoot back at the cops. That just common sense. That's common sense. Not to mention, anytime, I know young men that can have access to guns when they can't make a cell phone call (pause) on a CELL PHONE but they'll show me eight different guns in a thirty-day radius.

This didn't happen because he was (pause) he had money. It happened because, somewhere, they put guns, they, whoever you want. Guns are flooded in the Black community. They not in, flooded in Palatine. I bought my gun at a grocery store in Englewood, a corner store, a TWENTY-FIVE automatic from an Arab at the grocery store off [...] street. That's MY testimony.

Love

Washington DC, early 1980s

MALCOLM I was about four or five and I was in, like uh, kindergarten and ya know, well, it was around the holidays and the teacher was telling the kids (his voice shifts a bit to perform the teacher's voice and mannerisms), "Now, some people celebrate Christmas, and some people celebrate Hanukkah," and she explained a little bit more (he laughs slightly as if he could see the image in his mind). She then asks the class (Malcolm embodies the teacher again), "Does anybody here celebrate something else?" I raised my hand and she's like, "Yes, Malcolm?" And I say, "Kwanza." (His voice demonstrates a sense of pride in his remembrance of his response at age five.) Everyone looked at me like I was crazy, and the teacher was like, "WHAT'S that?" I was like, "This is what Black folk celebrate." (He laughs, and I laugh with him.)

Oh, and I HATED nursery rhymes, ya know, like the ones like, "row, row, row, your boat" and stuff like that. I HATED them (pause). I guess maybe I hated them because my mother never taught me them. Like (pause), she didn't read that to me before bed or sing them to me. I mean, she sang stuff like Marvin Gaye and Black pride songs, stuff like that, but not those nursery rhymes, and she read stuff to me about, ya know, me, Black folk and stuff. I remember we were going through those nursery rhymes in class, and, ya know, my kindergarten teacher was white, and she asks if anyone would like to share a nursery rhyme they know with the class, and there I was with my hand in the air, "I do!" (We both laugh aloud and, with a breadth of laughter as he speaks, Malcolm returns to his "teacher voice.") So, yeah, the teacher is like, "Yes, Malcolm."

(Malcolm breaks into song), "Power to the people, Black, Black power to the African people," and I had my little fist in the air, and I swear that teacher looked like she was going to die (we laugh again). Like I said, I was born into it, not sworn into it. You know, and, as I said before, it was a kind of countereducation my mother was teaching me, but it wasn't like one against the other—more like both.

Washington DC, 1980s and early 90s

How did the other kids react to your countereducation?

MALCOLM You know, it's funny I didn't feel much different when I was growin' up. Well, I mean, ya know, there were things that I wasn't gonna do. Like ya know, like smokin', robbin', hustlin'. I mean, brothers knew I was down, but there was a line that I wasn't gonna cross. So, ya know, I would be chillin', but I wasn't gonna go in no robbed car, 'cause then, mess around and get caught, I could be an accessory. So, brothers would be like, "Yo Malcolm. Ya wanna go do this right quick?" and I'd be like, "Yo, I'm chillin'." So, you know, I would chill, but there were times that I was like, "This is as far as I'm gonna wanna go." And, brothers would be like, "Yo, we're gonna go break in here, and I would be like, no, I'm chillin'."

So yeah, nah, I never really saw myself as different. I was always down to role, but, you know, there were things that I was still like, nah, I am not down with all that foolishness. But, ya know, yeah, it wasn't until about during my senior year of high school that dudes were like, "You know, Malcolm. You were always kind of different, yeah, you were always kind of (pause) good." Even when I go back NOW, I still hear this. Like, I would go into the barbershop, and, the barber would be like, "Ya know, you were always a good guy not like these other knuckleheads."

Ya know, not to say that I was good and other dudes were knuckleheads 'cause ya know, the difference was not that I was SO DIFERENT THAN THEM BUT the MAIN difference I would have to say was, IS, my mother, putting ideas into my head: the countereducation that others weren't getting. I mean, I can't explain it 'cause I didn't feel different, but, ya know, I still hear, "Yeah, you always was the good one." But that wasn't until the time where, ya know, you get older, changes start to occur. I mean, we all came up in the same neighborhood, chillin', ya know, so I would have to say it was that countereducation that I got from my mother.

Harlem, New York City, mid-1940s

MRS. M I started first grade; it was P.S. 170 and that was between Fifth and Lenox. That was the school, white, Black, you know, whatever, but um, there, the majority were Black because that was near Lenox. From 5th to Lenox, 6th, 7th, 8th [Avenues] was just Black. The majority were Black. You know, there were maybe one or two Puerto Rican families, but they were majority was Black there, and um, I had trouble there because some of the Puerto Rican girls didn't like me too much. The Blacks didn't like me because they knew I was Puerto Rican, and the Puerto Ricans didn't like me because I used to speak English.

They knew you were Puerto Rican?

MRS. M Yeah, they know, but because I spoke English, they didn't like it. I can count the, I didn't have many Spanish friends. Because the Hispanics in those days were really, really, Puerto Rican; they didn't speak English. I was born and raised here. So, to them I was, they thought I was, better because I spoke English. No, it's just that I was born here. I went to school here, they didn't. They were born in the island, and a lot of them kids didn't go to school. You know, so, when they came here, it was just Spanish, so it was difficult for them, but still. Because that's the way you would have to live, whether or not it was a Puerto Rican or a Black [person], never with the white person. I spoke English, and of course, then, my hair was long and whatnot, you know, so they thought I was cute, and I used to wear, like, two braids here, you know, like that, and I never forget (pause) one time, these two girls, they were Black girls; they were twins. One of them came and cut one of my braids off. Literally CUT IT OFF.

Oh, my Goodness.

MRS. M I came home, oh, oh my God, my mother wanted to kill me! So, I told my mother, "Hey, there were two of them. What could I do?" You know, but I had a girlfriend, her name was Emma, Emma McBride, may she rest in peace, and, uh, she was Black, so she, the next day, when she came to the house and saw me, I was crying, and I told her what happened. I told her. She said what happened? I told her one of the twins cut my hair. She said one of the twins? I said yeah, so next day she went to school with me. She beat the hell out of both of them (laughter). Both! Yup, two. She beat them so badly it was ridiculous. After that, every day, those girls used to wait for me outside my door to take me to school, and Emma used to tell them, "Don't let her fall, don't let her even trip 'cause if she's gonna trip, you better fall before she falls."

So, then what happened? Did the twins become your friends?

MRS. M Oh, after that they never ever, ever, bothered me again. NEVER. And, where I went, Emma was with me and the two girls. Emma used to tell them don't (Mrs. M does not finish her sentence and looks as if she is recalling something), and Emma became my best friend until the day she died. She only had one daughter, one daughter, and she named her after me (long pause).

One time I will never forget, we were going to a party—another party that we were sneaking out to, and I wanted this dress, so my mother told me, "You know I don't have the money to buy that," 'cause my mother, you know, uh, my father was dead; we had no kinda money like that. My mother said, "I don't have no money for no party; you can't get a dress," so Emma went to, uh, 113th, 114th and Park Avenue. In those days the stores were down in the basement; you know, the places like you open like that? (Mrs. M gestures with her hands and acts as if she is opening one of the metal cellar doors on the street).

Those were stores where they sell material, where they used to sell clothing; no food but clothes mostly, so Emma went, and she stole this dress.

No, she didn't!

MRS. M Yes, she did! She stole this dress for me! It was beautiful! It was the material that you could shrink and it, when you shake it, it comes back out. So, she stole this dress for me. So, I like, I was naïve, I didn't, it didn't dawn that it was such a bad thing that she gave me this dress. So, when my mother saw this dress, she say, "Where you get that dress from?" "Oh," I said, "Emma gave it to me." She said, "What do you mean Emma gave it to you?" I said, Emma bought it for me, so my mother took the dress, she took me to Emma's house, and my mother told her mother that Emma bought me that dress. So, her mother said, "But where did Emma get money? 'Cause that dress must have cost a good $5." In those days, at $5 honey, it was a dress that was $50 today, you know! (I laugh while nodding in agreement.)

So, her mother beat the hell out of Emma, and she took the dress and Emma back to the damn basement and she told the man, "This dress belongs to you, 'cause Emma took it, this dress, and I'm sorry." So, I went home, and I cried 'cause I love that dress, and I didn't have nothing for the party. About two hours later, there was a knock on my door; I say, "Who the heck is it now?" Emma. "Emma, what are you doing here?" "Look at what I got." She went back to the store and stole the same dress.

Oh no she didn't.

MRS. M (Laughs) Yes, she did! Yes, she did! (I laugh with her while stating a long dragged out, "Oh!") What? Yes, she did! So, I went out to the little party with my rinky dinky dress that I had, that my mother had for me. I got outside; I took that off; I shaked that little dress, put it on. I did it, and I was the queen of the ball!

So, Emma stole the dress for you but not for herself?

MRS. M She was very plain, and, because she was NOT a pretty girl. She wasn't uh, she not. Um, she had very short hair, she was very dark, she wasn't a pretty girl. But inside, oh God, that girl was gorgeous. To me she was gorgeous, because she had a heart of gold, and she was so sweet. I mean, there was nothing that I didn't want that she didn't get for me.

She didn't um, she would go party with me, but she wouldn't dance; she wouldn't, you know, try to make time with a boy or nothin' because she was so plain. She wasn't pretty. So, she would just stand in the corner. She would go with me to make sure nothing happened to me, and that was how it was with Emma and me, you know. Even when I had my boyfriend, she would, you know, go with me, make sure that nothing happened to me, and you know, that he might [get funny]. No, no. She would say "I'ma wait for you here." She would never dance in a party, she would never participate in the party.

But she would go with, just to take care of me, you know. That's why I always said, to me, she was my best friend I ever had. Because she was a true friend; she would do anything for me, you know. And when I heard that she had killed herself, I felt so bad 'cause, you know, she was a nice person. To me, she was gorgeous.

Conclusion

Mrs. M is in her nineties, her hair is short and fine with a slight wave, and white—a shiny, glistening white that she attributes to chemotherapy after her fight with cancer almost two decades before. She said, "When my hair grew back, it grew back this shade of white, and I just left it alone ever since." Images of her before the cancer showed her with darker hair and only the front white. Mrs. M is a couple of inches over five feet tall and, although not thin, she is not heavy. Her face is wrinkle-free and, though she looks senior, she can easily be mistaken for being in her early seventies.

When Mrs. M walks, she does so with a significantly noticeable limp and, as she sits, she lets out a few consecutive "ouches" as she endures the pain from her legs. "I have bad legs," she tells me. "My knees hurt, my feet. The doctor wants to give me an operation on both of my legs, but I said, 'No way. Uh, uh. Not this old bitch. I can do just fine. Thank you.'" The pain she suffers was quite visible, so I told her once, "You know, you might want to ask your doctor for a cane or a walker to help you with the pain." She gave me a swift cut with her eyes and clicked her teeth, "Don't get fresh, Lisi." She looked me up and down with her eyes, shook her head, then paused to look at me again. "Are you fuckin' crazy?"

I responded with an outburst of laughter and, while laughing, I asked her, "Why not?" Mrs. M. leaned in toward me, her eyes stared straight into my eyes, and she said in a soft whisper, "'Cause, (long pause) in case this nigga ever gotta run." She laughed, and then I laughed. We laughed together, and I never asked her about using a cane again.

I chose these stories and these residents because they represent how stories move people. These stories affect those who are telling them and those who listen. These stories attempt to capture the incommunicable nature of experiences of blackness as relational identification, creations of relations of homespace. They are mobile even when those who tell them may not be, and these stories also move as their story-tellers move listeners. Flowing through spaces and bodies in ways that cannot be controlled, they touch and move those who have listened to them in ways that may or may not have been the objective. At the wake of power, these stories embody resistance and empowerment, and the strategies of their telling add to the experiential excess.

These stories, as productive aspects of lived life from the internal exile, are errant performances that enable identification to occur but not in any rooted or universal way; their identifications move by their relational particulars of homespace.[3] These relation exchanges are materialism in the flesh as our bodies carry with them experiences of, and tactics against, racism in storied form.[4] I have approached these conversations with the aim of intimate conversation, dialogue, and, at times, materialized exchange.[5] Through the methods of critical performance ethnography, I have engaged in the practice of active listening and sharing and made myself vulnerable to encounter other perspectives, sharing and disrupting my own. This process of engagement is what D. Soyini Madison calls the dialogic performative, which not only asks the ethnographer to engage with but also reflect upon her actions (reflectivity) and to also push further to think critically about how her actions are reflected (reflexivity).[6]

Storied exchanges allow us as scholars to engage in and with *who* matters in sincere acts of communicative exchange: the people, the internal exiles, those who are included by their exclusion (the included excluded). The dialogic performative as a performance of exchange asks that knowing through doing is also doing something "to open up possibilities of alternative actions and behaviors."[7] Storied performances are enactments of "doing through saying: on investing the future with the past, re-marking history with previously excluded subjectivities, and challenging the conventional frameworks of historical knowledge with other ways of knowing."[8] The interdependence of storytelling, functionality, and racial memory compresses the past and present into a temporal existence that is also no longer reliant on the uncovering of past as truth but looks toward multiple possibilities of the future.[9]

5

Classroom Caravan

Popularizing Pedagogical
Performances of Disorder

What do we owe such men and women
who rain down revolutions and set
themselves aflame and who set aflame
the souls of millions to create a spring of
change? What is performance praxis in
the face of the problems that beset our
world and where do we position
ourselves within it; can we? How is
performance implicated in the ethical
labor that is within the tensions and
simultaneities of existential truths and
factual truths? How do we re-cast and
re-dress the bad trouble while taking care
to watch one another's backs in the
process? How do we assist in the small
stories—the Davids and their
slingshots—against the Goliaths of those
who order, dictate, discipline, and
punish our labors.
—D. Soyini Madison

In 2000, I entered the graduate program in communication studies at the University of North Carolina at Chapel Hill with a passion for cultural studies, yet I knew from before I was accepted that I wanted to study under D. Soyini Madison. Three years earlier, I met Madison as a Moore Undergraduate Research Apprenticeship Program (MURAP) fellow, a ten-week summer program housed on the Chapel Hill campus and designed to provide graduate-level research experience to minority students who demonstrated an interest in and potential for a career in the academy. At the time, I was a fourth-year undergraduate student at City University of New York, Brooklyn College, which was referred to as "Harvard for the working class," and I most certainly embodied the sentiment—at least, the working-class part. Although I did not study under Madison as a MURAP fellow, a dear friend and colleague of mine introduced us, and, from that moment, we were connected.

I watched Madison present her research alongside the MURAP mentors of color—William A. (Sandy) Darity, Jr., James Coleman (my advisor), Charlene Regester, Reginald Hildebrand, and Karla Slocum, among others, and after each presentation, we witnessed them discuss each other's research and exchange ideas. As we listened and watched their exchanges, we witnessed performances, and fights, on their work and also the meaning of being faculty of color who were dedicated to issues of race. At times, these viewpoints were shaped by their specialized fields, and at times, they were shaped by their experiential knowledge as academics of color; all conversations were informed by Black diasporic scholarship. We would break after their impassioned debates, and the mentors would walk and laugh with each other as if those exchanges were par for the course. For many of the MURAP participants, Madison, like her colleagues, embodied the promise of and the commitment to race politics in academia.

The dialogic exchanges of our MURAP mentors told us, albeit indirectly, that we, too, can be a "necessary irritant" within the academy unafraid "to speak truth to conventional knowledge."[1] Through their dialogue and their thoughts, bouncing off of one another, retracting, extending, shifting in real-time, continuous and constant during our summer with them, we understood that they were, indeed, differences that made a difference.[2] Their dialogic presence moved us. I visited Madison during those ten weeks more often than my appointed advisor and, at the time, I had never heard of performance or communication studies. As my summer in Chapel Hill was coming to an end, Madison encouraged me to apply to the master's program in the Communication Studies Department and work with her.

I applied two years later and moved to Carrboro, North Carolina, where I would stay during my graduate education. I entered the doctoral program another two years later (the combined MA/PhD program did not exist until after my first year as a doctoral student in the same department). It was during my graduate work in communication studies with Madison when I began to understand performance as a possible and practical method, theory, and object. Performance encompasses what Stuart Hall once described as the impetus of articulation: the methods and modes of resistance and survival (at times these are one and the same) within the rituals of the everyday.[3]

Similar to E. Patrick Johnson's pedagogical performance experience at Carolina, I also learned "the how" of performance pedagogy from Madison.[4] Before I taught my own performance course, Madison allowed me to attend and observe her interactions with her students. I learned, as Johnson did, how to interweave cultural context with Black literature and have students workshop what they have read, heard, and said into a variety of improvisational and staged performances. These lessons were reinforced by her investment in us in the graduate program through her teaching, scholarship, and mentorship. Later, I would again have the opportunity to witness Madison in the classroom and apply those same pedagogical performance methods to courses rooted in her ethnographic work in Ghana, West Africa. It was not until my first position as an Assistant Professor that I applied all that I learned about critical performance pedagogy to my own courses.

One of the courses was originally structured to highlight performance work that consisted of social change and, in turn, have students then perform the text they have learned. For me, this course was an opportunity to integrate performance pedagogy with performance ethnography and cultural studies with decolonization at its core. Such a project encompassed a theory-practice nexus to identify and theorize upon the included exclusion politics of the everyday in order to call into fruition social solidarity and change.[5] Taken from what I learned from Madison, I transformed the class into a community-based learning course that carried out this call of praxis through performed community engagement derived from critical ethnographical performance. This epistemological and ontological practice of knowing and active being helped to transform those who participated in the course, including me, and the classroom into a space of engaged action and agency.

Performance ethnographic methods have been practiced in the classroom in rigorous critical ways and does in fact expand pedagogical practices in general and of a cultural studies project in particular beyond the classroom to work with, listen to, and learn from others. As Édouard Glissant highlights, "All political activity is theater" and if politics provides us with representational meaning then "theater can be considered as representation (or the signifying expression of politics."[6] Theatrical expression is an intricate part of critical consciousness that can both present popular expression and its critical reflection, a twofold act that is often lost in popular representations of the people. Performance can aid in our critical reflection on actions, experiences, and activities of everyday life and then be acted upon to shape new forms of community and combat the limits of representation. For Glissant, "experimentation for us is the only alternative."[7]

To use performance as expressive politics of, for, and to form the people is a process of decolonization with "an ethical responsibility to address processes of unfairness and injustice within a particular *lived* domain."[8] This engagement with the people rests on a commitment to social justice and reaches beyond self-exploration; it illustrates a multilayered process of conscious and conscientious acts toward solidarity and social change. It allows those who are not directly affected by marginalization and oppression to *risk their face*, that is, one's common sense understanding, imagination, and representation of self, Other(ed), and the world around them.[9] What then does it mean to apply critical ethnographic performance to the localized politics of the classroom and community? How does decolonization continue in a classroom housed in a predominantly white institution that may seemingly work against antiracist strategies for belonging notwithstanding continued underlying and (not always) unconsciously acted upon racist/supremacist aggressions?

My community-engaged performance courses embodied the answers to these questions and have influenced the theoretical approaches in this chapter. As discussed previously, the move to incorporate community-based learning to my course underscored how Dwight Conquergood perceived performance as a means to "do," and position one's self in unison with rather than observe from a distance.[10] My goal for community engagement was a student-community relationship derived from socializing embodied exchanges of empathy through dialogue and presence. I had two necessary requests: First, I wanted my students to engage with a social justice organization that battled racist oppression and was linked to hyper-incarceration and police brutality. Although the organization did not have to be directly linked to hyper-incarceration or police brutality, its impact had to be one that was productive and opposed to these issues. This focus stemmed from the prominent role white sovereign policing plays in the containment, surveillance, and (social and actual) death of Black and Brown residents in urban communities.

Second, the students had to complete their service in the same organization in order to produce a necessary sense of organized affective investment in both the class and the act of engaged learning with the organization. This narrowed down my organization options immensely as it was difficult to get an organization who was willing to work with a group of approximately twenty students. With the help of the university's center to support community service, engagement, and learning throughout the curriculum, my class was "matched" with an organization. The students in these courses worked with a local Chicago organization that was established in the early seventies and combatted wrongful imprisonment and police crimes. The students were tasked to work under the guidance of two organizers, both of which have dedicated over thirty years to community activism and social justice against racism and oppression. Each student was required to complete at least twenty hours of service within a nine-week time period (one school quarter); and, during the first week of class, the students were visited by a University liaison who directed them on the logistics of service learning such as how to record their service hours and what is expected of them from all the institutional partners involved (the university, the instructor, and the organization).

The students, at the same time, met the representatives from the organization who served as the student's organization contacts. During this visit the organization representatives provided the class with the background of the organization and some examples of the Chicago cases they worked on throughout the years. As the students worked with the organization, they read texts related to racist oppression, hyper-incarceration, and police brutality. Through performance workshops, the students explored the intersections of the readings, their community engagement, and their critical reflections of the two. The courses culminated in a public performance that included members of the organization as a final mode of student-performers risking their face.

In this face-risking finale, student-performers always included a call to action that ranged from signing petitions to working directly with the organization. The public performances also included a talk-back session that allowed audience members to continue the dialogic engagement with the student-performers and organization. These courses, and Madison, have shaped this chapter and my understanding of what I call pedagogical performances of disorder, a performance pedagogy approach to community engagement that highlights the politics of included exclusion. This approach theorizes upon critical Black Diaspora and performance ethnography applied to the classroom with the goal of moving students to new points of identification that connect to critical self-awareness, agency, and relations of homespace.

Pedagogical performances of disorder are the core of this chapter. Previous chapters have emphasized western circulation as primary to white sovereignty and its sociogenic territorialization. Western practices of knowing have also depended on methods of extraction, expansion, and accumulation to gain, produce, and possess knowledge. In this chapter, I explore how performance-based, community-engaged learning can create embodied knowledges that are alternative to western practices of knowing and create possibilities of agency, community, and solidarity. These perspectives stem from my own engaged work in multiple classrooms and ethnographic work in urban spaces, now represented as its own circulated relation of homespace.

Service Stop 1: Classroom Caravan

My efforts to incorporate the radical turn in performance ethnography into performance pedagogy take seriously the effects of western circulation derived from the modernity-coloniality relationship in order to reframe these power trajectories and make possible future alternative political frameworks.[11] This shift to pedagogical practices recognizes the call of cultural studies in its rethinking of the political to describe the culture of everyday life;[12] it takes seriously the struggle of white sovereignty as one that rests in the intellectual realm as well as the economic, and acts, particularly within the realm of publics with the understanding that the pedagogical takes place beyond the educational institution.[13] Cultural studies in the classroom foregrounds how people "are empowered and disempowered by the particular structures and forces that organize their lives, always in contradictory ways, and how their ordinary lives are themselves articulated to and by the trajectories of economic and political power."[14] This call to action is one that can be carried out through performance possibilities within critical performance ethnography and applied to performance pedagogy.

Approaching the classroom as a structured space, already constituted by relations of white power and control *and* as a relational space where disalienation and disorder can take place, aligns with how performance ethnography understands "most simply, how culture is done in the body."[15] It stems from the premise "1) that identity and daily interactions are a series of conscious and unconscious choices improvised within culturally and socially specific guidelines, and 2) that people learn through participation."[16] Performed engagements act as a check and balance to ensure that we pay attention to people as well as the power relations that, through dynamic symbolic and ritualistic processes, naturalize and normalize ways of communicating and performing everyday life. Dwight Conquergood's metaphor of the caravan centers the possibilities of performance, which hold at the core a theory-practice nexus that depends on real-life engagement and on identifying and theorizing upon those practical, practiced everyday lived experiences.[17]

Conquergood's caravan, "a heterogenous ensemble of ideas and methods on the move," locates performance pedagogy as possessing the ability to move, disrupt, and cut through discursive formations even within the confines of officially mapped spaces.[18] The caravan encompasses how the transformation of storied, sincere exchanges become "the organization of a process of representation that allows the community to reflect, to criticize, and to take shape."[19] As such, I extend Glissant's theatre of disorder to community-engaged learning and performance-based pedagogy. I use the metaphor of the caravan as the performance dynamic in the classroom that moves through the terrain of pedagogical performances of disorder. For Glissant, the actions, experiences, and activities of everyday life can be critically reflected and acted upon through theatrical expression to shape new forms of community.[20]

These new formations, dynamic and unencumbered by representational limits of temporal colonialities and sociogenic marginalization, can be brought about by pedagogical performances of disorder.[21] Such performances of disorder "help destroy alienated forms of representation" and can create critical consciousness that opens possibilities and new creativities of relations.[22] The cultural politics of engaged subjective ideas, positions, and objective aims, formed in one shared spatial and temporal experience, transforms the classroom into a caravan for disorder. This collective praxis, concretized by the structures of the university but utilized to rearticulate our positions and intrapositional exchanges, can unveil and articulate shifts, disruptions, articulations, and disarticulations. Such movements of disorder critically interrogate sociogenic logics and western motivity to create social interaction and political action with, instead of for, the people.

Those of the classroom caravan move together to penetrate beyond the surface and uncover those hidden relations and structures of western sovereignty and, in this collective revelation, disrupt it.[23] This movement toward cultural political activity encompasses the circulation of ideas that occurs through classroom discussions between the speakers and listeners, a practice Glissant describes as a "dramatic dialogue."[24] The classroom becomes a space where the doing of critical theory represents itself and continues the conversations, a recirculation of newly articulated stories, critically embodied and transformed through space, time, and connectivity. The performance ethnographic paradigm, applied to the classroom, positions all who enter the space within "the delicately negotiated and fragile 'face-work' that is part of the intricate nuanced dramaturgy of everyday life."[25] Critical ethnographic performance (as) pedagogy is an embodied epistemology that intertwines the act of doing with the act of knowing and demands its participants, who are both inside and outside of the classroom, to reflexively consider their positions in and knowledges of the world around them.

This pedagogical performance of disorder not only "opens a space for disputing conventional academic borders" but transforms space itself.[26] It reconstitutes discursive knowledge and circulates these reconstitutions through the constant repetition of layered and connected acts of performing and performed community engagement. The classroom as a transformative space of disorder where dialectical processes of power are at play requires engaged and continuing dialogue with others as well as ethical acts toward social justice.[27] Dialogic performance, those engaged conversations, is not the end but the starting point and, within pedagogical performances of disorder, it is a multitemporal and spatial process of embodied practice of knowing and also active being through doing.[28]

Dramatic dialogic performances interweave a politics into class content, moves from class content to engagement, and actually doubles-down on performance possibilities through experiences that are brought back to the classroom, collectively embodied, and continuously re-presented. Performance, as an embodied performed practice of disorder, helps students and instructors alike to critically think through discursive formations that they typically take for granted. As Madison argues, "Performance becomes the vehicle by which we travel to worlds of subjects and enter domains of intersubjectivity that problematizes how we categorize who is us and who is them and how we see ourselves with other and different eyes."[29] Community-based learning pushes forth a co-performative witnessing to "work with real people instead of printed texts" and go beyond the surface and the self toward a space of connectedness.[30] Using the classroom as an introductory space of listening, the addition of community engagement disrupts the invisible borders typically drawn between college campuses and the local that are often utilized to serve the university and are excluded from entering university grounds.

The dialogical performance requires a displacement of seeing as the primary source of knowledge with an understanding that, "in the absence of profound listening," seeing reaffirms sociogenic included exclusion and logics of white sovereignty.[31] Through their engagement with community organizers and community residents, students again enact in dramatic dialogue to reflect on and frame the content of their experiences.[32] Madison defines this pedagogical and dialectical process of performance disorder as the mirror and the hammer.[33] The reflection is not enough on its own as it needs the hammer "to disturb performatively or trouble its content, its center space."[34] The hammer to the mirror pushes the students to discomfort to unveil their common sense articulations of seeing and knowing into a critical awareness of how discourse is personalized, memorized and memorialized, naturalized, and embedded into our very beings.

Through pedagogical dramatic dialogue, the hammer disorders and moves "past the borders of a framed reflection and moves into the center space for performed and rhetorical imaginings, artistry, symbols, and embodiments that smash the violent, bigoted, and historical hegemonies that are reflected in mere mirrors."[35] The performative hammer introduces the possibilities of relation that transcend the rootedness of sociogenic politics. The classroom caravan as a collective site where students reflect upon their fieldwork, share, disrupt, and transform motivity into a continuous constant access to agency as students engage outside of the classroom, return to the classroom for further reflection, and circulate self-reflexive thought through performed action.[36] The telling and listening within dramatic dialogue become primary pedagogical techniques within the course and both inside and outside of the classroom as students begin to grapple with the layered complexities of what and how they learn and know.

As the classroom is transformed into shared time and space, theories of the flesh, those subjugated embodied knowledges, articulate "affect and emotion as theory and polemic" in order "to deepen feelings even more" with the power of presence and proximity.[37] The space welcomes students to position themselves as co-performative witnesses in the process of speaking with and bearing witness to extraordinary acts of the everyday.[38] Like relations of homespace, disconnected to organized space, pedagogical performances of disorder transform the focus of community engagement to on-the-ground identifications that occur regardless of and, at times, outside of organizational space.[39] They can "link one's critical imagination with the possibility of activism in the public sphere."[40]

The classroom can produce a necessary shared sense of a collective, organized affective investment in both the class and the act of engaged learning with community members and organizations. Affective investment plays a primary role in the embodiment of everyday life, performance, and its relationship to disorder. Affect refers to those particular experiential qualities and effects of lived embodied experience that are conditioned by the historical complexities and processes of the world around us; a politics of affect is contextual and "always articulated by and to other registers, including the discursive, the cognitive, the ideological, the bio-political, etc."[41] It is a politics of feeling "that attaches subjects to objects and experiences, that stitches bodies and subjects into formations and organizations of social (rather than individual) experience . . . and binds relations together into larger and larger spaces, each with its own sense of coalescence, coherence or consistency."[42] Through an engaged, continuous encounter and performed experiences of those moments of engagement, students can reorganize what matters to them.

Service Stop 2: Moving Pedagogical Performances of Disorder

Pedagogical performances of disorder demand student engagement center, recognize, and attend to the people's politics and their desires, demands, and needs that "are always and already occurring."[43] As neoliberal structural and discursive practices solidified within the university, market "demands of privatized pleasures and the ready-made individual choices" have replaced "all modes of social responsibility, commitment, and action."[44] Academic processes mimic the market logic of consumer satisfaction in the student-university relationship, and expectations of immediate gratification are projected onto the academic body. These neoliberal discourses, rooted in western mobility and white sovereignty, cloud productive engagement and often influence how students interpret their experience and affective investment.[45] Students learn to approach community-based learning as extractive, an opportunity for them to learn first-hand how to become activists and create social change.

Although students gain and foster critical and creative skills with engaged learning, the focus on solely student impact reproduces communicative exchanges that are deeply rooted in western motivity. Extraction as a repetitive practiced form of engagement often invites rituals of paternalism and self-aggrandizement. Students often come to community-engaged courses all too ready to encounter imagined authentic experiences deeply embedded in sociogenic identifications, positive and negative, which occur even when the intentions behind such perceptions are admirable. Much like in fieldwork, a performance paradigm to pedagogical community engagement aims to break through these limited understandings and feelings of sociogenic relations to self through centering ethical dialogic encounters.[46] The field for the students is their engagement hours as they interact with the members of organizations and the people they may encounter as they are in and with multiple local communities.

To combat the community-engaged learning approaches that center on such neoliberal logics, the focus on people and performative communicative exchanges redirects community-based learning as an active ongoing practice of listening, sharing, and enacting. The students coexperience time as they share their time with others who have chosen to make their work and experience available and vulnerable to the students. Students often will not engage in the ways they have imagined with the communities as they will experience, instead, the everyday tediousness of organizing—the mundane tasks of paperwork, phone calls, list making, data collecting, and, if their engagement entails, cooking, cleaning, or whatever else is suitable to the course. Trust-building begins at the starting point of the pedagogical encounter, and professors, tasked with the responsibility of guidance, map the path of the classroom caravan. Professors inform the engaged learners that their labor with communities and for the fulfillment of community needs and desires is the focal point.

The shifting of expectations from immediate, individualized gratification to a layered, complex commitment to deep expressive and active social sacrifice for the students promotes a position of dialogical exchange as a productive alternative to encounters governed by sociogenic discourses and ideologies. Students learn that community engagement is approached as a practice that might inform their needs and goals but is ultimately about learning from and investing in the people who entrust us with engagement. Shaping the student-organization interactions by informing the students what will be expected of them as opposed to what they should expect asks the students to (re)learn how to give rather than receive from their community engagement. This approach veers from western paternalism through the conscious reminders that are produced by the structures of the classroom caravan. It opens the possibilities of engagement rather than limits them to logics of gain and reframes exchange as one of sincerity and fairness against processes of thingification and mystification.[47]

The affective investment in dialogical exchanges is a performative position that "does not end with empathy."[48] Rather, the exchanges ask students and professors to think of themselves as communicators and focus primarily on speaking and listening to traverse and possibly disrupt western practices of surveillance, difference, and thingifying exchange.[49] "Listening is an interiorizing experience, a gathering together, a drawing in" that can be manifested in particular ways through an understanding of the performance paradigm.[50] Pedagogical performances of disorder push all involved as social actors to take seriously the embodied acts of situating oneself into the politics of everyday life. This often means that those community members have a voice in how engagement occurs inside of the classroom in addition to community relations and share the position of specialized knowledge with professors to coshape the path of the caravan.[51]

By sharing professorial authority with community members and concretizing that shared relationship in relational contracts, such as course syllabi and community-learning contracts between the students, community organization, professor, and the university, professors partake in the "making not faking" space of connectedness.[52] Participating and investing in the "communicative praxis of speaking and listening, conversation, demands copresence even as it decenters the categories of knower and known."[53] Shared performed acts of action help everyone understand that each engager is a significant actor in community conversation and in the process of relational connectedness; this kind of exchange can be humbling for faculty, with the stakes even higher for junior faculty of color who are women; BIPOC women faculty, and especially those who can be identified as Black, do not share the same privileges of authority within the classroom as their white (and) male counterparts.[54] As such, the position of precarity determines the level and risk of vulnerability, which is always an act of respect and reflexivity necessary in the process of sincere dialogic exchange.[55]

Pedagogical performances of disorder acknowledge that interactive educational processes provide students with a freedom to critically engage with, reflect upon, and create new truths.[56] This embodied acknowledgment also dissembles the professorial position as the professor guides and moves the students within the classroom rather than being the one who proclaims an authoritative, predetermined program.[57] The professor as a coperformer, engaged with the spontaneous dialogical performatives, is no longer in the position of classroom monitor, a derivative of colonial circulation. The professor, however, remains within the position of specialized knowledge with the ability to shape how students experience the text and community engagement through performance and how they perform dramatic dialogue that is theatrically experienced and expressed.[58] The professor, as coperformer and improviser, takes on the responsibility to create paths that enable students to respond, and it is in "this ability to respond or response(ability) where trust emanates and paves the way for freedom."[59]

Madison distinguishes between performance ethnography, the day-to-day performances of everyday life and the method utilized to engage with the people who make use of these daily practices—the theories and methods I have discussed in great length and applied to a pedagogical performance of disorder and performed ethnography.[60] Performed ethnography refers to the "dramatic scenarios, public staging, crafted theatricality, and improvisational enactments of fieldwork and ethnographic data that will *be* that have *been*, and that are *being* performed."[61] Performed ethnography practices and techniques encourage the detailed reflections of what community-engaged students have witnessed, what they learned, how they learned, and how they reflect. As such, pedagogical performances of disorder ask the students to participate in methods of performed ethnography to further interrogate these epistemological formations. Students probe for meaning and understanding through the application of performance concepts to improvisational scenes based on topics, questions, themes, and debates from course content. These improvisational performances are introduced in segments and workshopped in class to extend, clarify, and interrogate concepts and impressions emanating from class discussions, students' lived experiences, and their engaged work. Each configured and performed segment tells a new story through dramatic dialogue and also as another dramatic dialogic expression that can move toward collective consciousness.[62]

Students reflect upon the concepts, depictions, and arguments from the readings or fieldwork, (mirror) discuss their reflections with their peers in small groups (mirror circulation through dramatic dialogue), and then highlight the themes and concepts of their shared discussion through improvisational performed images.[63] Students repeat this improvisational action in sequences and collectively choose performed quotes and phrases highlighted within their discussions. Bound by a theme, students communicate abstract images through their bodies and must negotiate their reflected positions now as a group to complete the workshop segment (hammer through dramatic dialogue). These improvisational segments are timed to limit students' common sense tendency to thought and verbal communication. Time limits urge students to affectively invest in the performance of listening with their entire bodies and participate in the socializing, embodied cocreation of the collective image.

The improvisational engaged encounter of dialogic performance is complexly repeated as students then perform their workshopped performance to the class (constant hammer through performed dramatic dialogue).[64] As Madison highlights, "If responsibility is a hallmark of freedom, then responsibility and the ability to respond are also hallmarks of improvisation. In collaborative performance, the cycle of improvisational responses, from beginning to end, is based on each improviser's ability to respond to another improviser's response."[65] Coperformers and improvisers reward and critique with an objective of sharing knowledges of experience and spectatorship and become coparticipants in relation to each performer and the creation of each image with every response. Improvisational collaborative groups have agency to choose how they alter their workshopped performances, which marks the improvisers' abilities to act and make something materialize.[66] Through these improvisational, collaborative workshops, we become conscious of our positions as collective actors who have access to agency and can disrupt, recreate, and create images, imaginaries, and realities.[67]

Within the repetition of dramatic dialogue, improvisational workshops complicate performed images, and performers add transitions to connect their formerly separate images. Additional pedagogical performances of disorder focus on movement (all performers must be moving at all times) and sound (all performers embody a sound that advances the workshop sequence). The sound and movement workshops guide performers to embody alternative modes of communication that do not rely on language. In these workshops, performers "discover new ways of orienting oneself to the world" through their bodies as they realize the body's affective influence on the audience.[68] Against colonial temporality, these performed images are fragmented thematic interjections in and of time, seemingly unrelated, and account for coexperiences of time that have folded onto each other through purposeful, critical continuous performances of disorder.

Traditional forms of learning and assessment remind student-performers that these workshops are "play" with a purpose, and such performance embodiments are meant to be repeated and furthered through staged performances. Workshops prepare student-performers, and each performer guides fellow performers to create staged work. Although these collaborations begin in class, they, too, travel beyond the boundaries of the classroom and course requirements. The labor that exists outside of the frame of performance demands the student-performers reflect upon and revisit their community engagement, their encounters in the workshops, and their performed experiences in their staged performance. Through the collaborative process of scripting and rehearsing, they repeat performed dramatic dialogue and disorder. The mirror and hammer continue.

Service Stop 3: Circulating Relations of Homespace

As performers travel through the process of creating the final performance, our previous workshopped and staged performances aim to move through another series of pedagogical disorder. Collectively and collaboratively, performers script the final performance and interweave past performances into one longer sequence. Student performers are cast in performance roles they may not have previously performed, which releases them from authorship, and, in turn, disrupts territorialization. Performance building is layered with the multiple voices and perceptions of the creators with fragments of the taken past and envisioned by the future—a multiplicity of shared voices, ideas, goals, and ideologies in one creative product. It is not without tension; however, the demands of responsibility for the public performance, for the community organization, and for the performers ensure that the tensions do not stop the journey.

Performers decide together what stories are highlighted in the performance, choosing those that honor the labor and voice of community interlocutors and the student-performers; they add to these stories as the creation and performed parts move toward finalized script performance. Performers adjust the sequences accordingly as they rehearse and add scenes, new and old, as the scripts and rehearsals demand. Such tweaks are often even at the final rehearsal, which occurs immediately before the public performance. The public performance bears the fruit of their labor and continues the prescribed goals of reflecting and representing the affective investments generated throughout the course. The final performance becomes the site for storied embodiments and relations of homespace.

Final pedagogical performances of disorder ask student-performers as collective collaborators to share their learned knowledges with the public and specifically those they engaged with during their pedagogical journey. Returning to Glissant, dramatic dialogue is also the experience shared by the storyteller and the collective listeners in the same place and at the same moment in order to shape the relationship between cultural formation and political activity.[69] Real embodied experience shared through dramatic dialogue makes possible the solidarities that might not have otherwise existed. The performance both includes those community interlocutors who entrusted their time, politics, and voice to engaged learners and honors their presence in the community and their commitment to student-performer engagement. Invitations symbolize the risk of engagement that occurs for all involved and the trust that is ensured through the staged performance.

Through the continued dialogue, student-performers embody accountability as a public performed act and continue the promises of becoming through relations of homespace. The final performed act socializes as it holds the experiential interpretations of the creators responsible.[70] The representation of author and ownership are demystified and disordered in the ongoing communicative and productive act of performance. This kind of performed disorder was represented in a community-engaged final performance when student-performers recreated the biographical function of the program page and replaced "Performers' Bios" with their experiences. To follow are selected excerpts from the program:[71]

SOPHOMORE AT [THE] UNIVERSITY

Whether it's to represent beauty or to inform the audience of underlying political issues performance and art can always hold powerful messages, and this course undoubtedly widened my vision of what performance can be and how to achieve a specific goal while effectively communicating with the audience.

SENIOR AT [THE] UNIVERSITY

This class has meant more to me than most of the ones I have taken at [the] University. I was engaged with the Chicago community and tackled issues that face many of our youth, men, and women today, specifically those of color. I hope this performance causes people to think about their own lives and those around them. We are all part of the problem and as a result, disposable.

SENIOR AT [THE] UNIVERSITY

As someone who is passionate about working with youth in the high-risk neighborhoods, it is my duty to continue to educate myself on these issues. This class taught me so much both mentally and emotionally about history that continues to haunt us, specifically here in Chicago. I hope this is a wake-up call for everyone in the audience.

The final performance produces questions rather than answers to continue dialogic engagement and move toward agency. Rooted in the colonial (limited to no) mobility, terror, and violence specific to the American postindustrial prison complex, the next two scenes illustrate student-performers' performances of disorder in relation to identifications of included exclusion. In the first scene, Performer 1 is an imprisoned transwoman who narrates her experiences of imprisonment, and the second scene centers on the daily routine of strip searches.

SCENE 9: Performer 1: transgender woman in prison; Performers 2, 3, 4, and 5: prison guards

Enter guards: Performers 2, 3, and 4. Enter fifth guard while shoving Performer 1 onstage; guards form a box around Performer 1.

P1: "I am a 28-year-old transgender woman who has been incarcerated in a men's state prison in Texas.

Here in Texas, there is something called "safekeeping," which is a setup for inmates that are considered vulnerable because they are gay, weak, scared, ex-gang members . . . or some other reason.

I have repeatedly asked to be transferred, but my attempts to get safety have been ignored. It is evident to the officers that I am having major safety problems in my current unit, but, still, they refuse to classify me into safekeeping.

I have been extorted.

I have had to do sexual favors for gang members.

I have had to ride with gang members for protection from another.

I am tired of being scared and having to do things against my will!

I no longer want to be anyone's god-damn property.

Because officers are not doing anything to protect me, I get into trouble on purpose so that I can be placed into solitary confinement.

Do you know what it's like to depend on solitary confinement for the sake of physical and mental survival?

5-second pause

TRANSITION: "What if I can't refuse?"

> **P1:** What if I **can't** refuse?
> **P2:** You can't refuse.
> **P2, 3, 4, 5:** You can't refuse.

Performer 1 is escorted offstage by the prison guards

SCENE 10: Prison rape: Performer 6: prisoner; Performer 7: prison guard

Performer 6 is escorted onstage by prison guard

> **P6:** Some of them put a finger in your rectum and vagina at the same time . . . I thought about refusing, but I sure as hell didn't want to get sent back to solitary. The internal search was as disgusting and as humiliating as it sounded.
> **P7:** Without the uniform, without the power of the state—it would have been sexual assault.
> **P6:** What if I refuse? The state deplores "unlawful" sexual assaults by its employees.
> **P7:** But it actually uses sexual assault as a means of control.
> **P6:** What if I refuse?

Prison guard escorts Performer 6 offstage.[72]

The final performance becomes a performance of disorder, not the truth of solitary confinement and imprisonment but the contestations of colonial mobility and its space. The scene centers on those who resist the normalcy of imprisonment and reinforces its meaning by their very being as prisoners, expendable and exploitable. In another scene, student-performers challenge discourses of drug addiction and their relationship to sociogenic logic through the popular trope of crack epidemic and "crack babies."

Crack Baby Scene: *Enter Performers 1, 2, 3, 4, and 5. They are crawling around on all fours and looking intently on the ground; they say their lines as they continue to crawl and search the ground.*

> **P4:** As crack made its entry into urban areas in the mid-1980s, reports began to surface about this new highly addictive and powerful drug.

P2: Cover stories appeared in *Newsweek, Time* and periodicals around the country.
P1: Reports of "crack babies" born to addicted mothers were among the most frightening to surface.

Performers freeze as each says the following lines:

P5: How could anyone fail to respond to this human tragedy?
P4: How could anyone fail to respond to this human tragedy?
P2: How could anyone fail to respond to this human tragedy?
P1: How could anyone fail to respond to this human tragedy?

Performer 3 rises while saying: Only later did information surface that indicated that there were, in fact, no data on crack-addicted babies.

Performer 4 rises while saying: The drugs are the enemy. Yet realistically, people have become the enemy, and rhetoric is used conveniently to hide this fact.

Performer 5 rises while saying: In the federal court system, Blacks have consistently represented about eighty-five percent of crack defendants for more than a decade.

Performer 1 rises while saying: . . . which is much higher than the proportions of actual Black crack users in 2002 and 2003.

Performer 2 rises while saying: Data from the Bureau of Justice statistics show that the chances of receiving a prison term after being arrested for a drug offense increased by 447 percent between 1980 and 1992.

ALL: We are the prisoners of the "War on Drugs."
P2: The fact is that more than one third of the people held in our prisons stand convicted of nonviolent, victimless crimes.

Two more performers enter, Performer 6 from stage right and Performer 7 from stage left. They cross each other, and Performer 6 stands center stage; Performer 7 stands stage right.

P6: In 2006, out the 5,067 people arrested on drug charges in Illinois . . .
P7: . . . 4,210 of the arrestees were Black.
ALL: We are the prisoners of the "War on Drugs."[73]

Pedagogical performances of disorder demand attention to the collaborative acts that occur right before our eyes and the communicative processes that give rise to them. They do not conclude with the performance but continue into the future with the post-performance "talk back" as one indicator of ongoing dialogue. The talk back symbolizes how the dialogue moves beyond the stage onto the audience and allows audience members to become performers within the dramatic dialogue. With the aforementioned performances, informational brochures and postcards on the community organization provided the audience with resources to get involved with the struggle against police torture and killings. A former student was in the audience and contacted me one year after the performance.

They wrote:

Hello, Professor:

Remember those postcards you handed out for the organization? I started volunteering for them soon after. The demonstration today against white supremacists was amazing; I can't believe how many people came together just from a few posters and many, many calls we made in a tiny office . . . I'm emailing you to ask you if you would talk to your students about joining to volunteer for extra credit or if they care to. The leaders of this organization are pushing 80 years old and do most of the work since there are so few volunteers. We need more people to help teach others to resist. Please let me know your thoughts.

Best,
[Former Student][74]

The unrootedness of performance manages to compel and circulate through affect and empathy, and dialogue illustrates how performances can move toward relations of homespace. As Glissant highlights, performance appears to be of "the greatest potential" for collective consciousness and relations of homespace.[75]

Concluding Reflection

Through performance pedagogy that stemmed from her ethnographic research in Ghana, I witnessed D. Soyini Madison embody the "on the ground politics" that her mentor, Dwight Conquergood, saw as a necessary praxis that aims toward social justice.[76] In fall 2004, I accompanied Madison as she directed a study abroad program that centered on the legacy of Kwame Nkrumah, Ghana's first president, who led the country to independence from Britain. The study abroad group was predominantly Black American undergraduate students, many of whom never traveled internationally and were housed at the University of Ghana in Legon. The study abroad program allowed the students to choose from the course offerings at the University of Ghana with a specific set of requirements that would shape their curriculum, contextualize their spatial experiences, and introduce them to Ghana's politics and culture. Madison scheduled weekly sessions with scholars inside and outside of the university to lecture to students on a variety of themes such as decolonization, pan-Africanism, and neocolonialism.

After each of these sessions, we would travel on the weekends as a collective. Most of these excursions were closely related to the themes discussed by the invited guests and involved going to historical tourist sites, such as the as the Cape Coast and Elmina Castles, the Kwame Nkrumah Mausoleum, and the W.E.B. DuBois Centre, as well as meeting activists housed at cities throughout the country who were continuing the legacy of Kwame Nkrumah. Within the classroom, Madison assigned West African and Black Diaspora literature alongside cultural texts primarily on decolonization, which helped students reflect on what they experienced outside of her classroom. Throughout the planned curriculum, we dealt with the less-planned, unstructured everyday life experiences: conflicting personalities, multiple bouts of malaria, weight gain, weight loss, heat rash, allergic reactions, love, and death.

I watched Madison transform the students' perspectives through improvisational performances that stemmed from journal entries (a requirement), assigned readings, and everyday experiences and engagements. Each week, students would piece together improvisational, collaborative small group images, adding, image by image, to the continuing workshops that were begun the class before. Madison helped the students interweave these improvisational images with repetitive transitions derived from the students' own words and performances. The students' final project was to engage with Ghanaian students, university workers, and local sellers encountered in and around the university to discuss their experiences with travelers to Ghana. Unlike their other excursions traversing, experiencing, and creating the space together, they were to do this final project alone, with their thoughts and with their engagements with the people they have come to know through local spaces.

The students, Madison, and I participated in the rehearsals of what culminated into a final staged performance by the student-performers at the outside theater of the University of Ghana's campus. For the final staged performance, the student-performers invited the people with whom they engaged, as well as the scholars and activists who shaped their performed perspectives of Ghana and the legacy of Nkrumah during the program. These invited guests were not only invited to bear witness to what they had helped to create but, through the allotted time for the audience to engage with the student-performers, were encouraged to continue the conversation. Madison created a space for further engagement between the performers and the people they had encountered as a point of accountability, labor, and reflection.

Within the talk back discussion, student-performers were pushed to reflect upon and challenge their own position on their engaged experiences. Finally, students-performers were required to reflect upon their overall experience and critically and reflexively discuss the entire study abroad program, including the performance and performance talk back, in their journals as their final assignment.[77] Only Madison knows what was written in all of the journals, but I have always interpreted this final account as Madison's investment in performance's resistance to conclusions, constantly sustaining conversation and accountability.[78] Madison never claimed credit or authorship of the study abroad program or her involvement in the final performance.

Just one year after the study abroad program in Ghana, I was back at the University of North Carolina, in Chapel Hill, and witnessed for a second time as Madison interwove performance, her ethnographic work, text, and pedagogy. At Chapel Hill, she directed a performance titled *Water Rites* and describes her performance as such: "Water Rites explored water democracy and our human relationship with water through a montage of digital imagery, comic satire, dramatic monologue, and stylized movement. Water Rites reflected how we all perform 'water rites' in our everyday lives variously pervade our lives and culture. Water Rites performed the questions, 'What is your first memory of water?' 'Does anyone have the right to own water?' 'What is the connection between local water and global profit?'"[79]

Although this was not the only staged performance from Madison's fieldwork, this was the first that I saw *how* she shared her fieldwork and the knowledge garnered from that work within the classroom. Much like what I learned from her in Ghana, I watched her teach students a politic through a theme and the context of that theme, but, unlike Ghana, I also watched her share her own conversations, intimate reflections in the field, and the experiences she bore witness to, and partook in, as they pertained to the politics of clean water access. Witnessing Madison's lived engagements unfold in the classroom as performed ethnography and performance pedagogy, transforming her students into performance actors for social change, once again, *moved* me. Student-performers and their interlocutors alike travel through lived spaces and engage with each other as travelers of and to varying terrain; they open performative possibilities of how we constitute meaning and action. Praxis, the expectation of performance work, requires the reflexive labor with and for real people in order "to widen the door of the caravan and clear more spaces for Others to Enter."[80] And, it is in this chapter that Glissant's errantry, a story of relation, is told as a power of poetic mobility—a caravan of performance pedagogy.[81]

Conclusion

Remembering "The Score"

Telling Stories of Blackness and Their Circulation

When I turn on my radio, when I hear that negroes have been lynched in America, I say we have been lied to: Hitler is not dead; when I turn on my radio when I learn that Jews have been insulted, mistreated, persecuted, I say that we have been lied to: Hitler is not dead; when, finally, I turn on my radio and hear that in Africa forced labor has been inaugurated and legalized, I say that we have certainly been lied to: Hitler is not dead.

—Aimé Césaire

Policies change, and programs change, according to time. But the objective never changes. Our objective is complete freedom, complete justice, complete equality, by any means necessary. That never changes. Complete and immediate recognition as human beings, that doesn't change, that's what all of us want.

—Malcolm X

On February 26, 2017, Warren Beatty and Faye Dunaway reunited as announcers of the best film at the eighty-ninth Academy Awards ceremony. They were chosen to represent the fiftieth anniversary of *Bonnie and Clyde*, which was nominated for multiple Oscar award categories including best film forty-nine years earlier. As Beatty and Dunaway opened the card to reveal the most awaited award of the night, Beatty read the card and then gave it to Dunaway to read. Excitedly, she announced *La La Land* as the Oscar winner for Best Picture. As the cast of *La La Land* reached the stage, buzzes both behind and on stage began. *La La Land* did not, in fact, win for Best Picture but, apparently through a card mix-up, was mistakenly announced as the film frontrunner instead of *Moonlight*. *Moonlight*, the real winner of the evening, features an all-Black cast and centers on Chiron, a gay Black American youth, and the difficulties he faces based on his identity. It was the first all-Black-cast film to win an Oscar for the Best Film category.

The card mix-up was also the first mistake of its kind since the first Academy Awards ceremony in 1929. The error marked not only an embarrassing moment for the awards ceremony but also the ongoing critique of Hollywood's repudiation of Black actors, a critique the Academy Awards seemingly aimed to resolve with the number of nominations and wins with its eighty-ninth ceremony as opposed to the last one, which consisted of zero nominations for Black Hollywood. Moreover, it marked the erasure of *Moonlight* and its win from popular memory as these representations of white privilege positioned whiteness at the forefront. The blunder would also be at the center of Jay-Z's song, "Moonlight," from his thirteenth album, *4:44*, released just four months after the Oscars. "Moonlight" tells a multifaceted story of blackness circulated through hip-hop music and centers on the limits of Black mobility.

The song underscores how sociogenic included exclusion and white sovereignty actively prevent Black freedom and inclusion even with the promise of Black (economic) mobility and bourgeois sensibility. The sound of "Moonlight" samples "Fu-Gee-La," the lead single from *The Score*, the second album of the successful nineties hip-hop group The Fugees. The sample includes part of the chorus with the voice of Lauryn Hill, who was a member of The Fugees alongside Wyclef Jean and Pras Michel, all of whom are of Haitian descent. Hill was the first female artist to win a Grammy for Best Rap Album for *The Score* in 1997 as part of the hip-hop group and, two years later, she would be the first rapper to win a Grammy award for Album of the Year for *The Miseducation of Lauryn Hill*. After her groundbreaking success, Hill was plagued with lawsuits that cited writers and producers were not properly credited in her solo album and was also indicted for failure to pay taxes on over $1.5 million earned between 2005 and 2007. In 2013, the hip-hop celebrity and mother of six was sentenced to three months in prison and three months on house arrest.

Jay-Z's use of "Fu-Gee-La"—Hill's initial catapult to fame with *The Score*— in "Moonlight" serves as a reminder of how white sovereign circulation limits Black mobility through colonial regulations of blackness, such as surveillance and policing, as Hill's own personal and professional woes demonstrated. In fact, Black mobility did not shelter any of The Fugees from modes of regulation but exacerbated them. John Forté, credited for cowriting and producing for The Fugees, was sentenced to fourteen years in prison for the possession of over one million dollars' worth of cocaine with the intent to distribute in 2001; he was pardoned by President Bush in 2008. A criminal investigation for fraud has haunted Wyclef Jean and his charity organization, Yele Haiti, since 2010, and Pras was indicted in 2019 on money laundering charges linked to contributions for the 2012 U.S. presidential campaign. Jay-Z himself faced criminal charges in 2001 for allegedly stabbing record producer Lance "Un" Rivera; he pled guilty to a lesser assault charge and received three years of probation.[1]

Indeed, Black mobility circulates the fate of blackness in white sovereignty, and, in his second verse, Jay-Z drives this point further, names Lauryn Hill, and depicts her as a victim of a structure that, through its modes of extraction, thingifies and capitalizes off of blackness. "We" in the first verse and "our" in the second mark a belonging to blackness and, with a sample of Hill singing "Ooo la la la," the chorus asserts, "We stuck in la la land; even when we win, we gon' lose."[2] Indeed, white sovereignty regulates Black mobility, limits and stops it in the struggle toward the path of freedom. The "Moonlight" video extends its theme of regulated Black mobility through an all-Black reenactment of the hit sitcom *Friends*.[3] The video of the two-minute and twenty-three-second song runs seven minutes and twenty-five seconds with credits, so much of the video is a reenactment of the *Friends* episode, "The One Where No One's Ready." Its video features the rising Black actors of its time with Jerrod Carmichael as Ross, Issa Rae as Rachel, Lil Rel Howery as Joey, Lakeith Stanfield as Chandler, Tessa Thompson as Monica, and Tiffany Haddish as Phoebe.

The introduction of *Moonlight's Friends* echoes the original with the cast in the same clothes as the television actors; they mimic the movements and gestures with similar props like the couch and the water fountain. Because of copyright use, Whodini's *Friends* replaced the original show's theme song, but the use of the hip-hop song furthers sociogenic differentiation of the Black performers from their white counterparts and articulates their bodies to hip hop and blackness in general.[4] Staged in Monica's New York apartment, with the same lines and scene as in the original episode, Jay-Z as the voice of Richard leaves a message for Tessa/Monica just as Tom Selleck did for Courtney Cox/Monica. The mimetic imagery of *Moonlight's Friends* suggests an ease of white mobility as comedian Hannibal Buress visits Carmichael on the set and tells Carmichael that the scene was "garbage."[5]

Buress continues, "It was terrible, man. It was whack as shit. It was just episodes of Seinfeld but with Black people."[6] Carmichael explains his decision to play Ross with the intention to create "something subversive, something that would turn the culture on its head."[7] Buress then quips that he "did a good job of subverting good comedy" and asks if he's "gonna do Black 'Full House' next?"[8] Buress then tells Carmichael that he just accepted a role as "a parrot with a bad attitude" on the Pirates of the Caribbean Cruise Line and states, "It's terrible, but it's way better than this shit."[9] The "Moonlight" video captures Black popular sentiment that unlimited Black mobility, its articulated freedom in western modernity, only occurs when its productive labor is extracted and articulated to white. As I have highlighted in Chapter 3, but it is worth repeating to underscore its significance in modernity-coloniality relations, white sovereignty always looks to blackness "for a little human sustenance," and, in its structures of mobility, this extractive measure is constant.[10]

"Moonlight" draws upon the Black popular understanding of *Friends* as the appropriation of *Living Single* with white actors, operating similarly to the western freedoms of mobility in other structural genres such as media, film, music, politics, education, and the academy. As the journalist Zeba Blay highlights, "Both shows are about a group of six friends living in the same apartment complex, and both have similar characters—Lisa Kudrow's Phoebe Buffet, for instance, has the same ditsy behavior and earthy style as Sinclair (played by Kim Coles)."[11] Queen Latifa, the lead actor of *Living Single*, also revealed that Warren Littlefield, who ran NBC, admitted to wanting *Living Single* as part of the network's television lineup and then shortly after created *Friends*.[12] Although this context speaks directly to "the tendency of white Hollywood to profit from and copy the ideas of black entertainment," it demonstrates that sociogenic included exclusion articulates and regulates how we see, how we are seen, and, in turn, our ability to move.[13] We are trapped in what Fanon identifies as an "hellish cycle" of hegemonic, sociogenic discourse regulated and circulated by the structural relations of coloniality and modernity.[14]

The sociogenic Black image and white image are imprinted with their colonial past and are always and already trapped within the coloniality-modernity relationship.[15] As such, each image's categorical possibility is limited and thereby also restricts the relations of identification between and among those who identify and are identified as Black and white. The limits of freedom have only heightened with the advancement of new technology that communicates blackened bodies as thingified value through identificatory seeing but not worthy speaking subjects.[16] The "closed circuit"[17] of coloniality demands limited blackness as it relates to white superiority even with positive and subversive disruptions that appear to always arrive "too soon or too late."[18]

Fanon's attention to temporality demonstrates how the movement of time itself functions against the material fact of blackness within western modernity. Even as Black performances on screen disrupt racist imaginaries of negation, Black images are regulated to sociogenic codes of included exclusion. This regime of visibility is evidenced by Buress' response to Carmichael that his "parrot with a bad attitude" is better than Black *Friends*, and, certainly, Buress' response echoes that his parrot is better than *Friends*, whose "terrible" and "shit" content is exposed only when the actors are Black. Jay-Z's storied Black consciousness directly confronts the limits of Black mobility in "The Story of O. J.," the second song listed in *4:44*.[19]

Popularized by the television miniseries *American Crime Story: The People vs. O. J.* and its trailer, Cuba Gooding, Jr. as O. J. Simpson in prison garb and awaiting trial for the murder of Nicole Simpson and Ronald Goldman says, "I'm not Black. I'm O. J."[20] Jay-Z redelivers the line and states sarcastically, "Okay."[21] Symbolic repetition is apparent throughout the song with samples of Nina Simone's "Four Women," played continuously throughout the song and heard in the background of the verses, emphasizes our hellish sociogenic cycle; it is Simone's remixed voice that is first heard, which sets the tone for the chorus that repeats twice each time it is introduced. The chorus itself covers a variety of binaries: light/dark, faux/real, rich/poor, house/field, and, with each category, "nigga" repeats and initially suggests its typical use in hip hop. The shift at the end of the chorus suggests the pejorative meaning, "still nigga, still nigga."[22] Its video centers the cyclical theme of our "Manicheism delirium," with historically racist cartoon caricatures of Black images, Jay-Z's and Simone's included.[23]

With Manichean logic threaded throughout the song, Jay-Z's two verses underscore Black liberation through the accumulation of wealth and credit—an ironic twist given its Simone-sampled score, video, and "Moonlight." According to *Forbes* in 2019, however, Shawn Carter, a.k.a. Jay-Z, has reached billionaire status, is one of the few entertainers to achieve this, and is the first hip-hop artist to do so with assets worth conservatively $1 billion at the time of this writing.[24] With financial freedom as the path to Black liberation, Jay-Z begs the question of how much financial freedom is demanded to liberate us from sociogenic bounds in the modernity-coloniality framework. For Fanon, there is one underlying principle: "A given society is either racist or it is not,"[25] and there is no amount of Black bourgeois mobility that can alleviate the circulation of racism's "infernal circle."[26] As the former leader of the Black Panther Party, Elaine Browne highlights in response to the resurgent sentiment: "There is no room for more than one Oprah. Everybody can't be America's Mammie."[27]

Western sovereign logic remains undeniably "assimilate or die," as applied to all, even billionaires.[28]

Conceivably, the logic of wealth accumulation was the impetus for Carter to sign with the NFL only three years after Colin Kaepernick first took a knee during the national anthem in protest against police brutality and killings. Carter's NFL deal occurred only one year after he, too, stood with Kaepernick. As Carter says, "[Colin Kaepernick] was done wrong. I would understand if it was three months ago. But it was three years ago, and someone needs to say, 'What do we do now, because people are still dying?'"[29]

In his own act of storied circulation, Kaepernick tweeted, "Reading always gives me clarity," with a picture of a highlighted excerpt from

Robert L. Allen's *Black Awakening in Capitalist America* in response to Carter's NFL deal.[30] A significant part of the excerpt is as follows:

> This reformist or bourgeois nationalism—through its chosen vehicle of black
> capitalism—may line the pockets and boost the social status of the black
> middle class and black intelligentsia, but it will not ease the oppression of the
> ordinary ghetto dweller ... They call themselves nationalists and exploit the
> legitimate nationalist feelings of black people in order to advance their own
> interests as a class.[31]

With the excerpt, Kaepernick reposted the line: "What [they] seek is not an
end to oppression, but the transfer of the oppressive apparatus into their own
hands."[32] Kaepernick's repost to Carter refers to his justification for his NFL
deal, which includes a social justice initiative. *Inspire Change* "focuses on 'education and economic advancement, police and community relations, and criminal justice reform' and $100 million dedicated to social justice outreach
groups over the next 10 years" at a rate of $10 million per year.[33] Perhaps in ten
years, we will see the positive results of Carter's deal or perhaps the most fit-
ting response is Jay-Z's, right after the infamous line from O. J., "Okay."[34]

The intended message behind the track "The Story of O. J." cannot contain
the performative excess made apparent through the sample of "Four Women;"
the affective sound of Simone, her repeated voice, and the visual imagery of the
racist caricatures are reminders of relations of homespace and their identificatory circulation. Simone's Black consciousness moved her to speak back to the
nation, which resulted in an industry backlash, the boycotting of her music and,
in turn, self-exile from which her career never recovered, at least in terms of
monetary gain.[35] Prior to Simone, there was a historical line of targeted direct
and indirect murder in Black movement toward freedom.

As Dave Chappelle made clear in his Netflix stand-up *The Bird Revelation*,
"[Kaepernick's] so light skinned. He didn't have to say he was Black. And yet,
he took a knee during that anthem for us. Thought about us when things were
going good, when his belly was full ... he didn't think about his livelihood or
any of that, and they took his livelihood away from him."[36] Certainly, indirect
death remains the case for Kaepernick, his price tag for his identification with
blackness.

Chappelle's message is significant as he also chose to walk away from his con-
tract, worth $50 million, with Comedy Central for The Chappelle Show in
2005 for similar reasons.[37] It also underscores the point of *Moving Blackness*:
out of the modernity-coloniality relationship, there is an emergence of a new
humanism, one that already resides in a circulating blackness.[38] Such emer-
gences appear in the unarchivable, silenced truths that not only exist and circulate but compel new relations of homespace outside the frame of sociogenic

representation and white sovereignty. These told stories move beyond the emptied symbols of western inclusion "in which life has no taste, in which the air is tainted in which the ideas and men are corrupt."[39] These story-tellings are revolutionary as they stand against white sovereignty and sociogenic erasure. And, in those moments that the fear of indirect death encourages and even compels us to silence, we should take note of what T. I. warned when he sampled Jay-Z, who quoted the Notorious B.I.G., which I will now retell: "It's [ONLY] hard to yell, when the barrel is in your mouth."[40]

Acknowledgments

Words cannot express my gratefulness to all the people I have encountered who have shaped my consciousness of who I have become. Each of you with your presence, your actions, and your shared memories and intellect continues to shape my becoming.

To the Department of Communication at The University of North Carolina, old and new, I could not have imagined better scholars to learn from and work with. Thank you for your support, conversations, passion, and sincerity. I am truly honored to be your colleague.

To some special graduate students who continue to teach me about knowledge production, solidarity, and equity, namely, Khari Johnson, Joey Richards, Kayla Corbin, Nic Gerstner, Miquell Shaw, Leah Ai Ling Woehr, X. Ramos-Lara, Vanessa Sanders Taboada, and especially Cree Noble and Stephanie Kaczynski who, since Chicago, continue to move me with their tenacity and creativity toward social justice. To my ride or die, Megan Foster, I have learned from your care for knowledge and equity in the most profound ways. Thank you!

For this project, many thanks go to Nicole Solano, my editor at Rutgers University Press, whose continued and enthusiastic support has made this book possible, the book reviewers who provided thorough and much-needed feedback, and the production team at Rutgers University Press for their work on materializing my ideas. Much gratitude to the Woodrow Wilson Career Enhancement Fellowship for its funding and mentorship support and to El Centro, the Center for Puerto Rican Studies at Hunter College, City University of New York, whose archivists aided in shaping the primary sources for my research. To the Department of Black Studies at Northwestern University, where, as a postdoctoral fellow, I benefited immensely from the community dialogues and debates on blackness, power, and the Black Diaspora. I am truly grateful for John D. Márquez, whose friendship, critical brilliance, and collegiality have been unwavering, as well as for Sherwin K. Bryant, particularly for providing detailed feedback on this manuscript. Richard Iton and Charles W. Mills, I carry your extraordinary insight and politically charged wisdom with me in my intellectual journey (Rest-in-Power, and Solidarity).

Thanks go to my larger Chicago community, especially my former students Gabriel C. Tyler, Evangeline Semark, Abigail Escatel, Kristen May, Rebecca Wooley, Yesica Tellez, F. Javier Arellano, Tatiana Acosta, Trent Lawrence, Tyler Butterfield, Fabiola Rosiles, Taylor Moody, Kiah Wilson, Leila Abdelrazaq, Mackenzie Carlock, Emma Davis, Estefania de la Torre, Lauren Gonzales, Dai'sha Jones, Colleen McMahon, Scimone Williams, and the amazing Raven Jackson. Much admiration and thanks go to the Chicago Alliance Against Racist and Political Repression for continuing to fight the good fight in both love and solidarity and the participants of the Juvenile Justice program in the northside. I deeply appreciate Tera Agyepong for her intellect, politics, and friendship and Jerry Bramwell of the Law Offices of Fitzgerald Bramwell for his wit, passion, and consciousness to do the right thing. To all my petition signers and each of my letter writers, most of whom remain anonymous to me, I am sincerely indebted to you for responding to the calls. Thank you for acting in my time of need! Finally, I am indebted to Terry Smith, for standing with me when many others refused (Rest-in-Power, and Solidarity).

At Brooklyn College, City University of New York, where my higher education began, I am forever grateful for the opportunities and overwhelming mentorship I received at the beginning of my academic journey. To the Search for Education, Elevation and Knowledge (SEEK) program, especially Ann Wheeler, my SEEK counselor, you inspired me to pursue critical race studies. To Robert Scott at the Honor's Academy, I continue to cherish every word of wisdom you have bestowed upon me. To my mentors and colleagues in the Ford Colloquium, especially Tucker Farley, my advisor, a brilliant scholar, and teacher, who shaped my critical approach to knowledge and inspired me to pursue cultural studies and BIPOC feminist theory. To the Mellon Mays Undergraduate Fellowship (MMUF) program, especially Margarite Fernández Olmos, who took a chance on me as a fellow and later pushed me to learn Spanish. And, finally, to María Pérez y González, in the Department of Puerto Rican and Latino Studies, who introduced me to my Black Diasporic Puerto Rican history and politics, you continue to be my role-model and thank you for always betting on me. Pa'lante!

My intellectual community at Brooklyn College paved the way toward my introduction to The University of North Carolina at Chapel Hill as a fellow in the Moore Undergraduate Research Apprenticeship Program (MURAP). At MURAP I encountered BIPOC scholars who transformed the course of my future and whose intellectual brilliance and political presence continue to shape my understanding of the world. Thank you, Sandy Darity, Reginald Hildebrand, Charlene Register, Karla Slocum, and the late James Coleman. Much respect and love to Leslie Clement Guitiérrez and Malcolm Woodland whose dedication to the Black Diaspora and activism remain my standard.

D. Soyini Madison, I first met you at MURAP and I have since strived to remain in your path with the deepest love and solidarity. You once wrote that I was your rock and your light, but it is you who are mine. Thank you for continuing to inspire, support, and teach me that we can always make a better world through love, one person, and one story at a time.

I am especially grateful to Kara Keeling and John L. Jackson for your academic integrity, brilliance, and always staying true to form. These qualities are quite rare in the academy.

Joshua Smicker, I continue to admire your critical awareness and deep sense of openness to learn.

Bernadette M. Calafell for continuing to fight for your belief in what's right even when you're not required to, for your years of friendship, and for reviewing an early version of this book.

Lawrence Grossberg, for reading and providing line-by-line feedback for this book, and especially for your continued mentorship and friendship. Your loyalty, brilliance, and kindness never cease to amaze me.

KaDarra Lowe, my Bronx sis, your enduring commitment to love, creativity, and friendship cannot be surpassed.

To my best friend, sis, and everything else, Guadalupe García, for reading and re-reading all the versions of this book and especially for standing with me throughout my entire intellectual journey. With the deepest gratitude, love, and admiration, you are truly my fam in solidarity, always.

My intellectual journey began well before my arrival in the academy in my godparents' home where friends and family would gather on the weekends. These collective moments brought me true joy and I will cherish them and those who made them forever. In this spirit, I especially want to thank my godmother, Gloria Morales, my father's cousin, who has been such a significant presence in my life. You have all my love, loyalty, and respect.

I want to thank my godmother's children especially Antonia Martinez, for all the family labor and care that you have done across generations, and Michelle Mimms for being sincerely good-hearted and continuing to make time for me when I come home—thanks, cuz. You are both blessings to our family.

I am indebted to the Brooklyn neighborhoods where young people like me shared a sense of home when we could not find any. For those who provided me a sense of homespace on Church, Ditmas, and Prospect Avenues, at Brighten 6, P.S. 160, Cortelyou Road, Sunset and Prospect Parks, Glenwood, Nostrand, and Sheepshead Houses, I cherish all the memories of love, care, community and joy you gave me.

To my godfather, Luis Santiago Morales, and my paternal grandfather, Alberto Calvente, who instilled in me a love for and a connection to the island. Puerto Rico will always be rich with pride. Harry Calvente and Judah Nasir Williams, you are with me always. My beautiful paternal grandmother, Consuelo Leon Calvente, a true hustler with a heart of gold, I love you. My practices of homespace come from the memories of you all.

To my extraordinary, remarkable mother, Lien Sang thi Dang Calvente, whose bravery, intelligence, and stubbornness continue to provide me with the strength and commitment to ride that tiger's back in the struggle for justice.

To my forever, Timothy Ryan Williams, for reading and providing feedback on this book. You are the embodiment of how "real G's move in silence." Thank you for continuing to help me be a better version of myself, for holding me down with enduring love and care, and for always betting on Black!

Finally, to my beautiful and brilliant little dragon, Luna Manye Williams, for speaking truth even when I am not ready to accept it. With the deepest of love, the world is yours. Mama, gotch'ur back, always.

Notes

Introduction

Epigraphs: Rachel Z. Rivera, *New York Ricans from the Hip Hop Zone* (New York: Palgrave, 2003), 26.

Know Your History: Jesus Is Black, So Was Cleopatra, directed by Bart Phillips (2007; Los Angeles: Image Entertainment), DVD.

1 For an in-depth explanation of the opposing relationship between the citizen and the nigger, the blackened noncitizen, see Richard Iton, *In Search of the Black Fantastic: Politics and Popular Culture in the Post-Civil Rights Era* (New York: Oxford University Press, 2008); see also Richard Iton, "Still Life," *Small Axe* 17, no. 1 (March 2013): 22–39.

2 Iton, *In Search of.*

3 See Eric Williams, *Capitalism and Slavery* (London: Andre Deutsch, 1964) for an in-depth analysis of how racial difference and slavery were integral components of western economic growth, capital, and of the western world itself. See also Guadalupe García, "Producing Place: Colonialism and Governance in the Early Modern Caribbean," in *Beyond the Walled City* (Berkeley: University of California Press, 2015), 19–37, for illustrations of how racial difference and colonial exclusion played a primary role in the sixteenth century Spanish empire.

4 For an extended discussion on modernity as a project that relied heavily on race and racial discourse, see Barnor Hesse, "Racialized Modernity: An Analytics of White Mythologies," *Ethnic and Racial Studies* 30, no. 4 (July 2007): 643–663; see also Lisa B. Y. Calvente, "Decolonizing Revolution through Visual Articulations," in *Imprints of Revolution: Visual Representations of Resistance*, eds. Lisa B. Y. Calvente and Guadalupe García (London: Roman & Littlefield, 2016), 1–20.

5 See Calvente, "Decolonizing Revolution."

6 See García, *Beyond the Walled City.*

7 For an extended discussion on repeated colonial violence and racialization of power as white sovereignty, see Barnor Hesse. "White Sovereignty (. . .), Black Life Politics: 'The N****r They Couldn't Kill,'" *South Atlantic Quarterly* 116, no. 3 (2017): 581–604.

8 W.E.B. DuBois, "The Humor of Negroes," *Mark Twain Journal* 36, no. 1 (Spring 1998): 8.

9 DuBois, "Humor of Negroes," 8.

10 Henry Louis Gates, Jr., "The Black Letters on the Sign: W.E.B. DuBois and the Canon," in *The Oxford W.E.B. DuBois*, ed. Henry Louis Gates (New York: Oxford University Press, 2006).

11 See Frantz Fanon, *Black Skin White Masks*, rev. ed. (New York: Grove Press, 2008); see also Sylvia Wynter, "Towards the Sociogenic Principle: Fanon, Identity, the Puzzle of Conscious Experience, and What It Is Like to be "Black," in *National Identities and Socio-Political Changes in Latin America*, eds. Antonio Gomez-Moriana and Mercedes Duran-Cogan (New York: Routledge, 2001), 30–66.

12 For more on American modernity see Lawrence Grossberg, *Caught in the Crossfire: Kids, Politics, and America's Future* (Boulder, CO: Paradigm, 2005), 197–217.

13 Grossberg, *Caught in the Crossfire*.

14 Calvente, "Decolonizing Revolution."

15 Calvente, "Decolonizing Revolution;" see Eric Williams, *Capitalism and Slavery*; see also Susan Buck-Morss, *Hegel, Haiti, and Universal History* (Pittsburgh: University of Pittsburgh Press, 2009).

16 Anders Stephanson, *Manifest Destiny: American Expansion and the Empire of Right* (New York: Hill and Wang, 1995).

17 See Richard Slotkin, *Regeneration through Violence: The Mythology of the American Frontier, 1600–1860* (Norman: University of Oklahoma Press, 2000); see Harold Innis, *The Bias of Communication* (Toronto: University of Toronto Press, 1950) and *Empire and Communications* (Toronto: University of Toronto Press, 1950); see also James W. Carey, *Communication as Culture*, rev. ed. (New York: Routledge, 2009).

18 See Reginald Horsman, *Race and Manifest Destiny: Origins of American Racial Anglo-Saxonism* (Cambridge, MA: Harvard University Press, 1981); see also Richard Steven Street, *Beasts of the Field: A Narrative History of California Farm Workers, 1769–1913* (Stanford: Stanford University Press, 2004).

19 See W.E.B. DuBois, *Black Reconstruction in America: An Essay toward a History of the Part Which Black Folk Played on the Attempt to Reconstruct Democracy in America, 1860–1880* (New York: Oxford University Press, 2007); see also David Roediger, *The Wages of Whiteness: Race and the Making of the American Working Class* (New York: Verso, 2007).

20 Grossberg, *Caught in the Crossfire*, 197–217.

21 For an in-depth critical analysis of the United States, Reconstruction, and abolition democracy, see DuBois, *Black Reconstruction in America*; see also Grossberg, *Caught in the Crossfire*, 197–217.

22 See, for example, Ida B. Wells-Barnett, "Lynch Law in America," *The Arena* 23 (January 1900): 15–24 and "Lynching: A National Crime" (lecture, National Negro Conference, New York, June 1, 1909); see also Richard Delgado, "The Law of the Noose: A History of Latino Lynching," *Harvard Civil Rights-Civil Liberties Law Review* 44 (2009); see also Angela Y. Davis, *Abolition Democracy: Beyond Empire, Prisons, and Torture* (New York: Seven Stories Press, 2005).

23 Barnor Hesse, "Self-Fulfilling Prophecy: The Post-Racial Horizon," *South Atlantic Quarterly* 110, no. 1 (Winter 2011): 155–178.

24 Sylvia Wynter, "Sambos and Minstrels," *Social Text* no. 1 (Winter 1979): 149–156.

25 See Stuart Hall, "What Is This 'Black' in Black Popular Culture?" in *Stuart Hall: Critical Dialogues in Cultural Studies*, eds. David Morley and Kuan-Hsing Chen (New York: Routledge, 1996); Paul Gilroy, *The Black Atlantic: Modernity and Double Consciousness* (Cambridge, MA: Harvard University Press, 1993); Richard Iton, *In Search of*.

26 See Félix Guattari, *The Three Ecologies*, trans. Ian Pindar and Paul Sutton (London: The Athlone Press, 2000); see also Stuart Hall, "On Postmodernism and Articulation: An Interview with Stuart Hall," Lawrence Grossberg, ed., in *Stuart Hall: Critical Dialogues in Cultural Studies*, eds. David Morley and Kuan-Hsing Chen (New York: Routledge, 1996), 131–150.

27 Lawrence Grossberg, *Dancing in Spite of Myself: Essays on Popular Culture* (Durham, NC: Duke University Press, 1997).

28 Wynter, "Sambos and Minstrels," 149.

29 bell hooks, *Black Looks: Race and Representation* (Boston: South End Press, 1992).

30 James Scott, *Domination and the Art of Resistance: Hidden Transcripts* (New Haven, CT: Yale University Press, 1990).

31 For the history of the relationship between politics, communication, and Black humor in the United States, see Mel Watkins, *On the Real Side: A History of African American Comedy from Slavery to Chris Rock* (New York: Simon & Schuster, 1994); for a comprehensive analysis on the political agenda of Black comedy in television, see Christine Acham, *Revolution Televised: Prime Time and the Struggle for Black Power* (Minneapolis: University of Minnesota Press, 2004); for a history of humor rooted in communication studies and western critical thought, see J. Jerome Zolten, "Black Comedians: Forging an Ethnic Image," *Journal of American Culture* 16 (Summer 1993): 65–75.

32 Antonio Gramsci, *Selections from the Prison Notebooks*, trans. Quentin Hoare and Geoffrey Nowell Smith (New York: International Publishers, 1971).

33 See Stuart Hall, "Gramsci's Relevance for the Study of Race and Ethnicity," in *Stuart Hall: Critical Dialogues in Cultural Studies*, eds. David Morley and Kuan-Hsing Chen (New York: Routledge, 1996): 411–440.

34 Meaghan Morris, "Banality in Cultural Studies," *Discourse: Journal for Theoretical Studies in Media and Culture* 10, no. 2 (1988): 3–29.

35 Morris, "Banality in Cultural Studies."

36 For dialogical performance see Dwight Conquergood, "Performing as a Moral Act: Ethical Dimensions of the Ethnography of Performance," *Literature in Performance*, 5 no. 2 (1985): 1–13; see also D. Soyini Madison, *Acts of Activism: Human Rights as Radical Performance* (Cambridge: Cambridge University Press, 2010): 47–48.

37 See Della Pollock, "Introduction," in *Remembering: Oral History Performance*, ed. Della Pollock (London: Palgrave MacMillan, 2005), 1–17.

38 Madison, *Acts of Activism*.

39 Madison, *Acts of Activism*, 49.

40 Gyanendra Pandey, "Unarchived Histories: The 'Mad' and the 'Trifling,'" in *Unarchived Histories: The Mad and the Trifling in the Colonial and Postcolonial World*, ed. Gyanendra Pandey (New York: Routledge, 2014), 3–19.

41 Hall, "What is this?"

42 Gloria Anzaldúa and Cherríe Moraga, eds. *This Bridge Called My Back* (New York: Kitchen Table, Women of Color Press, 1984), 34.

43 Charles W. Mills, "White Ignorance," in *Race and Epistemologies of Ignorance*, eds. Shannon Sullivan and Nancy Tuana (Albany: SUNY Press, 2007), 13–38.

44 Homi K. Bhabha, *The Location of Culture* (London: Routledge, 1994).

45 Latin American migrant workers in the Southeast continue to rely heavily on word of mouth for everyday life necessities such as employment, housing, and community building; even though they had access to social media, they used it only to interact for leisure. Steven Alvarez, "Research Overview Presentation" (lecture, Career Enhancement Fellows Retreat, Wesley Chapel, FL, August 2015).

46 For the difference between public and hidden transcripts, see James C. Scott, *Domination and the Arts of Resistance* (New Haven, CT: Yale University Press, 1992); see also Erving Goffman, *The Presentation of Self in Everyday Life* (Norwell, MA: Anchor, 1959).

47 Stuart Hall, Chas Critcher, Tony Jefferson, John Clarke, and Brian Roberts, *Policing the Crisis: Mugging, the State and Law and Order* (London: Palgrave, 1978).

48 Hall et al., 135–136.

49 Scott, *Domination*, 146–148.

50 See Mills, "White Ignorance;" see also Delgado, "Law of the Noose."

51 Tricia Rose, *Black Noise: Rap Music and Black Culture in Contemporary America* (Middletown, CT: Wesleyan University Press, 1994), 7–8.

52 Rose, *Black Noise*, 8.

53 For a more in-depth understanding of how colonial mimicry can disrupt power through the double articulation and intensification of surveillance, see Bhabha, *Location of Culture*.

54 Mills, "White Ignorance."

55 Mills, "White Ignorance."

56 Mills, "White Ignorance."

57 bell hooks, *Talking Back: Thinking Feminist, Thinking Black* (Boston: South End Press, 1989).

58 See part 3 of Michel de Certeau, *The Practice of Everyday Life* (Berkeley: University of California Press, 1984), 91–130. See also Meaghan Morris, "At Henry Parkes Motel," in *Too Soon Too Late: History in Popular Culture* (Bloomington: Indiana University Press, 1998), 31–63.

59 See Katherine McKittrick, *Demonic Grounds: Black Women and the Cartographies of Struggle* (Minneapolis: University of Minnesota Press, 2006), xi, ix–xxx.

60 See Stuart Hall, "Notes on Deconstructing the 'Popular,'" in *People's History and Socialist Theory*, ed. Raphael Samuel (London: Routledge and Kegan Paul, 1981), 227–240.

61 Hall, "Notes on Deconstructing," 234.

62 See Cedric J. Robinson, *Black Marxism: The Making of the Black Radical Tradition* (Chapel Hill: The University of North Carolina Press, 1983); see Fred Moten, *In the Break: The Aesthetics of the Black Radical Tradition* (Minneapolis: University of Minnesota Press, 2003); see also Daphne A. Brooks, *Bodies in Dissent: Spectacular Performances of Race and Freedom, 1850–1910* (Durham, NC: Duke University Press, 2006).

63 Hall, "On Postmodernism and Articulation," 135–136.

64 Hall "Gramsci's Relevance," 432.

65 For a discussion of mattering maps, see Lawrence Grossberg, *We Gotta Get Out of This Place* (New York: Routledge, 1992); see also Lawrence Grossberg, on the task of cultural analysts, *Caught in the Crossfire*, and "We All Want to Change the

World: The Paradox of the U.S. Left (A Polemic)," accessed May 23, 2024, https://www.academia.edu/13048909/We_all_want_to_change_the_world_The _paradox_of_the_U_S_left_A_polemic_.

66 Hall, "On Postmodernism and Articulation," 140.

67 Gramsci, *Selections from the Prison Notebooks*.

68 See E. Patrick Johnson, "Black Performance Studies: Genealogies, Politics, Futures," in *The SAGE Handbook of Performance Studies*, eds. D. Soyini Madison and Judith Hamera (Los Angeles: Sage Publishing, 2006), 446–463.

Chapter 1 Nation-Place

Epigraphs: Barnor Hesse, "Racialized Modernity: An Analytics of White Mythologies," *Ethnic and Racial Studies* 30, no. 4 (2007): 659–660.

See Jill Toliver Richardson, "Writing Her Legacy: A Conversation with María (Mariposa) Teresa Fernández," *Interview/Entrevista, Centro Journal*, 28, no. 2 (Fall 2005): 126.

1 "Executive Order no. 9981 of July 26, 1948," General Records of the United States Government, record group 11, U.S. National Archives.

2 W.E.B. Du Bois, "The Souls of Black Folk," in *Writings: The Suppression of the African Slave Trade, The Souls of Black Folk, Dusk of Dawn, Essays* (New York: The Library of America, 1986), 357–547.

3 Frantz Fanon, *Black Skin White Masks*, trans. Charles Lam Markmann (London: Pluto, 1986), 111.

4 Sharon Holland, *Raising the Dead: Readings of Death and Black Subjectivity* (Durham, NC: Duke University Press, 2000).

5 See W.E.B. Du Bois, *Black Reconstruction in America: An Essay toward a History of the Part Which Black Folk Played on the Attempt to Reconstruct Democracy in America, 1860–1880* (New York: Oxford University Press, 2007); see also David R. Roediger, *The Wages of Whiteness: Race and the Making of the American Working Class* (London: Verso, 1999); see Linda Martín Alcoff, "Latino/as, Asian Americans, and the Black-White Binary," *The Journal of Ethics* 7 (2003): 5–27.

6 Frantz Fanon, *The Wretched of the Earth* (New York: Grove, 1963), 40.

7 See Stuart Hall, "Race, Articulation, and Societies Structured in Dominance," in *Sociological Theories: Race and Colonialism* (Paris: UNESCO, 1980), 303–45; see also David Theo Goldberg, *The Racial State* (Hoboken, NJ: Wiley Blackwell, 2001).

8 Hall, "Race, Articulation, and Societies," 329.

9 Hesse, "Racialized Modernity," 659.

10 Hall, "Race, Articulation and Societies," 340.

11 Guadalupe García, "Topographies of Slavery and Freedom" (presentation, University of Warwick, Coventry, UK, May 2014). See also Sherwin K. Bryant, *Rivers of Gold, Lives of Bondage: Governing Through Slavery in Colonial Quito* (Chapel Hill: The University of North Carolina Press, 2014).

12 See Achilles Mbembe, *The Critique of Black Reason*, trans. Laurent Du Bois (Durham, NC: Duke University Press, 2017).

13 See Fanon, *Black Skin, White Mask*. See Sylvia Wynter, "Unsettling the Coloniality of Being/Power/Truth/Freedom: Towards the Human, After Man, Its Overrepresentation—An Argument" in *CR: The New Centennial Review 3*, no. 3 (2003): 257–337. See also Sylvia Wynter, "Towards the Sociogenic Principle: Fanon, Identity, the Puzzle of Conscious Experience and What it Is Like to Be

'Black,'" in *National Identities and Sociopolitical Changes in Latin America*, ed. Mercedes E. Durán-Cogan and Antonio Gómez Moriana (New York: Routledge, 2001), 30–66. For white sovereignty, see Barnor Hesse, "White Sovereignty (. . .), Black Life Politics: 'The N****r They Couldn't Kill,'" *South Atlantic Quarterly* 116, no. 3 (2017): 581–604.

14 Paul Gilroy, *Postcolonial Melancholia* (New York: Columbia University Press, 2005), 8–9, 14.

15 W.E.B. Du Bois, "The Souls of Black Folk," 357.

16 Stuart Hall, "Old and New Identities, Old and New Ethnicities," in *Culture, Globalization, and the World System: Contemporary Conditions for the Representation of Identity*, ed. Anthony D. King (Minneapolis: University of Minnesota Press, 1997), 54.

17 See Fanon, *Black Skin, White Mask*, 4. See Sylvia Wynter, "Unsettling the Coloniality" and "Towards the Sociogenic Principle."

18 See Frantz Fanon, *Black Skin, White Mask*.

19 See Hall, "Race, Articulation, and Societies."

20 Fanon, *Wretched of the Earth*, 37.

21 Édouard Glissant, *Poetics of Relation*, trans. Betsy Wing (Ann Arbor: University of Michigan Press, 2010), 11.

22 Oliver C. Cox, *Caste, Class, and Race: A Study in Social Dynamics* (New York: Monthly Review, 1948), 360.

23 See Eric Williams, *Capitalism and Slavery* (London: Andre Deutsch Limited, 1983); Walter Rodney, *How Europe Underdeveloped Africa* (Washington, DC: Howard University Press, 1982). See also Fanon, *Wretched of the Earth*, and Aimé Césaire, *Discourse on Colonialism* (New York: Monthly Review Press, 2000).

24 Glissant, *Poetics of Relation*, 14. See also Aimé Césaire, *Discourse on Colonialism*.

25 For sociogeny see Fanon, *Black Skin, White Masks*. For the process by which a sociodiagnostic assessment of this new world order is structured, see Fanon, *Wretched of the Earth*. For further details on the sociogenic principle see Wynter, "Unsettling the Coloniality" and "Towards the Sociogenic Principle." See also Sylvia Wynter and Katherine McKittrick, "Unparalleled Catastrophe for Our Species? Or to Give Humanness a Different Future: Conversations," in *Sylvia Wynter: On Being Human as Praxis*, ed. Katherine McKittrick (Durham, NC: Duke University Press, 2015), 9–89. See also Hall, "Race, Articulation, and Societies."

26 Wynter, "On How We Mistook the Map for the Territory and Reimprisoned Ourselves in Our Unbearable Wrongness of Being, of Désêtre: Black Studies Toward the Human Project," in *Not Only the Master's Tools: African American Studies in Theory and Practice*, ed. Lewis Gordon and Jane Anna Gordon (New York: Paradigm Press, 2006), 107–169.

27 Wynter, "On How We Mistook" and Sylvia Wynter, "Beyond Miranda's Meanings: UnSilencing the 'Demonic Ground' of Caliban's Women," in *Out of the Kumbla: Caribbean Women and Literature*, ed. Carole Boyce Davies and Elaine Savory Fido (Trenton, NJ: Africa World Press, 1990), 255–372. See also Alexander Weheliye, *Habeas Viscus: Racializing Assemblages, Biopolitics, and Black Feminist Theories of the Human* (Durham, NC: Duke University Press, 2014).

28 Fanon, *Black Skin, White Mask*. For white sovereignty, see Barnor Hesse, "White Sovereignty." For disciplinary and regulatory violence in the colonial world, see Fanon, *Wretched of the Earth*. For such practices in the West, see also Michel Foucault, *The Birth of Biopolitics Lectures at the Collège de France, 1978–1979*

(New York: Palgrave Macmillan, 2008) and *"Society Must Be Defended": Lectures at the College de France 1975–1976* (New York: Picador, 2003).

29 See Fanon, *Wretched of the Earth*; Achille Mbembe, "Necropolitics," trans. Libby Meintjes, *Public Culture* 15, no. 1 (2003): 11–40; see also Foucault, *"Society Must Be Defended."*

30 Hortense J. Spillers, "'Mama's Baby, Papa's Maybe:' An American Grammar Book," *Diacritics* 17, no. 2 (1987): 64–81.

31 See Spillers, "'Mama's Baby, Papa's Maybe'" and Angela Y. Davis, *Women, Race, and Class* (New York: Vintage, 1981).

32 Fanon, *Wretched of the Earth*, 41. Mbembe, "Necropolitics," 25.

33 Césaire, *Discourse on Colonialism* 42. For colonial violence and the enslaved as commodity and worker, see Mbembe, "Necropolitics," 21. See also Fred Moten, *In the Break: The Aesthetics of the Black Radical Tradition* (Minneapolis: University of Minnesota Press, 2003).

34 Spillers, "'Mama's Baby, Papa's Maybe,'" 67.

35 See Saidiya V. Hartman, *Scenes of Subjection: Terror, Slavery, and Self-Making in Nineteenth Century America* (New York: Oxford University Press, 1997).

36 Gerald Horne, *The Dawning of the Apocalypse: The Roots of Slavery, White Supremacy, Settler Colonialism and Capitalism in the Long Sixteenth Century* (New York: Monthly Review Press, 2020) and *The Apocalypse of Settler Colonialism: The Roots of Slavery, White Supremacy, and Capitalism in Seventeenth Century North America and the Caribbean* (New York: Monthly Review Press, 2018); Hugh Thomas, *The Slave Trade* (New York: Simon & Schuster, 1997).

37 Tinker, Tink and Mark Freeland. "Thief, Slave Trader, Murderer: Christopher Columbus and Caribbean Population Decline," *Wičazo Ša Review* 23, no. 1 (2008), 33.

38 Horne, Dawning of the Apocalypse, 12.

39 Brett Rushforth *Bonds of Alliance: Indigenous and Atlantic Slaveries in New France* (Chapel Hill: The University of North Carolina Press, 2012). See also Horne, *Apocalypse of Settler Colonialism* and Erin Woodruff Stone "Indian Harvest: The Rise of the Indigenous Slave Trade and Diaspora from Española to the Circum-Caribbean" (PhD diss., Vanderbilt University, 2014).

40 Horne, *Dawning of the Apocalypse*, 13.

41 Woodruff Stone, "Indian Harvest."

42 Woodruff Stone, "Indian Harvest," 6.

43 Jason M. Yaremko, *Indigenous Passages to Cuba, 1515–1900* (Gainesville: University Press of Florida, 2016); Woodruff Stone, "Indian Harvest."

44 See Bryant, *Rivers of Gold*.

45 See Peter Hulme, *Colonial Encounters: Europe and the Native Caribbean 1492–1797* (London: Routledge, 1992).

46 Herman L. Bennett, *Colonial Blackness: A History of Afro-Mexico* (Bloomington: Indiana University Press, 2009), 4–5.

47 Bennett, *Colonial Blackness*, 5.

48 Gabino La Rosa Corzo, *Runaway Slave Settlements in Cuba: Resistance and Repression*, trans. Mary Todd (Chapel Hill: The University of North Carolina Press, 2003); Yaremko, *Indigenous Passages*.

49 Corzo, *Runaway Slave*; Yaremko, Indigenous Passages; for an in-depth analysis on the relationship between space and colonial exclusion, see also Guadalupe García, *Beyond the Walled City: Colonial Exclusion in Havana* (Oakland: University of California Press, 2015).

50 Corzo, *Runaway Slave.*
51 Gerald Horne, *Black and Brown: African Americans and the Mexican Revolution 1910–1920* (New York: New York University Press, 2005), 14.
52 Francisco S. Scarano, *Sugar and Slavery in Puerto Rico: The Plantation Economy of Ponce, 1800–1850* (Madison: The University of Wisconsin Press, 1984).
53 Scarano, *Sugar and Slavery.*
54 Horne, *Dawning of the Apocalypse.*
55 Christopher Schmidt-Nowara, *Empire and Anti-Slavery: Spain, Cuba, and Puerto Rico, 1833–1874* (Pittsburgh: University of Pittsburgh Press, 1999).
56 William B. Griffen, *Apaches at War and Peace, The Janos Presidio, 1750–1858* (Norman: University of Oklahoma Press, 1998). See also Yaremko, *Indigenous Passages.*
57 Yaremko, *Indigenous Passages.*
58 Gerald Horne, *The White Pacific: U.S. Imperialism and Black Slavery After the Civil War* (Honolulu: University of Hawai'i Press, 2007).
59 Horne, *White Pacific.*
60 See Horne, *Dawning of the Apocalypse and The Apocalypse of Settler Colonialism: The Roots of Slavery, White Supremacy, and Capitalism in Seventeenth Century North America and the Caribbean* (New York: Monthly Review Press, 2018) and Eric Williams, *Capitalism and Slavery.* See also Michel Foucault, *Birth of Biopolitics Lectures*, 232.
61 See Arnaldo de León, *They Called Them Greasers: Anglo Attitudes towards Mexicans in Texas 1826–1836* (Austin: University of Texas Press, 1983).
62 For a discussion on how modern nation-states are built on the premise of defense, threat, and fear, see Michel Foucault, *Security, Territory, Population: Lectures at the Collège de France, 1977–1978* (New York: Picador, 2009); see also Foucault, *"Society Must Be Defended;"* see also D. Soyini Madison, "Critical Ethnography as Street Performance: Reflections of Home, Race, Murder, and Justice," in *The Sage Handbook of Qualitative Research*, ed. Norman K. Denzin and Yvonna S. Lincoln (Thousand Oaks, CA: Sage, 2005), 537–546.
63 Quoted in Wynter "On How We Mistook," 114.
64 See Madison, "Critical Ethnography;" see also Lisa B. Y. Calvente, "'This is One Line You Won't Have to Worry about Crossing': Crossing Borders and Becoming," in *Latina/o Discourse in Vernacular Spaces: Somos de Una Voz?*, ed. Michelle Holling and Bernadette M. Calafell (Lanham, MD: Lexington Books, 2010).
65 See *Cargo*, directed by Ben Howling and Yolanda Ramke (Netflix, 2017), which is an Australian horror film on the zombie apocalypse.
66 See Calvente, "'This is One Line."
67 Walter Rodney, *Grounding with My Brothers* (New York: Verso, 1969; 2019), 9–18.
68 Rodney, *Grounding with My Brothers*, 24.
69 Homi K. Bhabha, *The Location of Culture* (New York: Routledge, 1994), 89.
70 Notes from an invited talk, box 1, folder 19, Juan Flores Papers, Archives of the Puerto Rican Diaspora, Center for Puerto Rican Studies, Hunter College, City University of New York.
71 Mexican and Mexican Americans make up over sixty percent of the Latina/o population and outnumber the second largest Latina/o group by approximately 27.2 million people. Puerto Ricans, the second major Latina/o group, reach upwards of 5.4 million with 3.4 on the island, and other groups, such as Dominicans, Cubans, Guatemalans, Salvadorans, and Colombians, reach approximately

one million each. See Antonio Flores, "How the U.S. Hispanic population is changing," *Pew Research Center*, September 18, 2017, http://www.pewresearch.org/fact-tank/2017/09/18/how-the-u-s-hispanic-population-is-changing/. See also Gustavo López and Eilleen Patton, "Hispanics of Puerto Rican Origin in the United States, 2013: Statistical Profile," *Pew Research Center*, September 15, 2015, http://www.pewhispanic.org/2015/09/15/hispanics-of-puerto-rican-origin-in-the-united-states-2013/.

72 Stuart Hall, "The Meaning of New Times," in *Stuart Hall: Critical Dialogues in Cultural Studies*, ed. David Morley and Kuan-Hsing Chen (New York: Routledge, 1996), 232.

73 On Thatcherism, see Hall, "Meaning," 231–232.

74 See John D. Márquez, *Black-Brown Solidarity: Racial Politics in the New Gulf South* (Austin: University of Texas Press, 2014); see also Lisa B. Y. Calvente, "From the Rotten Apple to the States of Empire: Neoliberalism, Hip Hop, and New York City's Crisis," *Souls* 19, no. 2 (2017): 126–143 and "'I'm Ready to Die': The Notorious B.I.G., Black Love, and Death," in *The Oxford Handbook of Hip Hop Music*, ed. Justin D. Burton and Jason Lee Oakes (Oxford: Oxford University Press, 2018), 1–17.

75 Juan Flores, "Nueva York-Diaspora City U.S. Latinos between and beyond," *NACLA Report on the Americas* 35, no. 6. (May/June 2002); see also box 2, folder 62, Juan Flores Papers, Archives of the Puerto Rican Diaspora, Center for Puerto Rican Studies. See also Frances Negrón-Muntaner, *Boricua Pop: Puerto Ricans and the Latinization of American Culture* (New York: New York University Press, 2004) and Arlene Dávila, *Latino Spin: Public Image and the Whitewashing of Race* (New York: New York University Press, 2008). See also Isabel Molina-Guzmán, *Dangerous Curves: Latina Bodies in the Media* (New York: New York University Press, 2010) and "Part Two: The Stage We Call Our Lives," in Bernadette M. Calafell, *Latina/o Communication Studies: Theorizing Performance* (New York: Peter Lang, 2007).

76 See for example Martha E. Gimenez, "Latinos, Hispanics . . . What Next: Some Reflections on the Politics of Identity," *Heresies* 7, no. 27 (1993); see also José Calderón, "'Hispanic' and 'Latino': The Viability of Categories for Panethnic Unity," *Latin American Perspectives* 19, no. 4 (Autumn, 1992): 37–44.

77 Gimenez, "Latinos, Hispanics;" Calderón, "'Hispanic' and 'Latino.'".

78 See G. Cristina Mora, *Making Hispanics: How Activists, Bureaucrats, and Media Constructed a New American* (Chicago: University of Chicago Press, 2014).

79 See Darrel Wanzer-Serrano, *The New York Young Lords and the Struggle for Liberation* (Philadelphia: Temple University Press, 2015), 2.

80 See Mora, *Making Hispanics*; see also Calderón, "'Hispanic' and 'Latino.'"

81 Mora, *Making Hispanics*, 49.

82 Mora, *Making Hispanics*, 49.

83 Mora, *Making Hispanics*, 50–82.

84 Mora, *Making Hispanics*, 50–82.

85 Susan Pearson, "Birth Certificates Have Always Been a Weapon for White Supremacists: Policing the Color Line Through Vital Documents," *The Washington Post*, September 11, 2018, https://www.washingtonpost.com/outlook/2018/09/11/birth-certificates-have-always-been-weapon-white-supremacists/?noredirect=on&utm_term=.55546d37c6eb.

86 See Calderón, "'Hispanic' and 'Latino.'"

87 Linda Martín Alcoff states, "We have no homogenous culture, we come in every conceivable color, and identities such as "mestizo" signify the absence of boundaries."

See Linda Martín Alcoff, "Latinos and the Category of Race," in *Visible Identities: Race, Gender, and the Self* (New York: Oxford University Press, 2005), 229.

88 "Race, Culture, and Identity: Locating Afro-Latin@," box 2, folder 54, Juan Flores Papers, Archives of the Puerto Rican Diaspora, Center for Puerto Rican Studies.

89 "Nueva York-Diaspora City U.S. Latinos between and beyond," in *NACLA Report on the Americas* 35, no. 6. (May/June 2002): 47, box 2, folder 62, Juan Flores Papers, Archives of the Puerto Rican Diaspora, Center for Puerto Rican Studies.

90 See Miriam Jiménez Román and Juan Flores' "Introduction," in *The Afro-Latin@ Reader: History and Culture in the United States*, ed. Miriam Jiménez Roman and Juan Flores (Durham, NC: Duke University Press, 2010).

91 Walter Rodney, *Groundings with My Brothers*.

92 Jesús Colón, "Arthur Schomburg and Negro History," in *The Way It Was and Other Writings*, ed. Edna Acosta-Belén and Virginia Sánchez Korrol (Houston: Arte Público Press, 1993), 98; originally published in *The Worker* (February 11, 1962), 9. Schomburg was an archivist, historian, and activist who is popularly known for his work during the Harlem Renaissance, although his larger body of work and political investments for Black history and culture far surpass this moment. The Schomburg Center for Research in Black Culture in New York City is dedicated to his life commitments. For a synopsis of his life and a sample of his work, see "Arthur A. Schomburg (1874–1938)" and "A Negro Digs Up His Past," in *Norton Anthology of African American Literature*, 2nd ed., ed. Henry Louis Gates, Jr., Nellie Y. McKay, William L. Andrews, and Houston A. Baker (New York: W.W. Norton, 2003). See also Vanessa K Valdés, *Diasporic Blackness: The Life and Times of Arturo Alfonso Schomburg* (Albany: State University of New York Press, 2017).

93 Jesús Colón, "Hiawatha into Spanish" in *A Puerto Rican in New York and Other Sketches*, 2nd ed. (New York: International Publishers, 1982), 49–51.

94 See Juan Flores, *From Bomba to Hip Hop: Puerto Rican Culture and Latino Identity* (New York: Columbia University Press, 2000).

95 Horne, Dawning of the Apocalypse, 13.

96 Milagros Denis-Rosario. "Asserting Their Rights: Puerto Ricans in Their Quest for Social Justice," *Centro Journal* 24, no. 1 (2012): 46.

97 Elena R. Gutiérrez, *Fertile Matters: The Politics of Mexican Origin-Women's Reproduction* (Austin: University of Texas Austin, 2008).

98 Oscar Lewis, *La Vida a Puerto Rican Family in the Culture of Poverty—San Juan and New York* (New York: Ransom House, 1966).

99 Lewis, *La Vida*.

100 See Nathan Glazer, "One Kind of Life," review of *LA Vida: A Puerto Rican Family in the Culture of Poverty—San Juan and New York*, by Oscar Lewis, *Commentary Magazine*, February 1967, https://www.commentarymagazine.com/articles/la-vida-a-puerto-rican-family-in-the-culture-of-poverty-san-juan-and-new-york-by-oscar-lewis/.

101 Glazer, "One Kind of Life."

102 See William Darity, Jr., "Bleach in the Rainbow Revisited," in *The Afro-Latin@ Reader: History and Culture in the United States*, ed. Miriam Jiménez Roman and Juan Flores (Durham, NC: Duke University Press, 2010).

103 Haya El Nasser, "Black America's New Diversity: Immigrants from Africa, Caribbean's Make Their Voices Heard," *USA Today* (February 17, 2003). See also David Roediger, "The First Word in Whiteness: Early Twentieth Century

European Experiences," in *Critical White Studies: Looking Behind the Mirror*, ed. Richard Delgado and Jean Stefancic (Philadelphia: Temple University Press, 1997), 354.

104 Box 2, folder 62, Juan Flores Papers, Archives of the Puerto Rican Diaspora, Center for Puerto Rican Studies.

105 See Stuart Hall, "Cultural Identity and Diaspora" in *Identity: Community Culture Difference*, ed. Jonathan Rutherford (London: Lawrence &Wishart, 1990), 223–224.

106 For examples of identity as political resistance see Stuart Hall, "New Ethnicities," in *Stuart Hall: Critical Dialogues in Cultural Studies*, ed. David Morley and Kuan-Hsing Chen (New York: Routledge, 1996), 441–449; see also Gayatri Chakravorty Spivak, "Can the Subaltern Speak?" in *Marxism and the Interpretation of Culture*, ed. Cary Nelson and Lawrence Grossberg (Urbana: University of Illinois Press, 1988), 271–313.

107 Assata Shakur, *Assata: An Autobiography* (Chicago: Lawrence Hill Books, 1987).

108 Shakur, *Assata*, 28.

109 Cited in Milagros Denis, "Asserting Their Rights: Puerto Ricans and African Americans in Their Quest for Social Justice," December 3, 2009, Archives of The Puerto Rican Diaspora, Center for Puerto Rican Studies, Hunter College, CUNY.

110 Denis, "Asserting Their Rights," 8.

111 Denis, "Asserting Their Rights." 8.

112 Denis, "Asserting Their Rights," 8.

113 Denis, "Asserting Their Rights," 8.

114 Denis, "Asserting Their Rights," 8.

115 Hortense Spillers, Saidiya Hartman, Farah Jasmine Griffin, Shelley Eversley, and Jennifer L. Morgan, "'What Cha Gonna Do?' Revisiting 'Mama's Baby, Papa's Maybe': An American Grammar Book": A Conversation with Hortense Spillers, Saidiya Hartman, Farah Jasmine Griffin, Shelley Eversley, and Jennifer L. Morgan, *Women's Studies Quarterly* 35, nos. 1/2 (Spring-Summer 2007): 299–309.

116 Spillers, et al., "'What Cha Gonna Do?,'" 304.

117 bell hooks, "Homeplace (a site of resistance)," in *The Woman That I Am: The Literature and Culture of Contemporary Women of Color*, ed. Soyini Madison (New York: St. Martin's, 1994), 454.

118 Édouard Glissant, *Poetics of Relation*.

119 Achille Mbembé and Steven Randell, "African Modes of Self Writing," *Public Culture* 14, no. 1 (Winter 2002): 239–273.

120 Glissant, *Poetics of Relation*, 20.

121 Glissant, *Poetics of Relation*, 18.

122 Glissant, *Poetics of Relation*, 11. See Kwame Nkrumah, *Consciencism: Philosophy and Ideology for Decolonization* (New York: Monthly Review Press), 1970. See also Mbembé and Randell, "African Modes," 239–273.

123 Mbembé and Randell, "African Modes," 272.

124 Gilles Deleuze and Félix Guattari, *A Thousand Plateaus: Capitalism and Schizophrenia*, trans. Brian Massumi (Minneapolis: University of Minnesota Press, 1987), 291.

125 Deleuze and Guattari, *Thousand Plateaus*, 291. For Glissant, errantry is not produced from deterritorialization but from poetics of relation. See Glissant, *Poetics of Relation*, 18.

126 See Fanon, *Black Skin, White Masks*. See also Frantz Fanon, *A Dying Colonialism*, trans. Haakan Chevelier (New York: Grove Press, 1965).

127 Fanon, *Black Skin, White Masks*; Fanon, *A Dying Colonialism*.

128 Stuart Hall, "On Postmodernism and Articulation: An Interview with Stuart Hall," ed. Lawrence Grossberg, in *Stuart Hall: Critical Dialogues in Cultural Studies*, ed. David Morley and Kuan-Hsing Chen (New York: Routledge, 1996), 141.

129 Hall, "On Postmodernism and Articulation."

130 Hall, "On Postmodernism and Articulation."

131 Hall, "On Postmodernism and Articulation;" see "The Formation of a Diasporic Intellectual: An Interview with Stuart Hall by Kuan-Hsing Chen," in *Stuart Hall: Critical Dialogues*, 484–503; see also Stuart Hall, *Familiar Stranger: A Life between Two Islands* (Durham, NC: Duke University Press, 2017).

132 See "On Postmodernism and Articulation," 131–150.

133 See Stuart Hall's discussion on Rastafarianism in "On Postmodernism and Articulation," 143–144.

134 Hall, "On Postmodernism and Articulation." See also Édouard Glissant's discussion of Western history and transversality as a cultural formation in opposition to the practices that Western myth pushes forth. Édouard Glissant, "History— Histories—Stories," in *Caribbean Discourse: Selected Essays*, trans. J. Michael Dash (Charlottesville: University Press of Virginia, 1999), 61–97.

135 Glissant, "History—Histories—Stories," 64, 66.

136 See Dwight Conquergood, "Performance Studies: Interventions and Radical Research," *The Drama Review* 46, no. 2 (Summer 2002), 145–146.

137 Conquergood, "Performance Studies" 149.

138 See Hall, "On Postmodernism and Articulation," 150.

139 Hall, "On Postmodernism and Articulation." See also Conquergood, "Performance Studies."

140 Conquergood, "Performance Studies," 150.

Chapter 2   The Limits of Mobility

Epigraphs: Henri Bergson, *Matter and Memory*, trans. Nancy Margaret Paul and W. Scott Palmer (New York: Zone Books, 1991), 138.

Stuart Hall, *Familiar Stranger: A Life Between Two Islands* (Durham, NC: Duke University Press, 2017), 24.

1 Ira Berlin, *The Making of African America: The Four Great Migrations* (New York: Penguin Books, 2010), 3–9.

2 Mary C. Waters, *Black Identities: West Indian Immigrant Dreams and American Realities* (Cambridge, MA: Harvard University Press, 2001).

3 Waters, *Black Identities*; see Alana C. Hackshaw, "Black Ethnicity and Racial Community: African Americans and West Indian, Immigrants in the United States," in *Constructing Border/Crossing Boundaries: Race, Ethnicity, and Immigration*, eds. Caroline B. Brettell and Alexander X. Byrd (Lanham: Lexington Books, 2008); see also Juliana Maantay and Andrew Maroko, "Mapping Urban Risk: Flood Hazards, Race, and Environmental Justice in New York," in *Applied Geography* 29, no. 1 (January 2009): 111–124, and Juliana Maantay, "Asthma and Air Pollution in the Bronx: Methodological and Data Considerations in Using GIS for Environmental Justice and Health Research," in *Health and Place* 13, no. 1 (2007): 32–56.

4 For the racialization of space throughout the United States, see June Manning Thomas and Marsha Ritzdorf, eds. *Urban Planning and the African American Community: In the Shadows* (Thousand Oaks, CA: Sage, 1997).

5 These two-fare zones were where residents would have to pay double the cost for transfers for more than two buses or from the bus to the train in the city's transit system. For a narrative on the two-fare zone, the value of dollar vans, and New York City's Metro-Transit-Authority's MetroCard campaign, see Monte Williams, "One Fare Zone, With Transfers for All," *New York Times*, July 5, 1997. For a narrative on income inequality based on the subway, zones, and boroughs, see "Idea of the Week: Inequality and New York's Subway," *New Yorker*, April 15, 2013.

6 See Robert W. Bailey's *The Crisis Regime: The MAC, the EFCB, and the Political Impact of the New York City's Fiscal Crisis* (Albany: SUNY Press, 1984) and John Krinsky, "The Historical Dialectics of Participation and Cooptation: Notes from New York" (presentation, Democratizing Inequalities Conference, New York University, New York, October 15–16, 2010).

7 Williams, "One Fare Zone."

8 Paul Gilroy, *Darker than Blue: On the Economies of Black Atlantic Culture* (Cambridge, MA: Belknap Press, 2010).

9 Gilroy, *Darker than Blue*, 22.

10 For an alternative argument of Black automotivity and hip hop, see Adrienne Brown's "Driving Slow: Rehearing Hip Hop Automotivity," *Journal of Popular Music Studies* 24, no. 3 (2012): 265–275.

11 Victor Turner argues, "Liminal entities are neither here nor there; they are betwixt and between the positions assigned and arrayed by law, custom, convention, and the ceremonial." Victor Turner, *From Ritual to Theatre: The Human Seriousness of Play* (New York: PAJ Publications, 2001), 95.

12 For Black aesthetics as a site of struggle, see Paul Gilroy, *The Black Atlantic: Modernity and Double Consciousness* (Cambridge, MA: Harvard University Press, 1993); for Black geographies, see Katherine McKittrick's *Demonic Grounds: Black Women and the Cartographies of Struggle* (Minneapolis: University of Minnesota Press, 2006); for popular culture as the terrain of struggle see, Stuart Hall's "Notes on Deconstructing 'the Popular,'" in *People's History and Socialist Theory*, ed. Raphael Samuel (Boston: Routledge, 1981), 227–240.

13 See Stuart Hall, "Gramsci's Relevance for the Study of Race and Ethnicity," in *Stuart Hall: Critical Dialogues in Cultural Studies*, eds. David Morley and Kuan-Hsing Chen (New York: Routledge, 1996), 431.

14 For an example of how this depiction of national culture is enfolded into the infrastructural history of our nation, see Rodney P. Carlisle and G. Geoffrey Golson, eds. *Turning Points—Actual and Alternate Histories: Manifest Destiny and the Expansion of America* (Santa Barbara: ABC-CLIO, 2007), 65.

15 See Carey, *Communication as Culture Revised Edition* (New York: Routledge, 2009). As James Hay reminds us, James Carey introduced the "moral meaning of transportation" technology, which emphasizes the religious dimension of the spatial conception of communication in the United States and acknowledges both the cultural and territorial/territorializing Western dimension of communication as transportation." See James Hay, "Between Cultural Materialism and Spatial Materialism: James Carey's Writing about Communication," in *Thinking with James Carey: Essays on Communications, Transportation, History*, eds. Jeremy Packer and Craig Robertson (New York: Peter Lang, 2006), 33.

16 Sandra Richards, "What Is to Be Remembered? Tourism to Ghana's Slave Castle Dungeons" *Theater Journal* 57, no. 4 (December 2005), 623.

17 Richards, "What Is to Be Remembered?," 623.

18 Richard Wright, *Black Power: A Record of Reactions in a Land of Pathos* (New York: Harper Perennial, 1995), 384.

19 Stephanie Smallwood, *Saltwater Slavery: A Middle Passage to from Africa to American Diaspora* (Cambridge, MA: Harvard University Press, 2007), 33–64.

20 For an example of the monetary and judiciary investment needed to construct, maintain, utilize, and repurpose city walls throughout the trajectory of history, see Guadalupe García, *Beyond the Walled City* (Oakland: University of California Press, 2015).

21 Michel Foucault, *Security, Territory, Population: Lectures at the College de France 1977–1978*, ed. Michel Senellart, trans. Graham Burchell (New York: Palgrave Macmillan, 2007), 18.

22 Foucault, *Security, Territory, Population*, 18.

23 See García, *Beyond the Walled City*; see also Sherwin K. Bryant, *Rivers of Gold, Lives of Bondage: Governing through Slavery in Colonial Quito* (Chapel Hill: The University of North Carolina Press, 2014).

24 For analyses on the development of western empires that depended upon colonialism and slavery, see Eric Williams, *Capitalism and Slavery Capitalism and Slavery* (London: Andre Deutsch Limited, 1983) and Walter Rodney, *How Europe Underdeveloped Africa* (Washington, DC: Howard University Press, 1974).

25 Rodney, *How Europe Underdeveloped Africa*, 208–209.

26 Rodney, *How Europe Underdeveloped Africa*, 209.

27 Achilles Mbembe, "Necropolitics," trans. Libby Meintjes, *Public Culture* 15, no. 1 (2003), 26.

28 Mbembe, "Necropolitics," 26.

29 Michael Taussig, "Culture of Terror: Space of Death. Roger Casement's Putomayo Report and the Explanation of Torture," *Comparative Studies in Society and History* (1984): 467–497, 468. Similarly, Achilles Mbembe identifies colonialism and colonial slavery as spaces of death. Necropolitical life is where people become "the living dead" and society functions under the notion of "death worlds." See Mbembe, "Necropolitics," 40.

30 Césaire, *Discourse on Colonialism* (New York: Monthly Review Press, 2000); Wynter, "On How We Mistook the Map for the Territory and Re-Imprisoned Ourselves in Our Unbearable Wrongness of Being, of Désêtre: Black Studies toward the Human Project," in *Not Only the Master's Tools: African American Studies in Theory and Practice*, eds. Lewis R. Gordon and Jane Anna Gordon (Boulder: Paradigm Publishers, 2006), 112.

31 See Berlin, *Making of African America*, 56; See also Herbert S. Klein, Stanley L. Engerman, Robin Haines, and Ralph Shlomowitz, "Transoceanic Mortality: The Slave Trade in Comparative Perspective," *William & Mary Quarterly* 58, no. 1 (January 2001): 93–118.

32 Klein et al., "Transoceanic Mortality" 94.

33 Berlin, *Making of African America*, 57.

34 Berlin, *Making of African America*, 57.

35 Smallwood, *Saltwater Slavery*, 40.

36 Smallwood, *Saltwater Slavery*, 40.

37 Smallwood, *Saltwater Slavery*, 40.

38 Klein et al., "Transoceanic Mortality," 96.

39 For how colonization decivilizes the colonizer through the ritualized acts of violence, terror, surveillance, and murder, see Césaire, *Discourse of Colonialism*.

See also David R. Wrone and Russel S. Nelson, eds., *Who's the Savage: The Documentary History of the Mistreatment of the Native North Americans* (Malabar, FL: Robert Krieger, 1982), Michael Taussig, *Shamanism, Colonialism, and the Wild Man* (Chicago: University of Chicago Press, 1991), and David E. Stannard, *American Holocaust: The Conquest of the New World* (New York: Oxford University Press, 1993).

40 See Williams, *Capitalism and Slavery*, 51–84. See also Cedric Robinson, *Black Marxism: The Making of the Black Radical Tradition* (Chapel Hill, NC: University of North Carolina Press, 1983).

41 Joseph C. Miller, "Mortality in the Atlantic Slave Trade: Statistical Evidence on Causality," *The Journal of Interdisciplinary History* 11, no. 3 (Winter 1981): 403.

42 See Smallwood, *Saltwater Slavery*.

43 Smallwood, *Saltwater Slavery*, 137.

44 Smallwood, *Saltwater Slavery*, 152.

45 See Charlotte Sussman, "The Colonial Afterlife of Political Arithmetic: Swift, Demography, and Mobile Populations," *Cultural Critique* 56 (Winter 2004): 96–126.

46 Marcus Rediker, *The Slave Ship: A Human History* (New York: Penguin Books, 2008) and Berlin, *Making of African America*.

47 Rediker, *The Slave Ship*; Berlin, *Making of African America*.

48 See also Édouard Glissant. *Poetics of Relation*, trans. Betsy Wing (Ann Arbor: University of Michigan Press, 2010), 64.

49 Williams, *Capitalism and Slavery*, 54–56. See also Glissant, *Poetics of Relation*.

50 For the plantation management of enforced pleasure, such as song, to ensure enslaved labor productivity, see Saidiya V. Hartman, *Scenes of Subjection: Terror, Slavery, and Self-Making in Nineteenth Century America* (New York: Oxford University Press, 1997), 42–45.

51 See John Fiske, "Surveilling the City: Whiteness, the Black Man, and Democratic Totalitarianism," *Theory, Culture and Society* 15, no. 2 (1998): 67–88. See also Simone Browne, *Dark Matters: On the Surveillance of Blackness* (Durham, NC: Duke University Press, 2015).

52 Homi K. Bhabha, *The Location of Culture* (London: Routledge 1994).

53 Glissant, *Poetics of Relation*, 64.

54 Browne, *Dark Matters*, 53.

55 For more on tracking blackness, see Browne, *Dark Matters*, 63–88.

56 Cheryl Harris' seminal piece on whiteness as property demonstrates how property is contingent upon racial domination, Black subjugation and white exclusivity, and supremacy. See Cheryl Harris "Whiteness as Property," in *Critical Race Theory: The Key Writings That Formed the Movement*, eds. Kimberlé Williams Crenshaw, Neil T. Gotanda, Gary Peller, and Kendall Thomas (New York: The New Press, 1995), 276–291. See presentations of the United States Commission of Civil Rights, September 26–27, 1983, in *A Sheltered Crisis: The State of Fair Housing in the Eighties* (Washington, DC: United States Commission of Civil Rights, 1983). See also Yale Rabin's "Highways as a Barrier to Equal Access," *The Annals of the American Academy of Political and Social Science* 40, no. 1 (May 1973). For whiteness as property and value, see Harris "Whiteness as Property."

57 For a discussion of blackness-sexuality and hypersurveillance, see especially "Introduction: Transpositions," in C. Riley Snorton, *Nobody Is Supposed to Know: Black Sexuality on the Down Low* (Minneapolis: University of Minnesota Press, 2014), 1–36.

58 Glissant, *Poetics of Relation*, 21.

59 Gerald Horne, *Dawning of the Apocalypse: The Roots of Slavery, White Supremacy, Settler Colonialism, and Capitalism in the Long Sixteenth Century* (New York: Monthly Review, 2020) 13.

60 Richard Hart, *Slaves Who Abolished Slavery: Black in Rebellion* (Kingston, Jamaica: The University of the West Indies Press, 1980); Horne, *Dawning of the Apocalypse* and *The Apocalypse of Settler Colonialism: The Roots of Slavery, White Supremacy, and Capitalism in Seventeenth Century North America and the Caribbean* (New York: Monthly Review Press, 2018).

61 Hart, *Slaves Who Abolished Slavery*, 4.

62 Horne, *Dawning of the Apocalypse*, 15.

63 For excerpts of letters, see Hart, *Slaves Who Abolished Slavery*; see also Francisco Morales Padrón, *Spanish Jamaica*, trans. Patrick E. Bryan, Michael G. Gronow, and Felix Oviedo Moral (Kingston, Jamaica: Ian Randle Publishers, 2003) and *Spanish Trinidad*, ed. and trans. Armando García de la Torre (Kingston, Jamaica: Ian Randle Publishers, 2014).

64 Morales Padrón, *Spanish Jamaica*; Morales Padrón, *Spanish Trinidad*; Hart, *Slaves Who Abolished Slavery*.

65 Frederick Douglass, *Narrative of the Life of Frederick Douglass, An American Slave, Written by Himself* (Boston: The Anti-Slavery Office, 1845), http://utc.iath .virginia.edu/abolitn/dougnarrhp.html.

66 Douglass, *Narrative of the Life*, 2.

67 Douglass, *Narrative of the Life*.

68 See Ida B. Wells, *Crusade for Justice: The Autobiography of Ida B. Wells*, 2nd ed., ed. Afreda M. Duster (Chicago: University of Chicago Press, 2020). See also "Ida Wells Case," Digital Public Library of America, accessed May 16, 2024, https://dp .la/item/8fdc4cecc932be68b7af2180ed2468d8.

69 Wells, *Crusade for Justice* and "Ida Wells Case," 4.

70 "Ida Wells Case," 5.

71 "Ida Wells Case," 5.

72 See Wells, *Crusade for Justice*

73 Wells, *Crusade for Justice*.

74 Zora Neal Hurston, *Their Eyes Were Watching God* (New York: Harper & Row, 2001); originally published in 1937.

75 Hurston, *Their Eyes Were Watching*, 111.

76 Hurston, *Their Eyes Were Watching God*, 113–114.

77 Hurston, *Their Eyes Were Watching*, 114.

78 Hurston, *Their Eyes Were Watching*, 114.

79 Hurston, *Their Eyes Were Watching*, 114.

80 See Frederick Douglass, *My Bondage and My Freedom* (New York: Miller, Orton, & Mulligan, 1855). See also Douglass, *Narrative of the Life*.

81 Douglass, *My Bondage*, 323.

82 Douglass, *My Bondage*, 326.

83 Douglass, *My Bondage*, 326.

84 See George J. Sánchez, *Becoming Mexican American: Ethnicity, Culture, and Identity in Chicano Los Angeles, 1900–1945* (London: Oxford University Press, 1995).

85 Sánchez, *Becoming Mexican American*, 97.

86 For an example of transporting migrant workers without their consent, see Jesús Colón, "Puerto Rican Migrant Labor," in *The Way It Was and Other Writings*,

eds. Edna Acosta-Belen and Virginia Sánchez Korrol (Houston: Arte Público Press, 1993), 96–97; originally published in *The Worker*, June 6, 1961.

87 Colón, "Puerto Rican Migrant Labor," 97.

88 Richard Wright, "The Ethics of Living Jim Crow: An Autobiographical Sketch (1937)," in *The Norton Anthology of African American Literature*, 2nd ed., eds. Henry Louis Gates, Jr. and Nellie Y. McKay (New York: W. W. Norton, 2004).

89 Wright, "Ethics of Living," 1412.

90 Jesús Colón, "Little Things Are Big," in *A Puerto Rican in New York and Other Sketches*, 2nd ed. (New York: International Publishers, 1981), 115; originally published in 1961.

91 Colón, "Little Things Are Big."

92 Snorton, *Nobody is Supposed to Know*, 22.

93 Snorton, *Nobody is Supposed to Know*, 22.

94 Colón, "Little Things Are Big," 116–117.

95 Zora Neal Hurston, "How it Feels to Be Colored Me (1928)," in *The Norton Anthology of African American Literature*, 2nd ed., eds. Henry Louis Gates, Jr. and Nellie Y. McKay (New York: W. W. Norton, 2004).

96 Hurston, "How it Feels," 1030.

97 See Alice Walker, "Definition of a Womanist," *Making Face, Making Soul Haciendo Caras: Creative and Critical Perspectives by Feminists of Color*, ed. Gloria Anzaldúa (San Francisco: Aunt Lute Books, 1990), 370.

98 See Raymond Williams, *Border Country* (London: Hogarth Press, 1988) and Paul Gilroy, *Darker than Blue*. See also Jeremy Packer, *Mobility without Mayhem: Safety, Cars and Citizenship* (Durham, NC: Duke University Press, 2008).

99 Ann Petry, *The Street* (New York: Houghton Mifflin, 1946), 155.

100 Hurston, *Their Eyes Were Watching*.

101 Petry, *Street*, 157.

102 See Ralph Ellison's "Cadillac Flambé," *Callaloo* 24, no. 2 (Spring 2001): 442–453; Gilroy, *Darker than Blue*; Packer, *Mobility without Mayhem*; Nathaniel Mills, "Playing the Dozens and Consuming the Cadillac: Ralph Ellison and Civil Rights Politics," *Twentieth Century Literature* 61, no. 2 (2015): 147–172. See also Petry, *Street*, 157.

103 Petry, *Street*, 157–158.

104 Petry, *Street*, 158.

105 Ben Fong-Torres, "Tales of Ike and Tina Turner: The World's Greatest Heartbreaker," *Rolling Stone*, October 14, 1971.

106 "Proud Mary," side 2, track 3 on Creedence Clearwater Revival, *Bayou Country*, RCA, 1969, LP.

107 See Gilroy, *Black Atlantic*; Fred Moten, *In the Break: The Aesthetics of the Black Radical Tradition* (Minneapolis: University of Minnesota Press, 2003); Alexander G. Weheliye, *Phonographies: Grooves in Sonic Afro-Modernity* (Durham, NC: Duke University Press, 2005). See also Daphne Brooks, *Bodies in Dissent: Spectacular Performances of Race and Freedom, 1850–1910* (Durham, NC: Duke University Press, 2006).

108 Raymond Williams describes "structures of feeling" as the lived and felt values that inform and reach beyond the discursive politics of everyday life. See Raymond Williams, "Structures of Feeling," *Marxism and Literature* (Oxford: Oxford University Press, 1977), 128–135. Also, Lawrence Grossberg highlights affect as the discursive and embodied ways in which people and practices become

empowered act(or)s of a given context. See Lawrence Grossberg, *Dancing in Spite of Myself: Essays on Popular Culture* (Durham, NC: Duke University Press, 1997).

109 For Grossberg, affective alliances are produced through popular discourses, empower and disempower, and "operate in and produce different 'mattering maps.'" Grossberg, *Dancing in Spite of Myself*, 13.

110 Lawrence Grossberg, "Another Boring Day in Paradise: Rock and Roll and the Empowerment of Everyday Life," in Grossberg, *Dancing In Spite of Myself*, 42.

111 In his foundational text, Dick Hebdige argues that Blacks and white working-class youth are similar in terms of their practices of subcultural style, however, blacks will "never lose what is, in our society the disability of blackness." Dick Hebdige, *Subculture: The Meaning of Style* (London: Routledge, 1979), 131–132.

112 Fong-Torres, "Tales of Ike and Tina."

113 "Proud Mary."

114 I am referencing specifically Elvis Presley's rendition of the song where he, too, relies on the sounds created by Ike and Tina Turner, specifically the Ikettes. His live performances incorporated both the original sounds of the song and the gospel-like sounds evoked by the Turners and the Ikettes. The power of this song and Turner to affectively inform Black womanhood and empowerment is also found in more contemporary examples such as Beyonce's staged performances and more specifically Beyonce's performance of "Proud Mary" at the 2005 Kennedy Center Honors for Tina Turner, as well as at her performances of the song with Tina Turner in multiple venues, including at the 2008 Grammy awards. In the former, Beyonce spoke to how inspiring Tina Turner's stage performances were for her when she was a child.

115 Stuart Hall, "What Is This 'Black' in Black Popular Culture?" in *Stuart Hall: Critical Dialogues in Cultural Studies*, ed. David Morley and Kuan-Hsing Chen (New York: Routledge, 1996), 474.

116 Fanon, *A Dying Colonialism*, trans. Haakon Chevalier (New York: Grove Press, 1994), 181.

Chapter 3   Movin' on Up

Epigraph: E. Franklin Frazier, "The Failure of the Negro Intellectual," in *The Death of White Sociology: Essays on Race and Culture*, ed. Joyce A. Ladner (Baltimore: Black Classic Press, 1998), 59.

1 See Adam Weddle, "Cardi B Wins Historic Best Rap Album Grammy for *Invasion of Privacy*," *Paste*, February 11, 2019, https://www.pastemagazine.com/articles/2019/02/cardi-b-wins-best-rap-album.html.

2 See Caitlin Kelley, "Cardi B: By the Numbers," *Forbes*, March 31, 2019, https://www.forbes.com/sites/caitlinkelley/2019/05/31/cardi-b-by-the-numbers/#233cb89377aa.

3 Kelley, "Cardi B."

4 Christopher Rosa, "Everything You Need to Know about Cardi B's Grammy Win Backlash," *Glamour*, February 13, 2019, https://www.glamour.com/story/cardi-b-grammy-win-backlash-fully-explained.

5 Rosa, "Everything You Need."

6 Rosa, "Everything You Need."

7 Gerrick D. Kennedy, "BET apologizes to Nicki Minaj after rapper drops out of Festival over offensive Tweet," *Los Angeles Times*, February 11, 2018, https://www

.latimes.com/entertainment/music/la-et-ms-bet-experience-nicki-minaj-cancel
-20190211-story.html.

8 See for example, Ron Dicker, "Cardi B Rails against People Who Say She Didn't
Deserve Grammy," *Huffington Post*, February 12, 2019, https://www.huffpost.com
/entry/cardi-b-rant-critics-instagram_n_5c629dafe4b04a5c2b3114ed; Joelle
Goldstein, "Cardi B Deactivates Her Instagram Account after Expletive-Filled
Rant Following Her Grammys Win," *People*, February 11, 2019, https://people
.com/music/cardi-b-deactivates-instagram-after-rant-grammy-win/; Natasha
Sporn, "Cardi B Deletes Instagram after Foul-Mouth Rant against Grammy
Critics," *Evening Standard*, February 12, 2019, https://www.standard.co.uk
/showbiz/celebrity-news/cardi-b-deletes-instagram-after-foulmouthed-rant
-against-grammy-critics-a4064056.html.

9 See TrueExclusives, "Cardi B Goes on Rant about Haters Dissing Her Grammy
Award Win," YouTube Video, February 11, 2019, https://www.youtube.com/watch
?v=vbPQLYyRsvA.

10 See Alexandra D'Aluisio, "Cardi B Deactivates her Instagram Account After
Grammys Rant: 'I F—king Worked My Ass Off,'" *Us Weekly*, February 12, 2019,
https://www.usmagazine.com/celebrity-news/news/cardi-b-deactivates-instagram
-after-grammys-2019-rant/.

11 Paul Gilroy, *The Black Atlantic: Modernity and Double Consciousness* (Cambridge,
MA: Harvard University Press, 1993), 198.

12 For more on non-rooted relations of identification, see Édouard Glissant, *Caribbean
Discourse: Selected Essays*, trans. J Michael Dash (Charlottesville: University of
Virginia, 1989).

13 For examples of the political potential of hip-hop artists' music and hip-hop
culture, see Michael Eric Dyson, *Reflecting Black: African-American Cultural
Criticism* (Minneapolis: University of Minnesota Press, 1993) and Tricia Rose
Black Noise: Rap Music and Black Culture in Contemporary America (Middletown: Wesleyan University Press, 1994); see Imani Perry, *Prophets of the Hood:
Politics and Poetics in Hip Hop* (Durham, NC: Duke University Press, 2004).
See also Kara Keeling, "'A Homegrown Revolutionary'?: Tupac Shakur and the
Legacy of the Black Panther Party," *The Black Scholar* 29, no. 2/3 (Summer/Fall
1999): 59–63 and Gil Rodman, "Race . . . and Other Four Letter words: Eminem
and the Cultural Politics of Authenticity," *Popular Communication* 4, no. 2
(2006): 95–121.

14 For how the temporal and spatial coincide in terms of new and old technologies of
entertainment and their effects, see Jody Berland's "Angel's Dancing: Cultural
Technologies and the Production of Space," in *Cultural Studies*, eds., Lawrence
Grossberg, Cary Nelson, and Paula Treichler (New York: Routledge, 1992), 38–55.

15 See Stuart Hall, "Notes on Deconstructing 'the Popular,'" in *People's History and
Socialist Theory*, ed. Raphael Samuel (Boston: Routledge and Keegan Paul, 1981)
and Stuart Hall, "What is This 'Black' in Black Popular Culture?" in *Stuart Hall:
Critical Dialogues in Cultural Studies*, ed. David Morley and Kuan-Hsing Chen
(New York: Routledge, 1996), 465–475.

16 See Herman Gray, "Subject(ed) to Recognition," *American Quarterly* 65, no. 4
(2013): 771–798.

17 For the "trap Selena" reference, see Migos, Nicki Minaj, & Cardi B, "Motorsport,"
track 17 on *Culture II*, Quality Control, 2018, digital stream; for other references,
see *Love & Hip Hop New York*, season 6, episode 2, "Cardi B Supercut (Part 1),

Best Moments from *Love & Hip Hop New York*," directed by David Wolfgang, Marcus Clarke, Josh Richards, and Pedro Feria Pino, aired December 21, 2015, on VH1.

18 See Herman Gray, "Television, Black Americans and the American Dream," *Critical Studies in Mass Communication* 6, no. 4 (1989): 376–386.

19 Gray, "Television, Black Americans."

20 Gray, "Television, Black Americans."

21 See Comments, "Cardi B Supercut (Part 1) Best Moments from *Love & Hip Hop New York* (Season 6) VH1," YouTube video, January 15, 2018, https://www .youtube.com/watch?v=Hw5-zxBRQKQ, and "Cardi B Supercut (Part 2) Best Moments from *Love & Hip Hop New York* (Season 7) VH1," YouTube video, January 21, 2018, https://www.youtube.com/watch?v=e52g2-lSqVo&t=319s.

22 Sara Benet-Weiser, *Authentic™: The Politics of Ambivalence in Brand Culture* (New York: New York University Press, 2012).

23 See "Cardi B Supercut (Part 1)."

24 See Lindsay Zoladz, "Bloody Slippers: The Fairy-Tale Come-Up of Cardi B," *The Ringer*, September 21, 2017, https://www.theringer.com/2017/9/21/16345124/cardi -b-bodak-yellow-career-rap-rise-nicki-minaj; see also D. Watkins, "All Hail Cardi B, a True 'Trap Cinderella,'" *Salon*, November 4, 2017, https://www.salon.com /2017/11/04/cardi-bs-trap-cinderella-story/; Vanessa Grigoriadis, "Cinderella Story: Cardi B Opens Up about Her 'Rags to Riches" Story,'" *Harper's Bazaar*, February 7, 2019, https://www.harpersbazaar.com/culture/features/a25996656/cardi-b -interview-2019/; see also "Cover Story," *Harper's Bazaar*, March 2019. For Cardi's reference to Cinderella, see Allie Gimmel, "Cardi B Sings 'Cinderella' from *The Cheetah Girls* as a 'Little Preview' of 'Invasion of Privacy,'" *Teen Vogue*, March 29, 2018, https://www.teenvogue.com/story/cardi-b-sings-cinderella-cheetah-girls.

25 For an example of hip hop as excessive commodification and objectification, see Paul Gilroy, *Against Race: Imagining Political Culture beyond the Color Line* (Cambridge: Belknap Press, 2002); for an example of nihilism and hip hop, see Cornell West, *Race Matters* (New York: Vintage Books, 1994), and as examples of hip hop and the end of civil rights politics and Black politics, see Todd Boyd, *The New HNIC: The Death of Civil Rights and the Reign of Hip Hop* (New York: New York University Press, 2002) and Paul Gilroy, *Darker than Blue: On the Moral Economies of Black Atlantic Culture* (Cambridge, MA: Harvard University Press, 2010). For an example of hip hop's relationship to neoliberalism, see Lester K. Spence, *Stare in the Darkness* (Minneapolis: University of Minnesota Press, 2013), and Lisa B. Y. Calvente, "From the Rotten Apple to the State of Empire: Neoliberalism, Hip Hop, and New York City's Crisis," *Souls: A Critical Journal of Black Politics, Culture, and Society* 19, no. 2 (April–June 2017), 126–143. See also Lisa B. Y. Calvente, "'I'm Ready to Die': The Notorious B.I.G., Black Love, and Death," in *Oxford Handbook of Hip Hop Music*, eds. Justin D. Burton and Jason Lee Oakes (New York: Oxford University Press, 2018), 1–17.

26 See Calvente, "From the Rotten Apple"; see also, "'I'm Ready to Die.'"

27 Stuart Hall, "Introduction," in *Paper Voices: The Popular Press and Social Change, 1935–1965*, eds. A. C. H. Smith, Elizabeth Immirzi, and Trevor Blackwell (Totowa, NJ: Rowman & Littlefield, 1975), 12, 18.

28 Walter Rodney, *Grounding with My Brothers* (New York: Verso, 2019; 1969).

29 For a discussion on crime and threat as equated to Black bodies see the Centre for Contemporary Cultural Studies, *Empire Strikes Back: Race and Racism in 1970s*

Britain (London: Routledge, 1992); see also D. Soyini Madison, "Critical Ethnography as Street Performance: Reflections of Home, Race, Murder, and Justice" in *The Sage Handbook of Qualitative Research*, ed. Norman K Denzin and Yvonna S. Lincoln (Thousand Oaks, CA: Sage, 2005), 537–546. For a discussion on how modern nation-states are built on the premise of defense, threat, and fear, see Michel Foucault, *Security, Territory, Population: Lectures at the Collège de France, 1977–1978* (New York: Picador, 2009) and Michel Foucault, *"Society Must Be Defended": Lectures at the Collège de France, 1975–1976* (New York: Picador, 2003).

30 See the Centre for Contemporary Cultural Studies, *Empire Strikes Back*; see also Herman Gray, "Television, Black Americans and the American Dream," *Critical Studies in Mass Communication* 6 (1989), 376–386.

31 Dicker, "Cardi B Rails;" Goldstein, "Cardi B Deactivates Her Instagram;" Sporn, "Cardi B Deletes;" D'Aluisio, "Cardi B Deactivates."

32 D'Aluisio, "Cardi B Deactivates."

33 Dicker, "Cardi B Rails."

34 These racist and mass-mediated processes of constructing the alien "enemy within" is not unique to the United States. See the Centre for Contemporary Cultural Studies, *Empire Strikes Back*, 21–35.

35 Centre for Contemporary Cultural Studies, *Empire Strikes Back*, 21–35.

36 See Hector Amaya, *Citizenship Excess: Latinos/os, Media and the Nation* (New York: New York University Press, 2013).

37 David E. Pitt, "Jogger's Attackers Terrorized at Least 9 in 2 Hours," *New York Times*, April 22, 1989, https://timesmachine.nytimes.com/timesmachine/1989/04/22/114889.html?pageNumber=1.

38 Pitt, "Jogger's Attackers."

39 Steven J. Mexel, "The Roots of 'Wilding': Black Literary Naturalism, the Language of Wilderness, and Hip Hop in the Central Park Jogger Rape," *African American Review* 46, no. 1, (Spring 2013): 101–115.

40 For this particular link, see Mexel, "Roots of Wilding;" see also Houston A. Baker, Jr., *Black Studies, Rap, and the Academy* (Chicago: University of Chicago Press, 1993).

41 See Linda S. Lichter, S. Robert Lichter, and Daniel Amundson, "The New York News Media and the Central Park Rape," Center for Media and Public Affairs, The American Jewish Committee, 1989; quoted in Mexel, "Roots of 'Wilding," footnote 2, 112.

42 Mexel, "Roots of Wilding," 106; for an image of Trump's 1989 advertisement see Jan Ransom, "Trump Will Not Apologize for Calling for Death Penalty over Central Park Five," *New York Times*, June 18, 2019, https://www.nytimes.com/2019/06/18/nyregion/central-park-five-trump.html.

43 Ransom, "Trump Will Not Apologize."

44 Ransom, "Trump Will Not Apologize."

45 See "New York City Police Corruption and Misconduct," Wikimedia Foundation, last modified December 12, 2019, https://en.wikipedia.org/wiki/New_York_City_Police_Department_corruption_and_misconduct.

46 See George James, "Cries of Police Brutality Follow Death," *New York Times*, February 4, 1989, https://timesmachine.nytimes.com/timesmachine/1989/02/04/837489.html?pageNumber=29.

47 Alen Feldman, "On Cultural Anesthesia: From Desert Storm to Rodney King," *American Ethnologist* 21, no. 2 (May 1994): 404–418.

48 For a synopsis of the crowd and this particular incident as an example, see Peter E. Tarlow's *Event Risk Management and Safety* (New York: John Wiley & Sons, 2002), 90–92.

49 Tarlow, *Event Risk Management*, 90–92. I attended this parade and was detoured by police barricades and officers to the park along with many young parade-goers; we were forced to go into the park out of sight of the parade. Although I was not one of the women assaulted or even accosted, I witnessed crowds of young men begin to shoot water at young women. I also saw lines of officers stand and laugh as these boys wet the girls who walked by.

50 See William Saletan, "The Central Park Rampage," *Slate*, June 22, 2000, https://slate.com/news-and-politics/2000/06/the-central-park-rampage.html; NYO Staff, "Puerto Rican Day Parade: Garbage and Trash," *Observer*, June 19, 2000, https://observer.com/2000/06/puerto-rican-day-parade-filth-and-garbage/; Bruce Shapiro, "Why Didn't the NYPD Stop the Central Park Wolf Pack?," *Salon*, June 15, 2000, https://www.salon.com/2000/06/15/central_park/; *The Washington Times*, "Wilding Victims Say Cops Ignored Them," June 16, 2000, https://www.washingtontimes.com/news/2000/jun/16/20000616-011442-2157r/; see also Larry Celona, "Three Molested at Dominican Parade," *NY Post*, August 14, 2000, https://nypost.com/2000/08/14/three-molested-at-dominican-parade/.

51 Shapiro, "Why Didn't the NYPD."

52 Shapiro, "Why Didn't the NYPD."

53 Lisa B. Y. Calvente and Josh Smicker, "Crisis Subjectivities: Resilient, Recuperable, and Abject Representations in the New Hard Times," *Social Identities: Journal for the Study of Race, Nation, and Culture* (Sept. 2017): 7, https://doi.org/10.1080/13504630.2017.1376277; see also Jamelle Bouie, "Michael Brown Wasn't a Superhuman Demon but Darren Wilson's Racial Prejudice Told Him Otherwise," *Slate*, November 26, 2014, https://slate.com/news-and-politics/2014/11/darren-wilsons-racial-portrayal-of-michael-brown-as-a-superhuman-demon-the-ferguson-police-officers-account-is-a-common-projection-of-racial-fears.html.

54 Quoted in Calvente, "From the Rotten Apple," 140.

55 Philip M. Stinson, "Charging a Police Officer in a Fatal Shooting is Rare, and a Conviction is Even Rarer," *Criminal Justice Faculty Publications*, Bowling Green State University, May 31, 2017, 80.

56 Stinson, "Charging a Police Officer," 80.

57 Stinson, "Charging a Police Officer," 80.

58 "Central Park Jogger Case," Wikimedia Foundation, last modified May 12, 2024, https://en.wikipedia.org/wiki/Central_Park_jogger_case.

59 "Central Park Jogger Case."

60 Kirk Johnson, "Levin's Injuries Are Described by a Physician," *New York Times*, February 10, 1988, https://www.nytimes.com/1988/02/10/nyregion/levin-s-injuries-are-described-by-a-physician.html.

61 "Robert Chambers (Criminal)," Wikimedia Foundation, last modified May 18, 2024, https://en.wikipedia.org/wiki/Robert_Chambers_(criminal).

62 "Robert Chambers."

63 Ross Barkan, "The Unnatural (and Possibly Doomed) Symbiosis between Bill de Blasio and Bratton," *Village Voice*, June 28, 2016, https://www.villagevoice.com/2016/06/28/the-unnatural-and-possibly-doomed-symbiosis-between-bills-de-blasio-and-bratton/.

64 Fanon, *Black Skin, White Masks* (New York: Grove Press, 2008), 98.

65 "Chapelle Show Extras Ask a Black Dude Deleted Scenes (Paul Mooney)," YouTube video, April 27, 2011, https://www.youtube.com/watch?v=fjTUZtpLLSc.

66 For representations of resilient, recuperative, and abject subjectivities (those who fall under the umbrella of blackness) within the neoliberal contemporary moment, see Calvente and Smicker, "Crisis Subjectivities."

67 See Keeling, *The Witch's Flight: The Cinematic, The Black Femme, and the Image of Common Sense* (Durham, NC: Duke University Press, 2007), 35; see also Fanon, *Black Skin White Masks*; see David Theo Goldberg, *Racist Culture: Philosophy and the Politics of Meaning* (Oxford, UK: Blackwell Publishers, 1993).

68 Stereo Williams, "The Racism of Respectability: Nicki Minaj's Disturbing Reaction to the Cardi B Fashion Week fight," *The Daily Beast*, September 14, 2018, https://www.thedailybeast.com/the-racism-of-respectability-nicki-minajs -disturbing-reaction-to-the-cardi-b-fashion-week-fight?ref=scroll.

69 See "Nicki Minaj Says She Was 'Mortified' and 'Humiliated' by Fashion Week Altercation with Cardi B," *ABC News Radio*, September 10, 2018, http:// abcnewsradioonline.com/music-news/2018/9/10/nicki-minaj-says-she-was -mortified-and-humiliated-by-fashion.html. See also Alyssa Bailey, "Cardi B Directly Addressed People Saying She's Over after Her Nicki Minaj Fashion Week Fight," *Elle*, September 26, 2018, https://www.elle.com/culture/celebrities /a23471564/cardi-b-over-nicki-minaj-fashion-week-fight-instagram-live/.

70 E. Franklin Frazier, *Black Bourgeoisie* (New York: The Free Press, 1997), 25–26.

71 Frazier, *Black Bourgeoisie*, 25–26.

72 Richard Iton, *In Search of the Black Fantastic: Politics & Popular Culture in the Post-Civil Rights* Era (New York: Oxford University Press 2008), 194.

73 Williams, "Racism of Respectability."

74 See Williams, "Racism of Respectability;" see also Jessica McKinney, "Ranking the Wildest Moments on Nicki Minaj's Queen Radio," *Complex*, August 22, 2019, https://www.complex.com/music/2019/08/nicki-minaj-quen-radio-wildest -moments/.

75 See Cardi B's address to Minaj titled, "Cardi Exposes Nicki Minaj on Instagram Rant," YouTube video, October 29, 2018, https://www.youtube.com/watch?v =cbbyxlX4ZEk.

76 Cardi B's address.

77 Audre Lorde, "The Transformation of Silence into Language and Action," *Sister Outsider* (Berkeley, CA: The Crossing Press, 2007), 42.

78 Lorde, "Transformation of Silence," 40–44.

79 Hall, "Notes on Deconstructing 'the Popular,'" 227–240.

80 See Hot 97 interview, "Cardi B Talks Leaving *Love & Hip Hop* and Getting Illegal Plastic Surgery," YouTube video, June 21, 2016, https://www.youtube.com /watch?v=230rFHrxdps.

81 Hot 97 interview.

82 "Cardi B Speaks on Getting Her Teeth Fixed Video Compilation," YouTube video, July 18, 2016, https://www.youtube.com/watch?v=BSTFbdL9GVQ.

83 "Cardi B's Funniest Moments Cured My Depression Part 1," YouTube video, August 8, 2018, https://www.youtube.com/watch?v=hxhFpMeojiA&t=1s.

84 "Cardi B's Funniest Moments."

85 For Cardi's Post and her video, see Peter A. Berry, "Cardi B Defends Her Use of the Word, Roach," *XXLmag*, August 10, 2017, https://www.xxlmag.com/video /2017/08/cardi-b-defends-use-the-word-roach/.

86   Berry, "Cardi B Defends."
87   "Cardi B Clears Up That She's Lightskin Black, not Mexican," YouTube video, June 25, 2019, https://www.youtube.com/watch?v=v8et4pK6neI.
88   "Cardi B's Funniest Moments."
89   For a discussion on the magical connectedness of the Black non-tradition tradition, see Paul Gilroy, *The Black Atlantic: Modernity and Double Consciousness* (Cambridge, MA: Harvard University Press, 1993); for the paradox of the slave condition, see Achille Mbembé, "Necropolitics," trans. Libby Meintjes, *Public Culture* 15, no. 1 (2003), 11–40.
90   Achille Mbembé and Steven Randell, "African Modes of Self Writing," *Public Culture* 14, no. 1 (2002): 272.
91   "Cardi B Supercut (Part 2)."
92   "Cardi B Supercut (Part 2)."
93   "Cardi B Supercut (Part 2)."
94   "Cardi Exposes the Darkside of the Music Industry." YouTube video, May 23, 2017, https://www.youtube.com/watch?v=ZCV-iKqde3Q&t=99s.
95   "Cardi Exposes the Darkside."
96   "Cardi Exposes the Darkside."
97   "Cardi Exposes the Darkside."
98   John D. Márquez, "The Black Mohicans: Representations of Everyday Violence in Postracial Urban America," *American Quarterly* 64, no. 3 (2012): 625–651.
99   Márquez, "Black Mohicans," 625–651.
100 bell hooks highlights how loving blackness is antithetical to how representations of blackness are perpetuated throughout society as symbols of fear and hatred; loving blackness in this sense is an embodied, social form of resistance. For more on this, see bell hooks, *Black Looks: Race and Representation* (Boston: South End Press, 1992). See also Richard Iton, *In Search of the Black Fantastic*.
101 "Cardi B. Exposes the Darkside."
102 Hall, "Notes on Deconstructing, 234.
103 Hall, "Notes on Deconstructing, 234.
104 "Cardi B's Funny Videos Will Cure Your Depression," YouTube video, December 15, 2018, https://www.youtube.com/watch?v=9k4wBUgodOk&t=816s.
105 Christopher Wallace, Jalacy Hawkins, and Christopher Martin, "Kick in the Door," track 4 on *Life After Death*, The Notorious B.I.G., Bad Boy, 1997, compact disc.
106 "Cardi B Clears Up."
107 "Cardi B Clears Up."
108 "Biggie & Tupac: Live at Trafalgar Square," YouTube video, April 1, 2013, https://www.youtube.com/watch?v=p-Mzj1z9aoI.
109 The film itself was panned by critics during its time, and these critiques centered on the film's supposed uncritical focus on youth gangs. See Critical Reception section of, "The Warriors (Film)," Wikimedia Foundation, last modified May 17, 2024, https://en.wikipedia.org/wiki/The_Warriors_(film).
110 *The Warriors*, directed by Walter Hill (Paramount Pictures, 1979).
111 For Cardi B in Flint, see Hot 97 interview, "Cardi B Talks Leaving;" see also Funkmaster Flex, "Cardi B Takes a Trip to Flint," InFlexWeTrust, March 3, 2016, https://www.inflexwetrust.com/2016/03/06/video-cardi-b-takes-a-trip-to-flint/.
112 "Cardi B Interview at The Breakfast Club Power 105.1," YouTube video, March 18, 2016, https://www.youtube.com/watch?v=dSkTtwYAFI8.

113 Caitlin O' Kane, "Cardi B Rants about Government Shutdown, Senators Wonder: Should We Retweet?" CBS News, January 17, 2019, https://www .cbsnews.com/news/cardi-b-rants-about-government-shutdown-sparks-debate -between-senators-on-twitter/.

114 C.L.R. James, "The Making of the Caribbean People," in *You Don't Play with Revolution: The Montreal Lectures of C.L.R. James*, ed. David Austin (Oakland, CA: AK Press, 2009), 29–49.

115 James, "Making of the Caribbean," 44.

116 Fanon, *Wretched of the Earth*.

117 James, "Making of the Caribbean," 44.

118 Frantz Fanon, *Wretched of the Earth*.

119 John D. Márquez, *Symposium on Violence* (presentation, DePaul University, Chicago, IL, April 14–15, 2014).

Chapter 4   Mobile Stories and Bounded Spaces

Audre Lorde, "The Transformations of Silence into Language and Action," *Sister Outsider: Essays and Speeches by Audre Lorde* (Berkeley, CA: Crossing Press, 2007), 40.

D. Soyini Madison, "'That Was My Occupation': Oral Narrative, Performance, and Black Feminist Thought," *Text and Performance Quarterly* 13, no. 3 (1993): 214.

1 See Bernadette M. Calafell, *Latina/o Communication Studies: Theorizing Performance* (New York: Peter Lang, 2007). See also Madison, "'That Was My Occupation,'" 213–232.

2 Madison, "'That Was My Occupation;'" see also Clifford Geertz, *The Interpretation of Cultures* (New York: Basic Books, 1977).

3 Édouard Glissant, *Poetics of Relation*, trans. Betsy Wing (Ann Arbor: University of Michigan Press, 2010).

4 Cherríe Moraga, "Preface" in Gloria Anzaldúa and Cherríe Moraga, eds. *This Bridge Called My Back*, (New York: Kitchen Table, Women of Color Press, 1984), xviii.

5 For an in-depth discussion on racial sincerity as a theoretical framework and a methodological practice for ethnographic fieldwork, see John L. Jackson, *Real Black: Adventure in Racial Sincerity* (Chicago: University of Chicago Press, 2005).

6 D. Soyini Madison, *Acts of Activism: Human Right as Radical Performance* (Cambridge: Cambridge University Press, 2010).

7 Madison, *Acts of Activism*.

8 Della Pollock, *Remembering: Oral History Performance* (New York: Palgrave Macmillan, 2005), 2.

9 See Pollock, *Remembering*. See also Della Pollock, *Telling Bodies, Performing Birth* (New York: Columbia University Press, 1999); Kristin Langellier, "Personal Narrative, Performance, Performativity: Two or Three Things I Know for Sure," *Text and Performance Quarterly* 19, no. 2 (1999): 125–144; Michelle Holling and Bernadette Marie Calafell, "Identities on Stage and Staging Identities: Chicano Brujo Performances as Emancipatory Practice," *Text and Performance Quarterly* 27, no. 1 (2007): 58–83.

Chapter 5   Classroom Caravan

D. Soyini Madison, "This Was Then and This is Now," *Text and Performance Quarterly* 33, no. 3 (2013): 210.

1 See Stuart Hall, "Race, Culture and Communications: Looking Backward and Forward at Cultural Studies," *Rethinking Marxism: A Journal of Economics, Culture, and Society* 5, no. 1(1992): 12, 11.
2 See Stuart Hall, "Community, Culture, Nation," *Cultural Studies* 7, no. 3 (1993): 353.
3 See Lawrence Grossberg, "On Postmodernism and Articulation: An Interview with Stuart Hall," in *Stuart Hall: Critical Dialogues in Cultural Studies*, eds. David Morley and Kuan Hsing Chen (New York: Routledge, 1989), 131–150.
4 For an example of Madison's performance pedagogy, see E. Patrick Johnson's *Appropriating Blackness: Performance and the Politics of Authenticity* (Durham, NC: Duke University Press, 2003), 219–255.
5 See *Selections from the Prison Notebooks of Antonio Gramsci*, ed. and trans. Quintin Hoare and Geoffrey Nowell Smith (New York: International Publishers, 2003).
6 Édouard Glissant, "Theatre: Consciousness of the People" in *Caribbean Discourse: Selected Essays*, trans. J. Michael Dash (Charlottesville, VA: University of Virginia, 1989), 209–210.
7 Glissant, "Theatre" 209.
8 D. Soyini Madison, *Critical Ethnography: Method, Ethics, and Performance*, 2nd ed. (Thousand Oaks, CA: Sage Publications, 2011), 5.
9 See Dwight Conquergood, "Performance Studies: Interventions and Radical Research," in *The Drama Review* 46, no. 2 (Summer 2002), 145–156.
10 Dwight Conquergood, "Performing as a Moral Act: Ethical Dimensions of the Ethnography of Performance," *Literature in Performance* 5, no. 2 (1985), 2.
11 See Conquergood, "Performance Studies." See also Stuart Hall, "Gramsci's Relevance for the Study of Race and Ethnicity," in *Stuart Hall: Critical Dialogues in Cultural Studies*, eds. David Morley and Kuan-Hsing Chen (New York: Routledge, 1996), 411–440.
12 See Henry A. Giroux, "Public Pedagogies and the Politics of Neoliberalism: Making the Political More Pedagogical," *Policy Futures in Education* 2, nos. 3/4 (2004): 494–503 and "Cultural Studies, Public Pedagogy, and the Responsibility of Intellectuals," *Communication and Critical/Cultural Studies* 1, no. 1 (March 2004): 59–79. See also Lawrence Grossberg, *We All Want to Change the World* (London: Lawrence & Wishart, 2015). https://www.lwbooks.co.uk/sites/default/files/free-book/we_all_want_to_change_the_world.pdf.
13 Grossberg.
14 Lawrence Grossberg, *Bringing it All Back Home: Essays on Cultural Studies* (Durham, NC: Duke University Press, 1997), 4.
15 Omi Osun Joni L. Jones, "Performance Ethnography: The Role of Embodiment in Cultural Authenticity," *Theatre Topics* 12, no. 1 (March 2002): 7. For disalienation, see Fanon, *Black Skin, White Masks* (New York: Grove Press, 2008) and *A Dying Colonialism*, trans. Haakon Chevalier (New York: Grove Press, 1994). For disorder, see Glissant "Theatre," 199–220.
16 Jones, "Performance Ethnography," 7. .
17 Dwight Conquergood, "Of Caravans and Carnivals: Performance Studies in Motion," *TDR* 49, no. 4 (Autumn 1995): 137–141. For a description of

theory-practice nexus, see *Selections from the Prison Notebooks of Antonio Gramsci*, ed. and trans. Quintin Hoare and Geoffrey Nowell Smith (New York: International Publishers, 2003).

18 Conquergood, "Of Caravans and Carnivals," 140.

19 Glissant, "Theatre," 209.

20 Glissant, "Theatre," 199–220.

21 Glissant, "Theatre," 199–220.

22 Glissant, "Theatre," 209.

23 D. Soyini Madison, *Critical Ethnography: Method, Ethics, and Performance*, 5.

24 Glissant, "Theatre," 211.

25 Dwight Conquergood, "Rethinking Ethnography: Towards a Critical Cultural Politics," in *The Sage Handbook of Performance Studies*, ed. D. Soyini Madison and Judith Hamera (Thousand Oaks, CA: SAGE, 2005), 359.

26 See Henry A. Giroux's "Cultural Studies as Performative Politics," *Cultural Studies ↔ Critical Methodologies* 1, no. 1 (2001): 5–23.

27 See Dwight Conquergood, "Performing as a Moral Act: Ethical Dimensions of the Ethnography of Performance," *Literature in Performance* 5, no. 2 (1985): 1–13; see also D. Soyini Madison, *Critical Ethnography: Method, Ethics, and Performance*.

28 Conquergood, "Performing as a Moral Act;" Madison, *Critical Ethnography*.

29 D. Soyini Madison, *Performed Ethnography and Communication: Improvisation and Embodied Experience* (New York: Routledge, 2018), xxv.

30 Conquergood, "Performing as a Moral Act," 2.

31 Madison, *Critical Ethnography*, 186.

32 See D. Soyini Madison, "Lost in Translation: The Mirror or The Hammer," *Text and Performance Quarterly* 34, no. 1 (2014): 111–112; see also Conquergood, "Performing as a Moral Act," 2.

33 Madison, "Lost in Translation."

34 D. Soyini Madison, "Lost in Translation," 112.

35 D. Soyini Madison, "Lost in Translation," 112.

36 See Nathan Stucky "Fieldwork in the Performance Studies Classroom: Learning Objectives and the Activist Curriculum" in *The Sage Handbook of Performance Studies*, eds. D. Soyini Madison and Judith Hamera (Thousand Oaks, CA: Sage, 2005), 261–267.

37 D. Soyini Madison, "Dwight Conquergood's 'Rethinking Ethnography,'" in *The Sage Handbook of Performance Studies*, eds. D. Soyini Madison and Judith Hamera (Thousand Oaks, CA: Sage, 2005), 347–349.

38 For a longer explanation of co-performative witnesses and performative witnessing, see D. S. Madison's *Acts of Activism: Human Rights as Radical Performance* (New York: Cambridge University Press, 2010); for an example of coperformative witnessing in the classroom, see Bernadette Marie Calafell and Andy Kai-chun Chuang, "From Me to We: Embracing Coperformative Witnessing and Critical Love in the Classroom," *Communication Education* 67, no. 1 (2017): 109–114.

39 Conquergood, "Performance Studies: Interventions and Radical Research."

40 Henry A. Giroux, "Cultural Studies, Public Pedagogy, and the Responsibility of Intellectuals," 77; see Bryant Alexander's "Performance and Pedagogy," in *The SAGE Handbook of Performance Studies*, eds. D. Soyini Madison and Judith Hamera (Thousand Oaks, CA: Sage Publications, 2005); see also Calafell and Chuang, "From Me to We," 109–114.

41 Lawrence Grossberg, *We All Want to Change*, 107. Although Grossberg has theorized affect in much of his scholarship, for a recent application of affect and affective investment, see also Lawrence Grossberg, *Under the Cover of Chaos: Trump and the Battle for the American Right* (London: Pluto Press, 2018).

42 Grossberg, *We All Want to Change*, 107.

43 Madison, *Performed Ethnography and Communication*, viii.

44 Henry A. Giroux, "Cultural Studies, Public Pedagogy," 75.

45 Giroux, "Cultural Studies, Public Pedagogy," 75.

46 See Conquergood, "Performing as a Moral Act," 1–13.

47 For a discussion on desirable and equal exchanges among people as well as a discussion on the colonialism as a process of thingification and mystification, see Aimé Césaire's *Discourse on Colonialism* (New York: Monthly Review Press, 2000). On methods of racial sincerity, see John L. Jackson Jr., *Real Black: Adventure in Racial Sincerity* (Chicago: University of Chicago Press, 2005).

48 Conquergood, "Performing as a Moral Act," 1–13.

49 See Conquergood, "Rethinking Ethnography," 351–365.

50 Conquergood, "Rethinking Ethnography," 355.

51 For the role of specialized knowledge, see D. Soyini Madison, "'That Was My Occupation': Oral Narrative, Performance, and Black Feminist Thought," *Text and Performance Quarterly* (1993): 213–232.

52 Victor Turner quoted in Dwight Conquergood, "Of Caravans and Carnivals," 138.

53 Conquergood, "Rethinking Ethnography," 355.

54 Studies on higher education have demonstrated that as faculty, Black and Latina faculty are burdened with racist and sexist expectations that characterize them as nurturing, subordinate, "mammie," and maid-like figures in the classroom. When their identifications navigate away from these expectations, they are often described as "hostile," "arrogant," "intimidating," and "silencing" in stark opposition to their white/male counterparts. See Kristina M. W. Mitchell and Jonathan Martin, "Gender Bias in Student Evaluations," *PS: Political Science and Politics* 5, no. 3 (July 2018): 648–652 and Chavella T. Pittman, "Race and Gender Oppression in the Classroom: The Experiences of Women Faculty of Color in the Classroom with White Male Students," *Teaching Sociology* 387, no. 3 (2010):183–196. See also Claude M. Steele, "A Threat in the Air: How Stereotypes Shape Intellectual Identity and Performance," *American Psychologist* 52, no. 6, (1997): 613–629. See Bernadette M. Calafell, "Mentoring and Love: An Open Letter" in *Cultural Studies ↔ Critical Methodologies* 7, no. 4 (2007): 425–441.

55 For more on vulnerability as empathy and respect see Ruth Behar, *The Vulnerable Observer: Anthropology that Breaks Your Heart* (Boston: Beacon Press, 1996); see also Sara Lawrence Lightfoot, *Respect: An Explanation* (Cambridge, MA: Perseus Books, 1999).

56 *Selections from the Prison Notebooks*, 33.

57 *Selections from the Prison Notebooks*, 26–47.

58 Glissant, "Theatre," 199–220. See also D. Soyini Madison, "'That Was My Occupation.'"

59 Madison, *Performed Ethnography and Communication*, 31.

60 Madison, *Performed Ethnography and Communication*, xvii–xxxi.

61 Madison, *Performed Ethnography and Communication*, xvii.

62 Glissant, "Theatre," 209.
63 See Augusto Boal, *Theatre of the Oppressed*, trans. Charles A. & Maria-Odilia Leal McBride (New York: Theatre Communications Group, 1985). See also Madison's discussion on the significance of improvisation in *Performed Ethnography and Communication*.
64 Madison, *Performed Ethnography and Communication*. See also Madison, *Acts of Activism*.
65 Madison, *Performed Ethnography and Communication*, 31.
66 For an in-depth understanding of performative labor, see D. Soyini Madison, "The Labor of Reflexivity," *Cultural Studies ↔ Critical Methodologies* 11, no. 2 (2011): 129–138; see also Madison's discussion on the significance of improvisation in *Performed Ethnography and Communication*.
67 Madison, *Performed Ethnography and Communication*.
68 Susan Leigh Foster, "Movement's Contagion: The Kinesthetic Impact of Performance," in *The Cambridge Companion to Performance Studies*, ed. Tracy C. Davis (Cambridge: Cambridge University Press, 2009), 51.
69 Glissant, "Theatre," 211.
70 Madison, *Performed Ethnography and Communication*, 31.
71 Program excerpts are taken from *Disposable: Bodies for Profit in the Age of Hyper-Incarceration*, dir. Lisa B. Y. Calvente, Performance for Social Change class, DePaul University, Chicago, IL (2015).
72 Scenes 9 and 10 are taken from the script of *Disposable: Bodies for Profit*.
73 "Crack Baby Scene" is taken from the script of dir. Lisa B. Y. Calvente, Performance for Social Change class, DePaul University, Chicago, IL., *The Prison Industrial Complex* (2016).
74 Former student, email message to author, August 16, 2017.
75 Glissant, "Theatre," 209.
76 See Dwight Conquergood, "Performance Studies: Interventions and Radical Research," in *The Drama Review* 46, no. 2 (Summer 2002): 145–156 and Conquergood, "Performing as a Moral Act," 1–13. See also D. Soyini Madison, "Co-Performative Witnessing," *Cultural Studies* 21, no. 6 (2007): 826–831.
77 For a conversation on reflexivity, see Barbara Myerhoff and Jay Ruby, "Introduction," *A Crack in the Mirror: Reflexive Perspectives in Anthropology*, ed. Jay Ruby (Philadelphia: University of Pennsylvania Press, 1981), 1–35; see also Charlotte Aull Davies, *Reflexive Ethnography* (London: Routledge, 1999).
78 For an analysis of performance studies, dialogue, and other, see D. Soyini Madison, *Critical Ethnography: Method, Ethics, and Performance*, 2nd ed. (Thousand Oaks, CA: Sage, 2012). See also Madison, *Acts of Activism*.
79 Madison, "Labor of Reflexivity," 129–138.
80 Madison, "Co-Performative Witnessing," 826.
81 Édouard Glissant, *Poetics of Relation*, trans. Betsy Wing (Ann Arbor, MI: University of Michigan Press, 2010), 18.

Conclusion

Epigraphs: Aimé Césaire, *Discours Politiques* of the election campaign of 1945, Fort-de-France, quoted in Frantz Fanon, *Black Skin, White Masks*, trans. Charles Lam Markman (London: Pluto Press, 2008).

Malcolm X, "I Don't Mean Bananas," in *The New Left Reader*, ed. Carl Oglesby (New York: Grove Press, 1969), 208.

1 Joe Dangelo, "Jay-Z Gets Three Years' Probation for 'Un' Rivera Stabbing," MTV, December 6, 2001, http://www.mtv.com/news/1451340/jay-z-gets-three-years-probation-for-un-rivera-stabbing/.
2 Jay-Z, "Moonlight," track 8 on *4:44*, Roc Nation, 2017, digital stream.
3 Jay-Z, "Jay-Z, Moonlight," directed by Alan Yang, August 10, 2017, music video, https://www.youtube.com/watch?v=FCSh48OlvMo.
4 See Dee Lockett, *"Master of None's* Alan Young on Directing the *Friends* Parody Video for 'Moonlight' and Making Jay-Z Cry," *Vulture*, August 8, 2017, https://www.vulture.com/2017/08/master-of-none-alan-yang-jay-z-moonlight-video.html.
5 Jay-Z, "Jay-Z, Moonlight."
6 Jay-Z, "Jay-Z, Moonlight."
7 Jay-Z, "Jay-Z, Moonlight."
8 Jay-Z, "Jay-Z, Moonlight."
9 Jay-Z, "Jay-Z, Moonlight."
10 Fanon, *Black Skin, White Masks*, 98.
11 See Zeba Blay, "This Detail about *Friends* Will Change the Way You Watch Jay Z's New Video," *HuffPost*, August 7, 2017, https://www.huffpost.com/entry/friends-jay-z-moonlight-living-single_n_59888c22e4b07e7f2150dc1b.
12 Blay, "This Detail."
13 Blay, "This Detail."
14 Fanon, *Black Skin, White Masks*, 107. See also Kara Keeling, *The Witch's Flight: The Cinematic, The Black Femme, and the Image of Common Sense* (Durham, NC: Duke University Press, 2007), 37.
15 Keeling, *Witch's Flight*, 34.
16 See also Richard Iton, *In Search of the Black Fantastic: Politics & Popular Culture in the Post-Civil Rights* Era (New York: Oxford University Press 2008), and Herman Gray, "Subject(ed) to Recognition," *American Quarterly* 65, no. 4 (2013), 771–798.
17 Keeling, *Witch's Flight*, 34.
18 Keeling, *Witch's Flight*, 35; see also Fanon, *Black Skin, White Masks*, 1.
19 Jay-Z, "The Story of O. J.," track 2 on *4:44*, Roc Nation, 2017, digital stream.
20 *American Crime Story: The People vs. O. J.*, directed by Ryan Murphy, aired February 2, 2016, on *FX*.
21 Jay-Z, "Story of O. J."
22 Jay-Z, "Story of O. J."
23 Fanon, *Black Skin, White Masks*, 141. For an example of Manichean delirium, see Fanon, *Black Skin, White Masks*, 149. See also See Iton, *In Search of*.
24 Zach O'Malley Greenburg, "Artist, Icon, Billionaire: How Jay-Z Created his $1 Billion Fortune," *Forbes*, June 3, 2019, https://www.forbes.com/sites/zackomalleygreenburg/2019/06/03/jay-z-billionaire-worth/#2d98042a3a5f.
25 Fanon, *Black Skin, White Masks*, 63.
26 Keeling, *Witch's Flight*, 37.
27 Elaine Browne, "The Rainbow Coalition: Unity in Action" (plenary address at the Young Lords 50th Anniversary Symposium, DePaul University, Chicago, IL, September 23, 2018).

28 For a discussion on neoliberalism and its practiced logic of, "assimilate or die," see Stuart Hall's "The Neoliberal Revolution," *Cultural Studies* 25, no. 6 (2011), 705–728.

29 Jordon Hoffman, "Jay-Z Talks Kaepernick, N.F.L. Deal on Super Bowl Eve," *Vanity Fair*, February 1, 2020, https://www.vanityfair.com/style/2020/02/jay-z -talks-kaepernick-nfl-deal-on-super-bowl-eve.

30 Colin Kaepernick (@Kaepernick7), "Reading always gives me clarity," Twitter, August 30, 2019, https://twitter.com/Kaepernick7/status/1167548687842762754.

31 Kaepernick.

32 Kaepernick.

33 Hoffman, "Jay-Z Talks Kaepernick."

34 Jay-Z, "Story of O. J."

35 John H. Johnson, "Nina Simone Reveals: 'Mississippi Goddam' Song 'Hurt My Career,'" *Jet*, March 24, 1986, 54–55; quoted in Jillian Murphy, "Nina Simone," *My Hero*, January 10, 2018, https://myhero.com/nina-simone.

36 Dave Chappelle, "*The Bird Revelation* (2017)—Transcript," *Scraps from the Loft*, January 3, 2018, https://scrapsfromtheloft.com/2018/01/03/dave-chappelle-the -bird-revelation-2017-full-transcript/.

37 For an interesting and more critical synopsis that ties Chappelle's decision to racial politics in the United States, see John L. Jackson, Jr.'s *Racial Paranoia: The Unintended Consequences of Political Correctness* (New York: Basic Civitas Books, 2008).

38 See Homi K. Bhabha, "Foreword: Remembering Fanon: Self, Psyche, and the Colonial Condition," in Fanon, *Black Skin White Mask*, xxi–xxvii.

39 Fanon, *Black Skin, White Masks*, 175.

40 See T. I. "Bring 'Em Out," track 13 on *Urban Legend*, Grand Hustle Records, 2004, digital stream; see Jay-Z, "What More Can I Say," track 3 on *The Black Album*, Roc Nation, 2003, digital stream; see also The Notorious B.I.G. (Featuring Method Man and Redman), "Rap Phenomenon," track 11, Born Again, Bad Boy, 1999, digital stream.

Index

About the Author

LISA B. Y. CALVENTE is an assistant professor of performance studies and cultural studies in the Department of Communication as well as adjunct faculty in the Department of African, African American and Diaspora Studies at the University of North Carolina at Chapel Hill. She is the coeditor of *Imprints of Revolution: Visual Representations of Resistance*.